BEATING THE DOW

Also by John Downes:

Barron's Finance and Investment Handbook

The Dictionary of Finance and Investment Terms

BEATING THE DOW

A HIGH-RETURN, LOW-RISK
METHOD FOR INVESTING IN THE
DOW JONES INDUSTRIAL STOCKS
WITH AS LITTLE AS $5,000

MICHAEL O'HIGGINS

WITH

JOHN DOWNES

HarperCollins*Publishers*

FIRST EDITION

Designed by Irv Perkins Associates

Library of Congress Cataloging-in-Publication Data

O'Higgins, Michael, 1947–
    Beating the Dow : a high-return, low-risk method for investing in
the Dow Jones industrial stocks with as little as $5,000 / by
Michael O'Higgins and John Downes. — 1st ed.
        p.   cm.
    Includes bibliographical references and index.
    ISBN 0-06-016479-4
    1. Investment analysis. 2. Investments. 3. Stock exchange.
I. Downes, John, 1936– . II. Title.
HG4529.037   1991
332.63'22—dc20   89-46551

91 92 93 94 95 CC/HC 10 9 8 7 6 5 4 3 2 1

TO

*Mimi and Dad for the gift of curiosity
and to Donna, Mark, Brendan, Colin and Sean
whose loving presence helps smooth out
the vicissitudes of investment life.*

—MICHAEL O'HIGGINS

Contents

Acknowledgments

I am grateful to many people, but especially the following:

John Downes, my coauthor, without whose talent, knowledge, and diligence this book never would have been written.

Bob Campbell for originally interesting me in the investment business.

Eddie Myers and Fred Milligan for giving me my first job in the field.

Gene Kaplan and Dom Izzo for teaching me to think for myself and do my own research.

Dick Adams and Harold Davis for introducing me to the idea of using Dow stocks exclusively.

David W. Oberting and Marie Hansen for the many hours, usually on evenings and weekends, of critical research and typing.

M. O'H.

We would like to give special thanks to the following people:

Senior Editor Thomas Ward Miller of HarperCollins for his superb conceptual and editorial contributions and his confidence in us; and Assistant Editor James Hornfischer for always being there with good advice.

Our agent, Faith Hornby Hamlin of Sanford J. Greenburger Associates, whose resourcefulness, energy, professionalism, and personal interest enhanced every aspect of the project.

Jordan Elliot Goodman for bringing us together.

Donna O'Higgins and Katie Downes for cheerfully having their husbands' collaborator underfoot as a house guest and for all the sacrifices a project like this imposes.

M. O'H. and J.D.

Introduction

I ENTERED the investment business in 1971 as an institutional research salesman for Spencer Trask and Company, one of Wall Street's oldest and most prestigious "research boutiques." My job was to convince banks, insurance companies, and other institutional investors that our research analysts, by virtue of their experience, analysis and insight, could help them beat the Dow. If they liked my pitch, we signed them up for our highly regarded research service at a price of over $50,000 a year.

In 1973, we were in the middle of a bear market. One day I sat talking with a bank investment manager I knew to be something of a market guru. Spread out in front of him was his bank's "approved list," a lengthy roster of top-quality common stocks that had received his investment committee's blessing as suitable for an institution entrusted with public funds.

An approved list is hardly where you'd go looking for excitement, but this respected professional had written something in the margin that made me intensely curious. Reading upside-down, my eye caught a little square box he had drawn in black ink. In it, he had jotted some numbers. Sure I must be onto something, I crossed my fingers and asked him for just a hint. What arcane investment wisdom did that mysterious box contain? His answer, given without hesitation, changed the course of my professional life.

The little black box, he explained almost apologetically, contained nothing mysterious at all; quite the contrary. It listed 30 of the most widely held and popularly followed stocks in the world—the 30 companies making up the Dow Jones Industrial Average. "If it were up to me," I can still hear him saying, "I would throw out the rest of the list and stick just with the 30 Dow Industrials."

This seasoned veteran of the investment wars, over a period encompassing many market cycles, had determined that it wasn't necessary to attempt, as most professional investors do, to follow hundreds of stocks in order to outperform the averages. Rather, by concentrating on these 30 very important companies, higher, steadier returns were available with relatively little risk and minimal effort.

Being a newcomer to the complex and often intimidating world of investments, the idea that an approach so simple and so safe could result in superior investment returns intrigued me. In any given period there would be Dow stocks that doubled and Dow stocks that went down, I reasoned, so why couldn't I look at the outperformers as a group, figure out what they had in common, and translate that into an investment strategy that beat the market as a whole—the goal of every money manager?

I started spending nights and weekends on research. Eventually I concluded that by periodically applying a few simple criteria to this small group of 30 top blue chips, I could achieve better results with less risk than the majority of independent money managers and mutual funds with their complex investment strategies.

And the idea that it could all be kept simple suited me just fine.

EARLY IN my career I made an observation about human nature and money—that *people tend to complicate something in direct proportion to its importance.* I'm sure I'm not the first person to observe this, but it's been such an important part of my life that as a private joke I call it O'Higgins' Law.

O'Higgins' Law helps explain why over two-thirds of professional investors fail to beat the market averages even though they spend heavily on research, employ economists, follow hundreds of companies, have sophisticated computer models and use techniques like program trading to try to enhance returns and limit losses.

In fairness to my fellow money managers, handling large corporate and institutional portfolios inevitably requires more complicated strategies than personal investing with smaller amounts of money. But most people, professionals included, make it more complicated than it has to be, which usually means making it more expensive and less profitable.

Investing *can* be too complicated. There are more economic variables and other imponderables involved in forecasting corporate earnings (which ultimately determine relative stock prices) and in anticipating market conditions (which move prices in general up and down) than analysts can possibly process with accuracy and consistency. Yet as long as there are computers, professionals will try to anticipate prices and markets. Some will succeed, most will fail, and that's enough to guarantee investment opportunities for personal investors who can see the forest for the trees.

Beating the Dow will show you how to see the forest for the trees.

I'm a contrarian. That means I look at things as they are, not as they might be in the future. Then I do the opposite of what everybody else is doing. In a market influenced by psychological factors, I usually win. When everybody moves to one side of the boat, I don't spend a lot of time trying to figure out what they're looking at; I know to move to the other side to keep dry.

What I'm saying would be simplistic rather than just simple if it weren't for the following premises basic to *Beating the Dow:*

1. Common stocks are the smartest investment alternative.
2. The Dow stocks are solid blue chip companies of enormous economic importance. All are good long-term investments.
3. A portfolio of out-of-favor Dow stocks has outperformed the Dow Jones Industrial Average consistently on an annual basis, an achievement that has eluded the majority of professional money managers.

In later chapters I will show you step-by-step how to structure and manage your own portfolio of five or ten out-of-favor stocks. Because they are Dow stocks, both portfolios are conservative, but a ten-stock portfolio offers greater safety. For the more adventuresome, I will also describe a one-stock strategy.

I am also going to prove that these portfolios have outperformed the Dow on an annual basis by margins that are not only impressive but often amazing.

The stock selection methods we'll use are time-tested, take only minutes, and cost the price of a newspaper.

Fair enough?

Method of Calculating Total Returns

UNLESS OTHERWISE specified, annual returns for the Dow components and the Dow Jones Industrial Average were calculated by taking year-end prices, subtracting them from the prices at the end of the following year (adjusting for any stock splits that might have occurred during the year) and adding dividends received for the period.

Historical total returns thus represent actual stocks and real time; they are the results you would have obtained had you been invested in those stocks in those years (as opposed to a retroactive reflection or back test of existing Dow components).

Total returns are compounded annually. (Quarterly compounding would have produced even higher returns).

All returns are expressed before commissions and taxes.

PART I

INTRODUCING THE DOW STOCK SYSTEM

CHAPTER 1

Keep It Simple!

In 1985, Texaco, America's third largest oil company, was ordered to pay Pennzoil Company a huge $10.3 billion judgment. In 1987 Texaco filed for bankruptcy. Its stock plunged 28 percent to $27 a share. In 1989, with the legal claim settled, a postbankruptcy share of a restructured Texaco sold at nearly $60, a new all-time high. Texaco has since gone even higher.

When deadly gas leaked from a pesticide plant in Bhopal, India, in 1984, killing over 3,300 people and injuring thousands more, Union Carbide Corporation, America's third largest chemical company and owner of 51 percent of the plant, was sued for over $3 billion. Its stock sank 21 percent to $11, but it bounced back in 1985. In 1989, the Bhopal litigation settled, Union Carbide shares hit an adjusted all-time high of $33 before entering an industry downcycle.

Early in 1989, the tanker Exxon Valdez, owned by America's third largest industrial corporation, ran aground in the pristine waters of Alaska's Prince William Sound. In a tragedy that inspired T-shirts reading "Tanker from Hell," it spilled enough crude oil to cover the state of Rhode Island. Exxon stock dropped 7 percent on the news but quickly rebounded. Today, even as Alaska pursues legal claims involving potential multibillions, Exxon shares are higher in relation to earnings than most other international oil company stocks.

I've made three long stories short, but these anecdotes—and I could cite many more—have a common lesson:

By virtue of sheer size and strength—call it raw staying power—blue chip companies tend to be survivors. The old adage "the bigger they are, the harder they fall" doesn't hold when you're talking about corporate giants. Blue chip stocks are usually safer investments than other kinds of stocks.

The investing public invariably overreacts to unfavorable developments. This creates special opportunities when you're dealing with blue chips: bad news is good news because it makes strong stocks cheap.

Here's another fact about today's financial markets:

Contrary to popular belief, large institutional investors, who dominate market volume and cause sharp volatility through program trading, have created more opportunities than disadvantages for personal investors.

Many individual investors turn to mutual funds as a solution to volatility, but the funds are actually part of the problem. Seventy-five percent of them fail to match, much less beat, the Dow and other market indexes. Their flexibility is seriously constrained by size, competitive pressures, liquidity responsibilities and diversification requirements. Together, these factors lower investment returns, increase transaction costs and necessitate trading practices that cause wide price swings, many of which are merely technical.

You can use the flexibility you have and that the mutual funds and institutional investors lack to actually capitalize on the volatility they create. *Beating the Dow* will show how you can outperform the pros, simply and conservatively, with your own portfolio of common stocks.

When it comes to accumulating wealth, common stocks historically have been unrivaled by any other investment alternative, including real estate and gold.

The uniquely simple system revealed in *Beating the Dow* has consistently outperformed the Dow Jones Industrial Average (DJIA). I make the 30 Dow industrial stocks—all leading blue chips—your total investment universe, and I identify the laggards and potential winners within it.

My approach to common stock investing is so simple anybody can use it and have fun doing it. It is a direct outgrowth of my personal philosophy, which I learned as a young broker before I became a professional money manager—keep it simple.

Within the small Dow stock universe there are dramatic profit opportunities for individual investors. The key is that *in relation to each other,* there are always Dow stocks that are doubling, moving sideways, or going down. *Beating the Dow* shows how to identify the winners when they are out-of-favor and can be bought at bargain prices.

The companies that make up the Dow are household names that are among the most publicized, analyzed, and widely held stocks. Their immense asset values, financial resources, and economic importance give them strength, adaptability and resilience. As a group, they include the most viable business enterprises on earth.

Part II of *Beating the Dow* includes profiles of the individual Dow stocks, showing how each has adapted to the modern economy and how each is positioned with reference to the megatrends of the 1990s. Although all of the Dow stocks are solid long-term investments, *Beating the Dow* does not involve a "buy and hold" strategy. As John Maynard Keynes once said, "In the long-term we're all dead." I don't know about you, but I prefer a shorter investment horizon.

Part III of *Beating the Dow* provides a step-by-step guide to structuring a portfolio of either one, five or ten Dow stocks (depending on your preference). Your individual portfolio can be self-managed with a minimum of time and expense and has an amazing history of beating the Dow Jones Industrial Average on an annual return basis.

My Beating the Dow–Basic Method incorporates my strategy in its simplest form. Requiring minimal investment, these income-producing portfolios have outperformed the Dow year in and year out. Even in 1987, when October's Black Monday saw a 508-point drop in the Dow Jones Industrial Average, the Beating the Dow—Basic Method made money for the year with an annual return nearly double that of the average as a whole.

My Beating the Dow–Advanced Method is designed for personal investors with a yen for more than vanilla. It covers more sophisticated strategies and shows the results of combining different selection tools with seasonal market timing techniques to produce outperforming returns, often with reduced risk.

Keep it simple—and make a bundle with *Beating the Dow*!

CHAPTER 2

Why Common Stocks Are the Best Investment for Accumulating Wealth

BUSINESS IS about risks and rewards. Since stocks represent shares of ownership in a business, you, as a shareholder, share those risks—and those rewards. But business is also about growth. Profitable companies, by retaining what they don't pay out in dividends, grow bigger. With more capital, they are able to generate increased sales and profits. Over time, the value of shares grows as the business grows. This is just as true of General Motors as it is of a smaller business. It's easy to forget that the world's major corporations, with their mind-boggling size and diversity, are businesses.

For these simple reasons, equities—stocks—have historically far outperformed bonds and other fixed-income securities.

One hundred dollars invested in common stocks (as represented by Standard & Poor's index of 500 stocks) in 1925 would have returned $53,345 by 1989. Invested in riskier small stocks, it would have grown by $162,759. The same investment in United States government bonds would have earned $1,630 and in Treasury bills (an indication of what a money market fund would have yielded) $867. Inflation alone would have increased the value to $703.

With an annual inflation rate averaging 3% and an annual total return on the S&P 500 of 10%, the resultant real return of 7% (before income taxes) is impressive evidence of the value of common stocks as a long-term inflation hedge.

A particular stock is as risky as a particular business, but even as most of the best stocks trend upward, they fluctuate in value. The word for that, of course, is volatility, and if you buy high and sell low you can lose money. Combine chronic bad corporate management with bad luck and stocks can become worthless.

STOCKS VS. BONDS AND TREASURY SECURITIES

A given company's bonds carry less risk than that same company's stock. I put it that way rather than categorically because it's safer to own General Motors stock than Fly-By-Night Bahamian Airline's junk bonds.

Whereas stock represents ownership and the risks that go with it, bondholders are creditors. If a company goes out of business and sells or otherwise liquidates its assets, it first repays its creditors, then the stockholders get whatever, if anything, is left over.

Stockholders, if they receive income at all, get dividends paid out of surplus earnings. Bondholders get interest, which is a contractual obligation of the company.

Bonds are subject to market risk, like stocks but to a more limited extent. General interest rate levels are always changing; the market prices of fixed-income securities go up or down to adjust the yield (the interest rate as a percentage of the market price) to market rate levels. Bond prices are also affected by supply and demand and by changes in credit quality. But, assuming the issuer is solvent, bonds repay their face value at maturity.

So bonds are generally *safer* than stocks, but in terms of total return—capital gains plus income—the wealth-building potential of stocks is infinitely greater.

INFLATION

Inflation is a major argument for owning stocks. Severe enough inflation can cause stocks to lose value, but over the long haul equities have outpaced the inflation rate. "Control of inflation" has come to mean an annual rate of 3 to 5 percent, so it looks like inflation is here to stay.

Bonds and Treasury bills, once issued, do not gain value with inflation. Although inflation expectations are taken into account when the rate of interest is originally determined, these investments become vulnerable to erosion of the dollar's purchasing power if inflation exceeds expectations.

REAL ESTATE AND GOLD

Real estate and gold have traditionally been viewed as inflation protection—"inflation-sensitive" is the buzzword—and are frequently touted as investments offering superior returns to common stocks.

Let's take real estate first. There are numerous ways to invest in it, from owning it physically to limited partnerships, to real estate investment trusts, to ordinary common stock in companies with real estate activities of various sorts.

I'm not going to say there's anything inherently wrong with investing in real estate. Immense fortunes have been made (and lost) in real estate. It can be an excellent place to put money if you know what you're doing and understand the tax ramifications of owning real estate in different ways.

But the charts and graphs you see around that show total returns of real estate investments over the last 35 years outperforming common stock deserve another look. They have a special credibility because so many of us are sitting with homes we bought in the 1960s and 1970s that have increased 1,000 percent in value, although there has been some devaluation in the soft real estate market of the past couple of years. What the promoters of real estate investments understandably don't point out is that the last 30 years are an aberration; the major factor in the real estate boom has been the baby boom.

The baby boom has moved through our economic system like a beach ball swallowed by a snake. The "baby boom babies" James Taylor sings about were born after World War II and married and formed families in the sixties and seventies, which is when the real estate boom started. As they gained upward mobility and upgraded their homes during the 1970s to mid-1980s, the boom escalated to a peak. As the nineties get under way, they are midfortyish and starting to think in terms of retirement planning. Now people talk of the "baby bust" and its implications for real estate.

Figure 1 shows that real estate, continuing a historical pattern, underperformed common stocks between 1960 and the early 1970s, then outperformed common stocks until the late 1980s when the traditional relationships resumed.

Real estate is *not* a better long-term investment than common stocks.

Gold has always been a popular doomsday hedge, the theory being that it is a store of absolute value whereas securities and currencies have relative value and are subject to loss. It has been true historically that when inflation or other anxieties have dominated market psychology, the price of gold has risen.

Like real estate, gold can be held in various physical forms, as well as by way of mutual funds and other securities.

The performance of gold was most dramatic in January 1980, when high international inflation led by rising oil prices, tension surrounding the American hostage crisis in Iran and civil disorder in oil-rich Saudi Arabia combined to drive the price per ounce to $887.50 before calmer times returned and gold stabilized at lower levels. It was a memorable lesson in how volatile this store of value can be.

In terms of total return compared with common stocks, however, forget it. Gold, including the common stocks of gold

Cumulative Wealth
Indices of Capital
Market Security
Groups

1960-1987

(Year-End 1959 = $1.00)

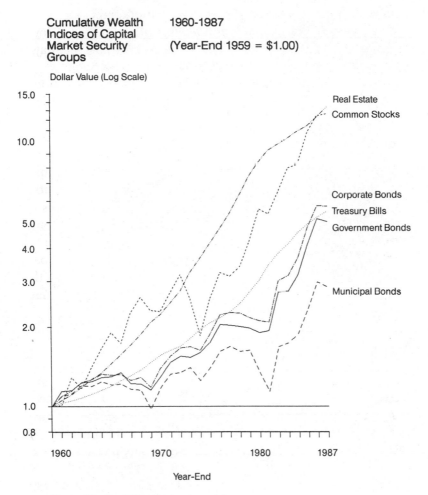

Source: The Asset Allocation Inputs module
of Ibbotson Associates' I/IDEAS software
and data package.

FIGURE 1

mining companies, has not provided total returns anywhere near those of general common stocks.

SHOULD *YOU* OWN COMMON STOCKS?

No other investment alternative rivals common stocks as a way of accumulating wealth. Unless you're flat broke, reading this from your death bed, and have no heirs, there will be a time in your life when it will make sense to hold common stocks.

To determine whether this is that time or not, I suggest putting yourself to the lifestyle test. *You shouldn't invest any more in common stocks than you can afford to forgo without significantly changing your lifestyle.* I don't mean to imply that putting money in stocks—particularly in Dow stocks—necessarily means risking a permanent and total loss of capital. All I'm saying is that stocks can go down as well as up, particularly in the short term, and some patience may be required at times to recoup losses. If that means you might need to do something as drastic as giving up your paramour, you might be better off in a money market fund or another investment that offers lower return and more short-term safety.

Beating the Dow assumes you have at least $5,000 to set aside for common stocks.

CHAPTER 3

Why Invest in the Dow Industrials?

FOR MOST of the last decade, the Dow Jones Industrial Average, fueled by the relatively recent phenomenon of institutional investing, has led the overall market, outperforming the broader Standard & Poor's 500 stock index by a significant margin and the indexes measuring the performance of smaller stocks by a much wider margin. Today's institution-dominated marketplace favors blue chip (high-capitalization) stocks and the Dow is the leading blue chip index.

As the most popular indicator of market activity, the Dow is itself an influential barometer of market and economic conditions. Individually, the 30 stocks that make up the Dow industrials are among the most widely held, widely analyzed, and widely publicized in the world. They are also among the biggest and the strongest. Combined, the 30 Dow components have assets of over a trillion dollars, nearly 4.5 million employees, and sales that exceed the gross national products of every country in the world except the United States, the Soviet Union and Japan.

These prime companies may gain, lose, spin off, acquire, merge, rename themselves, reorganize, even drop out of the Dow, but they are an integral and vital part of our economic system, and in one form or another they are here to stay.

The Dow companies and their products and services are

household names to most people. Here is the present list, with some recent name changes noted:

Allied-Signal Inc. (formerly Allied Corporation and Allied Chemical)
Aluminum Company of America (Alcoa)
American Express Company
American Telephone & Telegraph Company (AT&T)
Bethlehem Steel Corporation
The Boeing Company
Chevron Corporation
The Coca-Cola Company
E.I. du Pont de Nemours and Company
Eastman Kodak Company
Exxon Corporation
General Electric Company
General Motors Corporation
Goodyear Tire & Rubber Company
International Business Machines Corporation (IBM)
International Paper Company
McDonald's Corporation
Merck & Co., Inc.
Minnesota Mining and Manufacturing Company (3M)
Navistar International Corporation (formerly International Harvester)
Philip Morris Companies
Primerica Corporation (formerly American Can)
Procter & Gamble Company
Sears, Roebuck & Company
Texaco, Inc.
Union Carbide Corporation
United Technologies Corporation
USX Corporation (formerly U.S. Steel)
Westinghouse Electric Corporation
Woolworth Corporation

As we will see in Part II of *Beating the Dow,* the individual Dow companies have evolved in response to an ever-changing business environment. Their internal dynamism, together with mergers and substitutions, have made the current Dow Jones Industrial Average representative of virtually all important sectors of the American economy.

Multinational without exception, the Dow companies in their different ways are positioned to benefit from the megatrends of the 1990s—globalization of markets; cleaning up the environment; repairing the infrastructure; depletion of energy sources; revival of manufacturing; increased literacy rate; aging of the population; expansion of the free world.

Most important, however, our discussions of the individual companies will examine the kinds of problems these stalwart companies have encountered over the years—and solved. That even major corporations make mistakes and suffer from unforeseen adversity is a fact of life and always will be. That the investing public will always overreact to bad news is just as certain. The resilience the Dow companies have because of their immense financial, legal and human resources makes a portfolio of Dow stocks a conservative investment risk.

With companies of Dow stock caliber, there is more opportunity than risk. Bad news is usually good news because it makes strong stocks cheap.

FINDING BARGAINS IN THE DOW

Although I keep an eye on fundamentals, which is easy when you're holding stocks that Wall Street is constantly watching and that are in the news every day, as a contrarian I look for Dow stocks that are out of favor and selling at bargain prices.

Sooner rather than later, stocks that are "victims" of overreaction, whether to a news development or a business cycle, will regain a value appropriately reflecting their actual risk.

Cyclical stocks, by definition, are subject to good news and bad news and, by the same definition, to times when they're cheap and times when they're expensive.

In Part III, you'll learn how to identify Dow stocks when they are out of favor and most likely to outperform the average as a whole. Buy cheap, sell dear. Same old story, but this time with a twist in your favor. We're not dealing here with obscure, neglected or emerging companies. These stocks are in the lime- light all the time.

Which begins to answer some questions you were probably about to ask.

What if the stocks are cheap because the companies have real problems? Can't actual risks be important, even with Dow stocks?

The answer is yes, but because the Dow stocks are so highly visible and widely analyzed, the possibility of major adverse financial developments coming as a surprise is minimal. Even surprises with financial implications—Union Carbide's Bhopal disaster or Exxon's *Valdez* oil spill, to cite recent examples— were taken in stride financially (although the stocks dropped temporarily, providing an opportunity for contrarians).

In a worst-case scenario, such as a bankruptcy or near-bank- ruptcy, Dow stocks historically have become "turnaround situations," ultimately rewarding their holders with handsome, sometimes astonishing gains.

Have there been some exceptions? Yes, but they are very few and far between and more than offset by the diversification provided by the Dow portfolio. We'll be looking at actual cases in later chapters.

WHY HASN'T the world caught on to something this obvious? Won't the music stop once this book gets around?

My colleague owns a Saab. They're advertised as the "most intelligent cars ever built." When you open the hood and stand to the side, the oil stick, which in most cars is down among the belts and hoses, is located smack front and center and attached to a cap that is three inches in diameter, bright red in color, and marked (in English) "Motor Oil." He tells me that 100 miles outside the New York metropolitan area, the chances are better than even a station attendant will come around to say he can't for the life of him find the oil stick. The car may be intelligent, and so, no doubt, is the guy pumping gas. But the oil stick is too obvious to be seen.

The anomaly that there is more opportunity than risk in the Dow universe is partly explained, I am convinced, by the fact that it is so obvious it is overlooked or so simple it is suspect. I'm sure there are a few investors out there who see the opportunity in out-of-favor Dow stocks, and it's probably just my good luck that nobody has written a book about the subject. But don't forget who it is that dominates the stock market. It is the large institutional investors with huge pools of money, and as we have seen they are forced by liquidity and diversification requirements to operate in a larger universe than the Dow stocks provide. And if that weren't enough, the temptation to reach beyond the 30 Dow industrials for greater returns would be irresistible anyway to most professionals because of egos, competitive pressures and the need to legitimize fees.

The significance of this for you and other individual investors is that although they can and do hold DJIA stocks, institutional managers have different agendas. Their large portfolios require special strategies and involve special trading dictates.

The simple and relatively safe Dow portfolio is a luxury only individual investors can fully exploit. And even if everybody who reads this book went out and acted at once, it's unlikely you could eliminate the profit opportunities in the Dow universe. Not when you're outgunned three to one by institutions.

I've had an exceptional record as an investor because I've trained myself to think against the grain. Maybe you can train yourself to think in reverse too, but that isn't necessary to beat the market. All you have to do is learn to recognize the symptoms of opportunity and then have the courage to act against conventional wisdom. The courage should come easily when you see the results my simple approach has produced.

George Soros, who with Warren Buffett, Peter Lynch and a few others is one of the investment world's living legends, has said: "Investors operate with limited funds and limited intelligence: They do not need to know everything. As long as they understand something better than others, they have an edge."

I don't even go that far. I say if you can find the oil stick in a Saab you can beat the Dow. In an investment world addicted to complexity, it can almost be said that keeping it simple is in itself a form of contrarianism.

CHAPTER 4

How the Pros Try to Beat the Market—and Why Most Don't Succeed

MOST PROFESSIONAL money managers, 75 percent by most estimates, fail to beat the market averages. This fact startles most people, until they consider that the professionals we are talking about *are* the market. Their decisions account for three-quarters of all trading activity and determine which way the Dow and other major indexes move.

To understand why this is true and why keeping it simple can actually give you an edge over the pros, let's take a quick look at some basic approaches to portfolio management.

HOW THE PROS TRY TO BEAT THE MARKET

Every professional manager of common stock ("equity") portfolios tries to outperform the market—to achieve increases in a portfolio's value that exceed those of the market as a whole. Market ups and downs are measured by various stock indexes and averages composed of representative groups of stocks. The measure most widely followed is the DJIA of 30 stocks. A manager who can beat the Dow has had a successful year.

Independent investment advisers, mutual fund managers, bank trust departments and other professional investors follow hundreds of companies, employ staffs of analysts and economists, and use elaborate computerized trading techniques to try to beat the Dow performance—and most of them fail.

For example, Barron's/Lipper Gauge, in the quarterly mutual fund report published in Barron's in Spring 1990, shows the total reinvested cumulative performance of different categories of mutual funds for the decade ended March 31, 1990.

The category most fairly compared to the Dow stocks, Growth and Income Funds, which are made up of dividend-paying common stocks, had a total return of 351.19 percent. The total return of the Dow Jones Industrial Average for the same period was 450.31 percent. The funds underperformed the Dow by 22 percent.

The average of all five categories, which also included Capital Appreciation, Growth, Small Company Growth, and Equity Income Funds, was only 343.69 percent, over 100 percentage points lower than the Dow. (The comparable return on the S&P 500 was 409.91 percent.)

The message is clear: If you buy a mutual fund the chances are you will do significantly worse than the Dow.

Whatever their success, managers use variations of four basic investment approaches:

The *fundamental approach,* also called value investing, analyzes companies, industries, and the economic and market environments to identify stocks that are undervalued at their current market prices.

The *growth stock approach* tries to identify companies with high-growth potential before that potential is reflected in their market price.

The *contrarian approach* identifies established companies that are temporarily unpopular, selling at bargain prices and due to rebound.

The *market timing approach* holds that when the market goes up, most stocks go up, and when the market goes down, most stocks go down. It uses various indicators to anticipate market movements.

All these approaches work, although some are inherently more difficult to implement than others and each can get as complicated as one chooses to make it.

A fundamental or value investor, for example, would examine the daylights out of a company's financial statements and evaluate its earnings prospects in the context of its industry. That way, he or she would try to get an idea of the stock's real worth. If that is significantly below the stock's market value, the value investor concludes the stock has no real downside risk and will eventually rise to its proper market value. The legendary Warren Buffett set an all-time record by compounding money at 22 percent for 20 years as a value investor. Of course, it also helps that Mr. Buffett is a genius and didn't have clients breathing down his neck.

Growth stock managers are fundamental investors who seek out companies expected to enjoy rapid growth whose shares, based on that anticipated growth, are undervalued. These are usually, although not always, younger, smaller firms in emerging industries that carry a higher degree of risk than established companies. They usually do not pay big dividends, since their earnings are reinvested to finance their rapid growth.

Growth investing has its Houdini in the form of Peter Lynch, formerly of Fidelity's Magellan Fund, who garnered gains of 29 percent compounded over a ten-year period. When Lynch retired, he stated publicly that he had been working seven days a week and was afraid he was going to drop dead at 46 if he didn't quit. Enough said?

Growth companies require meticulous and constant analysis. To be sure, there are dramatic gains to be made in some growth stocks (although more efficient, computerized markets have reduced the number of what Mr. Lynch calls "ten-baggers"), but risk, generally speaking, equals return.

And although smaller stocks as a group have outperformed blue chips in alternating cycles historically, it's been the spectacular winners—the fledgling Apple Computers—that have tended to lift the growth stocks as a group. Growth stock investors in general have had the same experience relative to the market as value investors.

BEFORE I touch on contrarian investing and market timing, which are more up my alley, I want to emphasize that nothing in this business is pure. For example, there are growth companies that are among the most highly capitalized and long-established firms around. Philip Morris was considered one for most of the 1980s—an old-line, cash-rich tobacco company on an acquisition binge. And a Dow stock to boot.

Nor can any prudent investor afford to ignore fundamentals completely. If I heard hamburger was going to be declared illegal and immoral in addition to fattening, I'd sell my McDonald's.

Want to know what I'd really do? Knowing it would take a lot more than that to sink McDonald's (a Dow stock, after all), I'd sell it short. The market would kill it (not the company, the stock). I'd buy it for next to nothing. Then when the Big Mac came back in some edible and marketable reincarnation, I'd be on my way to the bank. But that's getting ahead of my story.

A CONTRARIAN, by definition, goes the opposite way the crowds do. When the light turns red, the contrarian steps on it (an imperfect metaphor since professional contrarian investors are quite sane and largely law-abiding). Contrarians capitalize on the part of market behavior that is psychological, but that is not to say there isn't a financially logical reason for going against the crowd.

Stock prices follow the laws of supply and demand. As real value becomes more widely recognized, demand increases and the price rises. And vice versa. But in the stock market there is only so much stock and so much money. Therefore, as more investors act on their anticipation that a stock is going up, the more purchasing power is exhausted, which means the market for that stock is closer to its peak. Conversely, when most investors sell, there is a liberation of cash to create upward pressure on a stock representing opportunity.

That's the theoretical rationale for contrarianism. In practice, real value only partly explains why stocks are bid up or bid down.

To the contrarian, just as axiomatic as the fact that the crowd always buys dear and sells cheap is the fact that it almost invariably overreacts to news, both good and bad. *The difference between real and perceived risk is opportunity.* This is an essential part of my Dow stock strategy, and we'll be talking a lot more about it.

How do contrarians stack up against value and growth investors?

There are contrarians and then there are *contrarians.* Everybody is trying to buy low and sell high, but the actions a true contrarian takes run contrary to conventional wisdom. That's really to say we have to act against our own human nature. Most people, *investment professionals included*, cannot do this.

The majority of professional contrarians take their cue from more courageous contrarians and wind up simply following a different crowd. In practical terms, that means they buy somewhere along the way up and sell somewhere along the way down. In other words, professional contrarian investors as a group are no exception to our rule. Most of them don't beat the market. *But the real ones do!*

MARKET TIMERS use technical analysis of historical price performance to try to predict future movements. In effect, they say:

"To hell with the facts, show me the charts." They use statistics and are guided by historical chart patterns, known by such picturesque names as "head and shoulders," "double tops," "triangles," "gaps," and "rising bottoms." (They daydream a lot, those guys.)

Cycles of various sorts have been a fact of market life throughout history. There are also seasonal and other historical market patterns that have a logical basis and recur with phenomenal consistency. But the past isn't necessarily prologue and history rarely repeats itself exactly. Investors who use a market timing approach exclusively have about the same record of beating the averages as other professionals.

Many market timing techniques nonetheless do have well-documented validity. The investor who doesn't make a point of becoming familiar with them is missing out on an opportunity to enhance returns. I'll show you the ones that work.

In the way of a subtotal, I want to emphasize that to underperform the market is not necessarily to lose money. In fairness to my fellow professionals, most managers of equity portfolios who have applied a consistent approach—whatever that approach is—with discipline have made money for their clients over the long term even when they haven't beaten the averages. As indeed they should have, since the market has risen over the long term.

Although there will be years, inevitably, when stock portfolios show losses rather than gains, the importance of avoiding losses—and the professionals who cause them—can't be overstressed. Imagine making money for a few years, then seeing it wiped out because somebody did something stupid. It is an arresting fact that to overcome a 50 percent portfolio loss, you need a 100 percent portfolio gain. Think about that! So try to avoid losing money.

IT'S A simple fact that unless you're Ivan Boesky (Mr. Boesky, you will remember, learned the hard way that insider trading meant trading pinstriped suits for striped pajamas), it's impossible to predict with certainty what a stock—or the stock market—is going to do in the short run. That's why discipline and patience are essential ingredients for successful investing.

But there are additional reasons why the majority of money managers fail to match, let alone beat the Dow or the S&P 500, and they are worth looking at because there are traps you as an individual investor can avoid.

One of them is the short-term focus that most investment professionals have developed in the last 20 years. Deregulation of the financial markets, rising personal incomes, a long-running bull market, IRAs and other tax legislation—these and many other factors worked to change the investment marketplace in two fundamental ways.

The first was to bring personal investing, formerly the province of the wealthy, within the reach of average people. That was, to be sure, a welcome development, but it vastly increased the market for investment services.

The second was a result of the first—the spawning of a financial services industry in which a dizzying assortment of investment professionals, including mutual funds, independent money managers, banks, insurance companies, financial planners and stockbrokers (some of whom have been renamed financial consultants), began competing for the investor's hard-earned dollar.

It's hardly surprising that the name of the competitive game has not been, "Who provides the best long-term investment returns through patience and discipline?" Instead, it has turned into, "Who outperformed the rest last quarter?" Speaking of the pressures the marketplace puts on mutual funds to produce quarterly performance, somebody has said it's as though they all worked for George Steinbrenner. The result, more often than not, has been short-term portfolio profits at the expense of higher long-term returns. That and a self-defeating attempt by investors to go with the hottest fund or money manager, thereby making buying high and selling low a virtual certainty (Peter Lynch and his miraculous Magellan Fund excepted).

Another important factor contributing to a short-term focus

has been the need to provide liquidity. A mutual fund, for example, must be able to meet shareholder redemptions if necessary, possibly in big numbers should the market decline or the fund's performance turn sour for other reasons. This requires flexibility, which means holding stocks that can be gotten in and out of with relative ease—namely, the largest companies with the largest number of shares outstanding. Not only do these high-cap stocks tend in general to be mature companies with less potential for sales-driven growth than younger, smaller-cap firms (there are exceptions, of course), but when a lot of huge institutional investors jam into relatively few large stocks, the result is less flexibility, not more. You can't just dump a whole position in GM, for example, on the market. It has to be done over time. This lack of flexibility has its effect in lower returns.

The problem a quarterly mentality brings to stock investing is not a lack of short-term opportunities, which exist in abundance even among the largest stocks. The problem is that investors forced into such a tight time frame are forced to take short-term losses along with their short-term gains and often have to forego better returns that could be had by following a disciplined approach.

As a personal investor free of institutional investors' constrictions, you have the best of both worlds—the opportunity to capitalize on relatively short-term price increases and the ability to follow a system that automatically ensures you will be buying low and selling high.

Professionals who actively trade and follow a lot of stocks also have high overhead. In addition to management fees (1 percent, typically), transaction costs, custodial fees and other legal and administrative expenses all take their toll, so that even those portfolios that match the market in terms of pure performance produce underperforming net returns to clients.

THERE IS one other reason most professionals underperform. It's my favorite so I've saved it for last: *They make the process too complicated.*

In fairness, part of the reason they make it complicated is that they have to. Either they are required by law to be widely diversified, as with mutual funds, or they feel extensive diversification is necessary to avoid criticism—or even lawsuits, should one of their heavy positions take a beating. I prefer to keep all my eggs in a few baskets—sometimes as few as one— and then keep a close eye on the baskets.

But no small part of the problem has to do with other stuff.

Like egos. How can you look like a genius if what you're doing isn't complicated?

Then there's the simple need to justify fees. How can an investment manager accept a percentage of the assets unless he or she looks busy?

And still another part of it is, I'm convinced, human nature. Remember O'Higgins' Law? If it's important—and money always is—we can't resist making it complicated. We're brought up that way.

PASSIVE "INDEX" INVESTING

Since most mutual funds and independent money managers fail to beat the averages, one way of outperforming the pros is to buy the averages. If you can't beat 'em, join 'em. This is done by buying one of a number of mutual funds that replicate indexes, such as the AMEX Major Market Index (of 20 stocks designed to correlate with the Dow), the S&P 500, the New York Stock Exchange (NYSE) Composite Index or the Value-Line Composite Index.

These funds simply buy and hold the stocks making up the index or a representative sampling thereof. An example of an index fund replicating the S&P 500 is the no-load Vanguard 500, which has no management fee and a very low expense ratio. Other index funds have nominal management fees.

Although expenses, however minimal, cause stock index funds slightly to underperform the market as they represent it, they nonetheless outperform some 75 percent of all general stock funds and money managers.

The most persuasive apologists for such "passive investing" are advocates of the so-called efficient market hypothesis, also known as the random walk theory. Its practitioners contend that past, present and future stock prices over a broad spectrum simply reflect information coming into the market at random. Thus while there may be for relatively short periods investors who overachieve and others who underachieve, over the long pull there is no knowledge or judgment an investor can add beyond what has already been perceived and reflected in prices.

In the words of Burton Malkiel, whose *A Random Walk Down Wall Street* advocates passive investing, "A blindfolded chimpanzee throwing darts at *The Wall Street Journal* can perform as well as the experts." Hence money spent on active portfolio management, including management fees and transaction costs, is money ultimately wasted, and the relatively small cost of passive investing is well justified.

The efficient market hypothesis has its staunch supporters and many detractors. The fact that the S&P 500 significantly *underperformed* active managers during the period from the mid-1970s through 1982 is cited as hard evidence by those, mainly investment professionals, who consider the theory academic nonsense. Proponents argue that the market's information-processing and pricing mechanisms were less efficient in the 1970s than in the 1980s, when computers became more widely used in a securities marketplace dominated by large institutions.

I'm a strong believer that no matter what people put into computers, stock prices reflect consensus, consensus means average and average means mediocrity. I've *beaten* the market and so can you.

As for indexing, it seems to me the most effective argument against it is that while you do no worse than the market, you do no better, either. Let's not forget you can do as well as the market and still go broke.

Between 1972 and 1974 the market lost 47 percent of its value. I'm not sure how consoled I would have been by the fact that my index fund had done as well as the market. Incidentally, my system produced positive returns for that period, as you will see later on.

Beating the Dow shows you how to *outperform* the market *and avoid losses* by managing your own *simple* portfolio of top-quality stocks. One of the benefits of self-management is that it eliminates the risk of getting involved with the wrong professional.

CHAPTER 5

The Dow Jones Industrial Average

HISTORY

Late in 1989, *The Wall Street Journal,* publisher of the Dow Jones Industrial Average, put out a special centennial edition to mark the anniversary of its founding. One part, titled "On the Average: How DJ Indicator Evolved," describes what times were like back in 1884 when Charles H. Dow first published the indicator of stock market profits that would become the DJIA. Wall Street was then about seven blocks of lower Manhattan. Offices had working fireplaces, but unlike the one Sanford Weill had installed in the 1980s when he was head of Shearson Lehman, the chimneys weren't poking through the towers of a World Trade Center.

The New York Stock Exchange listed just a few dozen companies (today it lists some 1,600), and a 300,000-share day was big volume (today 150 million is a moderate day). Instead of computers, news services and disclosure requirements were gossip, inside information and, according to the *Journal* article, "pools of financiers and plungers who would manipulate stocks up or down, leaving outsiders like shorn lambs. . . . A breath of rumor would bring riches or ruin." (That has a familiar ring, doesn't it?)

Charles Dow brought out his "index of active stocks" in a year that started well but ended in what became known as the Railway Panic of 1884. The first part of the year saw a blossoming of new enterprises and growing investor optimism. But as the months went on, rate wars between railroads, the exposure of some fraudulent market practices, and a sharp drop in Union Pacific shares caused disenchantment and loss of confidence on the part of investors. Eighteen eighty-four ended with bank failures and a market collapse.

Until then, it had been the practice of most investors to focus on individual companies rather than the overall market. Dow was one of the first to see that all boats rise and fall with the tides, and that the market as a whole was influenced by such factors as interest rates and changes affecting trade or agriculture. A man after my own heart, 32-year-old Charles Dow had an analytical bent combined with a love of simplicity. He set about trying to devise what the *Journal* described as "a systematic indicator that would isolate daily ripples from the waves, and the waves from the tide."

A New England farmboy, Dow had a talent for writing and was an avid reader of Horatio Alger's novels about young men who realized the American dream of rags to riches. He brought with him the sense of humor requisite to a Wall Street-related career, revealed in a piece he had written for the Providence and Stonington Steamship Company. After 84 years of excursions, he noted, "there was, proportionately, the same number of elderly ladies who constantly expected an explosion [and] of young people who sought the uppermost parts of the boat and sat quite unnecessarily close together, considering the amount of room there was to spare . . ."

According to a *Wall Street Journal* piece on Dow quoted in Richard J. Stillman's *Dow Jones Industrial Average:* "The men of the Street soon learned that this reticent, quiet-speaking man who took shorthand notes on his cuffs could be relied upon to quote them absolutely and without embellishment and moreover, that it was safe to tell him news in confidence . . ."

His talents led to a position with the Kiernan News Agency, where he met Edward D. Jones and Charles M. Bergstresser. The three left together several months later to found Dow, Jones & Company. That was in November 1882.

DOW, JONES & COMPANY

Dow, Jones & Company ("Financial News Agents") distributed daily financial news bulletins to subscribers and published the Customer's Afternoon Letter, predecessor to *The Wall Street Journal.* Although Dow was the only partner without a college education, he was the analytical mind and writer. Jones, a Brown University graduate, had editorial and managerial rather than analytical skills and evidently had nothing to do with developing the average. Bergstresser, who had graduated from Lafayette College, had a lot of contacts and was mainly the marketing man. Why Bergstresser's name wasn't part of the company name is a mystery; perhaps it was just too much of a mouthful.

The three worked out of "a ramshackle building next door to the entrance of the Stock Exchange" that reminded an employee of a scene from Dickens' Nicholas Nickelby: "It was such a crowded scene that at first Nicholas saw nothing at all. By degrees, however, the place resolved itself into a bare hole with a few forms . . ."

THE DOW JONES INDUSTRIAL AVERAGE

Charles Dow first came up with a list of eleven of the most actively traded stocks, including nine railroads, Pacific Mail Steamship and (a bit of real high-tech) Western Union. These he simply listed with their closing prices added up and divided by 11.

The resultant simple arithmetic average was published in the Customer's Afternoon Letter and then in *The Wall Street Journal* to become what is today the oldest continuously published index of stocks in the world.

During the next 12 years, much happened to change the business and economic landscape. These were the years leading up to the era of trust-busting that began with the Sherman Anti-trust Act of 1890. Small businesses were being consolidated into large corporations and trusts, which became the "action" for investors and speculators on Wall Street. Several changes in the average were made to reflect the new marketplace.

In 1896 the first purely industrial average was published in *The Wall Street Journal,* which was now seven years old. This average, published May 26, 1896, was composed of 12 stocks. They were:

American Cotton Oil	Laclede Gas
American Sugar	National Lead
American Tobacco	North American Company
Chicago Gas	Tennessee Coal & Iron
Distilling & Cattle Feeding	U.S. Leather Preferred
General Electric	U.S. Rubber

In 1902 Dow, Jones & Company was sold to Clarence W. Barron (founder of *Barron's National Business and Financial Weekly,* a Dow, Jones & Company publication), but Charles Dow, who appeared on *The Wall Street Journal's* masthead following the sale, died that same year.

In 1916, the industrial average was increased to 20 stocks and on October 1, 1928, it was expanded to 30—the number of stocks comprising the average ever since. The original 30 companies were:

Allied Chemical	American Smelting
American Can	American Sugar

American Tobacco
Atlantic Refining
Bethlehem Steel
Chrysler
General Electric
General Motors
General Railway Signal
Goodrich
International Harvester
International Nickel
Mack Trucks
Nash Motors
North American
Paramount Publix

Postum, Inc.
Radio Corporation of America (RCA)
Sears, Roebuck & Company
Standard Oil of New Jersey
Texas Corporation
Texas Gulf Sulphur
Union Carbide
United States Steel
Victor Talking Machine
Westinghouse Electric
Woolworth
Wright Aeronautical

Counting a number of name changes, 13 of that original list are in the Dow today. Actually, more than half the original list remains: Victor Talking Machine merged with RCA, which became part of General Electric, and Postum, Inc., changed its name to General Foods, which was acquired by Philip Morris. It is noteworthy how relatively few substitutions there have been between 1928 and now, especially considering that the Great Depression hadn't yet occurred. In fact, for two stretches of 17 consecutive years there were no changes whatsoever: between March 14, 1939, and July 3, 1956, and June 1, 1959, and August 8, 1976. In the last 50 years, there have been 13 substitutions. But allowing for substitutions that replaced substitutions, 20 stocks or ⅔ of the average have been constant for a 50-year period.

CALCULATION OF THE DJIA

It's important to understand how the Dow is computed because the equation affects its value as a yardstick of the market. In 1928 the present method of calculating the average was adopted. Until then, the average was computed the original way, simply by totaling up prices and dividing by the number of stocks. For a while, the only problem with that was that it gave more weight to higher-priced stocks than lower-priced stocks.

To this day, the Dow is a price-weighted average, meaning that a $120 stock like IBM moving 10 percent influences the average 30 times more than a $4 stock like Navistar with the same percentage change.

In 1928 a flexible divisor in place of the total number of stocks was introduced. This change became necessary when companies began splitting their stocks. As you probably know, a split occurs when a company increases its outstanding shares without increasing shareholders' equity. If a company whose stock was selling at $20 split it two for one (issued two shares for each existing share), the price per share would drop to $10. If the average were then to list the shares of that company at $10, it would reflect an artificial decline from $20. So instead of dividing by the number of shares, the publishers used a divisor that would make the average equal to what it was before the split.

The divisor in 1928 was 16.67. Today, after many adjustments made necessary not only by splits but by stock dividends, substitutions and mergers, the divisor is 0.450. The divisor is adjusted whenever an event would cause a distortion of 10 or more points in the average. Notice I say points. Another result of the flexible divisor was that changes became measured in terms of points rather than dollars, although dollar changes are, of course, what are being averaged.

Let me give you a simple illustration:

Assume the average consisted of only four stocks, selling for $10, $30, $60, and $80. Using the original formula, the total of the prices, $180, would be divided by the number of stocks, 4, to arrive at the average, $45.

$$
\begin{array}{r}
10 \\
30 \\
60 \\
\underline{80} \\
180 \div 4 = \$45
\end{array}
$$

But now suppose the $80 stock was split 2 for 1. The unadjusted average following the split, assuming closing prices remained unchanged, would be:

$$
\begin{array}{r}
10 \\
30 \\
60 \\
\underline{40} \\
140 \div 4 = \$35
\end{array}
$$

Since the market values of the companies didn't change but the average did, an adjustment must be made for the sake of continuity. One possibility would be to count twice the price of the stock that split, so it would look like this:

$$
\begin{array}{r}
10 \\
30 \\
60 \\
40 \\
\underline{40} \\
180 \div 4 = \$45
\end{array}
$$

But Dow, Jones & Company chose, instead, to get the same effect by changing the divisor, thus calculating as follows:

$$
\begin{array}{r}
10 \\
30 \\
60 \\
\underline{40} \\
140 \div 3.11 = 45 \text{ points}
\end{array}
$$

The formula for arriving at the divisor is:

$$\frac{140}{x} = 45; \; 45x = 140; \; x = 3.11$$

Because the divisor gets smaller with each stock split or stock dividend, there is an increasing disproportion between the change in the actual prices of the 30 stocks making up the average and the change in the average. Thus when you say the Dow ended the week up 10 points, you are talking about a much smaller rise in the dollar value of the shares.

But the average nonetheless makes it possible to compare the magnitude and direction of price changes from day to day and year to year—in fact, with today's computers, from minute to minute.

THE DOW COMPARED WITH
OTHER POPULAR INDEXES

The Dow Jones Industrial Average does have a few shortcomings, two of which we have already touched upon. The most serious, I think, is the fact of its being price-weighted. As we observed earlier, the same percentage change in an expensive stock like IBM moves the average more than in an inexpensive stock like Navistar. In an extreme case, this could cause a misleading indication. A huge move in a few high-priced components could send the average one way even though a majority of the components went the other way and the other way was the way of the broader market.

But even under normal circumstances, price weighting creates distortions. It is simply a fact of market life that lower-priced shares tend to register greater gains and losses than higher-priced shares. If Navistar is up or down a half a buck in a given day, which is 12½ percent of $4, it's hardly big news. But when IBM is up or down $15 (the same percentage) in one day, you can bet it will be a news item. This is a factor (among several others) in a phenomenon Wall Street calls the small firm effect.

An interesting result of this is that if you in effect "unweight" the Dow—that is, if you bought an equal dollar amount of each of the 30 stocks (the same $120 would buy one share of IBM but 30 shares of $4 Navistar)—the historical experience has been that you would outperform the average (and, of course, most professionals). This happens because lower-priced stocks simply tend to move more percentage-wise than higher-priced shares. We'll take a closer look at this phenomenon when we discuss strategies later on.

When used in relation to the Dow, "weighted" and "un-weighted" can be confusing. You'll see references to the un-weighted Dow—the phenomenon just described. But you'll also see the Dow referred to as an unweighted average. In that sense unweighted relates to the Dow's automatic price weighting as distinguished from other indexes that are deliberately adjusted to result in "market value" or "capitalization" weighting.

Let's look at some other major indexes.

By far the second most widely quoted stock index is the S&P 500 or just the S&P (although Standard & Poor's has less widely-used indexes of 400 stocks and 100 stocks). You'll usually see the performance of mutual funds and money managers compared to the S&P 500 because it is a broader measure of the overall market than the blue chip Dow. The S&P (as we'll call it throughout this book, unless otherwise specified) is made up approximately of 400 industrial, 60 transportation and utility and 40 financial stocks. Most of its components are listed on the New York Stock Exchange (it accounts for something like 80 percent of the market value of all shares traded on the big board), but it includes some American Stock Exchange companies and over-the-counter stocks.

It is market value- (capitalization-) weighted, which means that each of its components is given a weight proportionate to its market capitalization (its share price times its shares outstanding). The effect of this is to give big companies with high market capitalizations more weight than smaller-cap companies.

To understand what this means compared with the Dow's price weighting, compare Westinghouse, which has a market cap of $10 billion and a recent (pre-split) share price of $75, with Exxon, which has a market cap of $58 billion and a share price of $45. Given the same percentage change in price, Westinghouse would affect the Dow more than Exxon because of its higher price. But in the S&P, Exxon would have more clout because of its higher total market value.

The S&P is computed by multiplying the stock price of each component by the number of shares outstanding and dividing the total by the aggregate market value of all S&P stocks from 1941–1943, which was designated as a base period. The result is multiplied by 10 to get the value at any particular time.

In comparing different indexes, however, weighting methods do not make that much of a difference under normal conditions. The blue chip Dow and the broader S&P have tended to parallel each other's movements. This happens because large-capitalization companies tend to have higher-priced shares.

YOU SHOULD also be familiar with several other indexes.

The Value-Line Composite Index, like the S&P, is significant because it is widely used and the subject of abundant data. But whereas the Dow tracks the blue chips exclusively and the S&P tracks a broader group of blue chips and other mainly large ("secondary") stocks, the Value-Line attempts to reflect the "typical" industrial stock. It is neither price- nor market value-weighted, but rather is an equally-weighted geometric average of approximately 1,700 NYSE, Amex and over-the-counter stocks followed by the Value-Line Investment Survey. Changes are expressed in index numbers related to a base value of 100 established in 1961.

Insofar as the trading of indexers and large institutions has a disproportionate influence on the Dow and the S&P 500, the equally weighted and broader-based Value-Line is a more accurate measure of general investor sentiment. As this is being written, for example, the Value-Line has been trending downward as the Dow and, to a lesser extent, the S&P have been climbing. This would indicate sagging public confidence in the market even as the institutions, buying selected blue chips, would give the opposite impression.

The NASDAQ Composite Index is based on the National Association of Securities Dealers Automated Quotations National Market System, which includes all actively traded domestic over-the-counter stocks. It is thus most representative of more speculative, smaller, growing companies. It is a market value-weighted index introduced with a base value of 100 in 1971.

The Wilshire 5000 Equity Index is a market value-weighted index of 5,000 stocks. It is thus the broadest of all indexes, including all NYSE- and Amex-listed stocks as well as those over-the-counter stocks tracked by Value-Line, which run the gamut from large to small.

The above does not cover all the important stock indexes. Other major (nonspecialized) indexes include the aforementioned New York Stock Exchange Composite Index and the Amex Major Market Index (the latter is made up of 20 NYSE-listed blue chips, 15 of which are Dow components, and is designed to be a proxy for the DJIA); the relatively new (and market value-weighted) Dow Jones Equity Index; and the Amex Market Value Index of stocks traded on the American Stock Exchange.

AMONG THE stock averages published by Dow Jones, the Dow Jones Equity Average, a 700-stock index designed to measure broader market performance and essentially compete with the S&P 500, has its value, to be sure. But since it is new and has not historically been important, we will focus instead, where comparisons with the Dow are appropriate, on the S&P 500. The S&P has been widely used to measure investment performance as a surrogate for the broader big-stock market.

Other Dow stock averages include the specialized Utility and Transportation stock averages and the Dow Jones Composite Index of 65 stocks, which combines the Industrial, Utility and Transportation averages.

The Dow Jones Utility Average comprises the common stocks of 15 geographically representative gas and electric utilities. Public utilities are heavily government-regulated and are permitted to raise their rates in order to meet certain cash-flow requirements. This tends to assure (but does not guarantee) their ability to pay common-stock dividends with the result that utility common stocks—and the Dow Jones Utility Average— tend to behave like bond substitutes. Utility common stocks usually have lower yields than utility bonds because the public puts more importance on the potential of common stocks to rise in price than it puts on the greater safety of bonds.

A significant drop in the Dow utilities average is like a drop in bond prices and has the same significance for the stock market. That is, it means interest rates are trending higher, which normally is negative news for ordinary common stocks.

The Dow Jones Transportation Average is made up of 20 air, truck and rail shippers and its principal significance is its use in the Dow Theory—a time-honored if controversial formulation arguing that when both the DJIA and the Dow Jones Transportation Average reach new highs or new lows a market trend is afoot. Conversely, when they don't, the theory goes, the market, whatever it's doing, will resume its existing trading range. The underlying logic of the Dow Theory is that transportation companies, which ship raw materials to factories and finished goods to distributors, provide a confirming indication of manufacturing and business activity and thus of the direction of the stock market.

I've never been much of a Dow Theory man myself. I'm

really more interested in what stocks are going to do than what the market's going to do. Whatever you think of the Dow Theory, enough people believe in it for it to have some influence on market sentiment.

When it comes to sentiment, I reserve mine for Charlie Dow, the guy who gave us a Dow to beat.

SO TWO limitations of the Dow have to do with its being price-weighted (or, if you prefer, unweighted) and composed exclusively of blue chips, which are not always representative of the broader market.

A third limitation traditionally cited is that the 30 stocks don't adequately represent all the principal industrial sectors of the economy. Our discussions of the individual companies making up the Dow Industrials will show that the diversification of the component companies and recent substitutions have largely made that criticism anachronistic.

Until the mid-1980s, categories commonly cited as unrepresented included major U.S. banks; hotel and entertainment; media; transportation; and to a lesser extent electronics and health care.

I would point to General Electric's acquisition of RCA with its NBC subsidiary and Westinghouse Electric's Group W activities as giving the Dow strong representation in entertainment and media. Kodak's acquisition and expansion of Sterling Drug and Procter & Gamble's and du Pont's expanded activities in medical products and pharmaceuticals complement Merck's strength in the health-care areas. The substitution of Boeing in 1987 provides transportation representation. The addition of Coca-Cola in 1987 ties in generally to the hotel and entertainment sector.

The financial services industry has become so diversified and many Dow companies (American Express, Primerica, General Electric, Sears) so involved in financial services that there is hardly a lack of adequate representation there. Nor does there seem to be a serious lack of strength in electronics; General Motors' expanded activities have bolstered that representation.

It's my conviction that the Dow Jones Industrial Average well represents the important segments of today's economy and that its blue chip composition reflects a securities marketplace dominated by large institutional investors.

The Dow's preeminence as a market indicator is therefore based as much on current realism as on long tradition. But by virtue of its being the world's most widely watched measure of the stock market, the Dow not only provides a reading of the investor psychology driving the market but also influences the psychology that is likely to underlie its movement in the future.

An investment strategy based on the Dow and using the Dow components is thus focused on both the nerve center and the brain of the investment marketplace. What better place is there for a contrarian with a yen for simplicity to find himself? And in such good company!

PART II

THE DOW
INDUSTRIAL
STOCKS

IN THIS section we will gain an appreciation of the importance, the adaptability, and the resilience of the firms the Dow Jones Company has selected to comprise the average.

The Dow, as we know, is not without its critics, and one of their complaints is that by consisting mostly of "industrials" it inadequately reflects the American economy's service orientation and other recent developments and trends.

While it's true that the Dow Jones Company has put a higher priority over the years on continuity than on responding to short-term changes in the economic structure—that's how it has held on to its preeminence as a market barometer—this criticism ignores the dynamism of the companies themselves. Firms have themselves adapted to the changing economy even when the Dow has waited for opportunities created by mergers or other events to make substitutions reflective of the current business environment.

In response to shareholder expectations of profitability and growth, the Dow companies have modernized through internal diversification and through acquisitions and divestitures. They have recognized the need for globalization of their businesses and continue to expand their global vision. At the same time they are distinctly American enterprises, in most cases richly rooted in American tradition and yet often on the cutting edge

47

of modern technology. To the extent that the Dow retains a "smokestack America" bias, it is because manufacturing is the backbone of this country's economy. My strong belief, as I've said, is that we will see a revival of basic American industry in the 1990s. If we don't, I think we're in trouble.

THE DOW stocks can all be good investments, and the critical question of knowing when to buy and sell them for the greatest profit is the subject of later chapters.

You should read each of the following profiles as a way of becoming familiar with the Dow stocks, their history and especially their dynamism. Try to get a sense of the kinds of problems these stalwarts have encountered and solved, problems that, to contrarian investors, have been opportunities.

I've listed the companies' addresses and phone numbers at the end of this section, on pages 153–154, in case you wish to request annual reports or other company literature.

Consider each of them in the context of the megatrends of the 1990s I listed earlier—globalization of markets; cleaning up the environment; replacement and rejuvenation of the nation's crumbling highways, bridges, and other infrastructure systems; the growing need for sources of energy; revival of the manufacturing sector; increased literacy rate; the opening of Eastern European markets and expansion of the free world. I'm sure you'll think of some I haven't.

This may all sound kind of lofty for a book on how to make a buck. But it is the vital importance of the Dow companies in the larger economic and cultural framework that gives them their enormous viability. In practical terms, it turns any portfolio made up of them into a solid long-term investment. That they are run by humans, patronized by humans, and owned by humans guarantees that each and every one of them will have problems from time to time. And that's what every contrarian wakes up in the morning and thanks the good Lord for.

Here then, in capsule form, is the story of each of the 30 Dow stocks. Let's get to know them.

DJIA 30 COMPONENTS
MARKET CAPITALIZATION AND YIELD
AS OF JULY 30, 1990

Stock	Symbol	Share Price	Per-Share Div	Yield	Shares (in millions)	Market Cap
Allied-Signal	ALD	33.50	1.80	5.37%	144.00	4,824,000,000
Alcoa	AA	69.63	1.60	2.30	86.90	6,050,412,500
American Express	AXP	29.13	.92	3.16	446.70	13,010,137,500
AT&T	T	37.00	1.32	3.57	1089.00	40,293,000,000
Bethlehem Steel	BS	13.88	.40	2.88	75.70	1,050,337,500
Boeing	BA	58.63	1.00	1.71	346.20	20,295,975,000
Chevron	CHV	79.00	3.10	3.92	354.50	28,005,500,000
Coca-Cola	KO	45.75	.80	1.75	666.60	30,496,950,000
Du Pont	DD	41.63	1.60	3.84	678.40	28,238,400,000
Eastman Kodak	EK	38.50	2.00	5.19	324.40	12,489,400,000
Exxon	XON	50.75	2.40	4.73	1248.00	63,336,000,000
General Electric	GE	72.50	1.88	2.59	897.10	65,039,750,000
General Motors	GM	47.38	3.00	6.33	602.00	28,519,750,000
Goodyear	GT	27.75	1.80	6.49	58.00	1,609,500,000
IBM	IBM	112.13	4.84	4.32	574.70	64,438,237,500

Continued

(Continued)

Stock	Symbol	Share Price	Per-Share Div	Yield	Shares (in millions)	Market Cap
International Paper	IP	56.13	1.68	2.99	109.00	6,117,625,000
McDonald's	MCD	32.13	.34	1.06	358.50	11,516,812,500
Merck	MRK	89.50	2.24	2.50	391.80	35,066,100,000
3M	MMM	90.13	2.92	3.24	222.50	20,052,812,500
Navistar	NAV	4.00	.00	.00	251.30	1,005,200,000
Philip Morris	MO	47.50	1.37	2.88	923.80	43,880,500,000
Primerica	PA	31.63	.40	1.26	110.80	3,504,050,000
Procter & Gamble	PG	86.88	1.80	2.07	346.10	30,067,437,500
Sears	S	33.88	2.00	5.90	343.00	11,619,125,000
Texaco	TX	62.88	3.00	4.77	260.20	16,360,075,000
Union Carbide	UK	19.88	1.00	5.03	142.40	2,830,200,000
United Technologies	UTX	59.63	1.80	3.02	120.30	7,172,887,500
USX	X	34.38	1.40	4.07	254.80	8,758,750,000
Westinghouse	WX	36.25	1.40	3.86	291.60	10,570,500,000
Woolworth	Z	30.88	1.04	3.37	129.20	3,989,050,000

TOTAL RETURNS IN PERCENTAGES

Year	ALD	AA	AXP	T	BS	BA
1973	73.41%*	40.61	−31.24	.33	17.96	−48.96
1974	−38.97	−36.94	−39.72	−4.67	−17.65	33.00
1975	22.26	33.77	44.27	21.62	43.22	61.19
1976	24.63	51.84	12.83	32.09	28.90	88.57
1977	15.86	−16.18	−8.74	1.73	−43.96	29.54
1978	−32.01	6.49	−14.58	7.60	−2.37	287.69
1979	80.07	20.37	8.62	−5.74	15.29	9.32
1980	13.83	14.49	41.29	1.44	32.43	−10.08
1981	−14.51	−7.96	14.60	33.79	−5.78	−45.85
1982	−19.84	27.41	50.59	10.26	−11.61	56.76
1983	79.61	48.63	5.42	13.43	51.17	33.27
1984	−2.39	−14.87	19.25	15.80	−36.49	32.62
1985	40.72	7.30	44.32	34.36	−9.00	41.15
1986	−3.48	−8.90	9.41	4.80	−60.00	.14
1987	−25.11	41.55	−56.95	12.80	168.00	−30.37
1988	21.42	22.57	19.72	10.93	38.81	68.05
1989	12.86	38.79	33.67	62.43	−20.09	49.79
Cumulative	336.04%	673.74	90.50	791.80	29.61	3686.16

Year	CHV	KO	DD	EK	XON	GE
1973	−3.77%	−13.60	−7.18	−20.74	12.42	−11.57
1974	−8.44	−56.44	−38.53	−44.15	−25.99	−44.48
1975	26.50	59.49	41.47	72.08	45.13	43.00
1976	46.95	−.74	11.19	−17.01	26.93	24.15
1977	.57	−1.82	−6.65	−38.12	−4.66	−6.74
1978	27.19	22.46	10.70	19.03	8.98	−.69
1979	26.45	−16.92	2.65	−13.15	20.19	13.20
1980	82.88	3.00	10.84	51.29	56.05	26.76
1981	−9.38	11.13	−4.76	7.00	−15.06	−1.23
1982	−19.77	56.89	2.75	25.85	4.80	71.15
1983	15.70	8.08	51.64	−7.35	36.05	27.39
1984	−2.82	21.75	.77	−.91	29.39	.00
1985	29.68	40.28	43.18	10.99	30.19	32.36
1986	25.31	37.72	28.25	40.71	33.74	21.40
1987	−7.38	3.96	7.95	−24.93	−40.21	45.69
1988	21.89	20.20	5.25	−4.13	21.05	4.59
1989	54.21	76.16	44.29	−4.42	18.86	47.93
Cumulative	1020.46%	498.10	375.03	−18.74	601.05	236.81

*All stock returns throughout book exclude the effect of commissions and taxes.

Year	GM	GT	IBM	IP	MCD	MRK
1973	−36.67%	−48.54	−21.88	28.38	−25.25	−8.05
1974	−25.96	−8.82	−29.66	−27.87	−48.46	−16.09
1975	95.20	77.48	37.36	67.13	98.72	6.41
1976	45.82	14.25	28.04	22.73	−8.39	.37
1977	−11.24	−22.32	1.57	−33.58	−3.13	−16.33
1978	−4.95	1.01	13.35	−12.00	−9.60	24.87
1979	2.88	−12.09	−9.13	7.40	−5.12	9.68
1980	−4.10	34.37	10.78	20.00	14.26	19.94
1981	−9.11	27.25	−11.14	−1.13	36.18	3.50
1982	68.25	91.58	75.28	29.78	40.39	1.85
1983	23.73	−9.21	30.61	26.93	18.45	10.13
1984	17.47	−9.47	4.28	−4.62	11.47	7.33
1985	.80	26.35	29.87	−1.35	58.40	49.13
1986	.89	39.12	−20.00	52.76	14.50	82.93
1987	.57	47.10	−.08	−40.49	−26.51	29.94
1988	44.20	−11.96	9.33	12.79	10.64	11.73
1989	8.38	−11.39	−18.88	25.41	45.69	37.04
Cumulative	294.69%	256.42	118.76	181.95	261.11	665.97

Year	MMM	NAV	MO	PA	PG	S
1973	−7.67%	−28.99	−1.75	−10.04	−16.09	−29.3
1974	−39.25	−17.09	−14.95	19.62	−9.46	−37.5
1975	23.27	21.90	12.42	15.78	11.53	37.5
1976	4.66	22.38	18.62	31.51	7.51	9.4
1977	−11.35	−2.73	2.53	4.29	−5.71	−15.6
1978	34.29	26.78	17.04	−.35	6.64	−24.9
1979	−16.59	14.41	5.53	.95	−12.97	−2.3
1980	22.99	−28.75	24.36	−6.60	−2.66	−7.2
1981	−2.54	−70.75	17.16	22.72	22.21	14.6
1982	43.49	−40.35	27.84	−1.75	52.22	95.2
1983	14.40	170.59	24.25	23.73	.01	28.2
1984	−.58	−29.35	16.94	17.47	4.44	−9.7
1985	18.60	4.62	14.38	.80	26.93	28.3
1986	33.96	−44.12	67.75	.89	13.27	6.2
1987	−41.61	−10.53	22.96	.57	15.58	−10.1
1988	−.40	26.47	23.82	44.20	5.18	27.1
1989	32.63	−27.81	68.55	8.38	65.29	−1.1
Cumulative	72.26%	−85.94	1780.41	349.74	335.58	50.1

Year	TX	UK	UTX	X	WX	Z	DJIA
1973	−17.05%	−27.61	−43.71	28.62	−38.71	−37.36	−13.12
1974	−21.79	27.66	48.75	6.86	−56.73	−42.42	−23.14
1975	21.56	53.53	48.28	78.43	43.55	157.24	44.40
1976	27.27	5.30	72.73	−9.91	39.10	22.50	22.72
1977	2.70	−29.23	−3.47	−32.26	8.56	−22.04	−12.71
1978	−6.72	−10.29	13.94	−27.49	−2.87	10.07	2.69
1979	29.82	32.09	16.27	−10.08	26.95	36.90	10.52
1980	74.72	27.00	46.98	50.57	54.16	5.67	21.41
1981	−25.42	8.81	−27.62	28.79	−7.85	−20.00	−3.40
1982	3.41	9.32	41.38	−23.85	59.51	53.75	25.79
1983	24.90	25.09	32.56	49.40	45.47	42.71	25.65
1984	3.48	−36.03	3.81	−10.70	−1.02	10.46	1.08
1985	−3.30	102.08	24.55	6.12	74.74	67.51	32.78
1986	29.58	48.85	8.34	−14.37	28.31	32.53	26.92
1987	5.92	3.33	−23.32	43.95	−7.82	−7.39	6.02
1988	43.29	13.33	25.98	2.52	9.66	54.52	15.95
1989	37.11	3.19	35.81	27.01	44.99	27.44	31.71
Cumulative	466.85%	450.51	904.87	227.45	660.00	1007.55	499.35

ALLIED-SIGNAL INC. (ALD)

In his book *One Up on Wall Street,* Peter Lynch calls this company, formerly Allied Chemical, an example of "diworseification." *Moody's Industrial Manual* uses no fewer than 420 lines of fine print to record all its acquisitions and divestitures, most of them in the last ten years.

If corporate genealogy doesn't do it for you, try a little romance. Remember Mary Cunningham, the brainy Harvard MBA who helped young William Agee of Bendix Corporation attempt a hostile takeover of Martin Marietta, which then countertendered, adding the term "Pac-Man defense" to the colorful argot of high finance? Prior to their marriage in 1982, the pair had appeared as often in the gossip columns as in the financial pages.

Unlike Cunningham and Agee, Bendix and Martin Marietta never did merge. A white knight in the form of Allied came to the rescue, acquiring all of Bendix and 39 percent of Marietta, which was later spun off. Bendix, a world leader in brakes and other equipment for the aerospace and auto industries, is now Allied's most profitable division.

Allied-Signal was created in 1985 when Allied Corporation acquired The Signal Companies, a diversified group originally (but no longer) involved in oil and gas activities (Signal Oil & Gas Companies). In 1986, Allied spun off a collection of assorted businesses known now as The Henley Group (dubbed then "Dingman's Dogs," after the head of the management group that formed it). Even after that transaction, a *Wall Street Journal* headline read "Allied-Signal merger yields few benefits."

Allied-Signal had 1989 sales of $12 billion from three groups: Aerospace (40 percent), Automotive (35 percent) and Engineered Materials, which include synthetic carpet fibers, solvents and such (25 percent).

The Aerospace sector, which derives about 55 percent of its revenues from commercial customers and the balance from government contracts, is the world's leading manufacturer of auxiliary power units for commercial transports and high-performance military aircraft, and of environmental control systems for all types of aircraft. It also leads the world in aircraft wheels and brakes. It is among the top producers of turboprop and turbofan engines used in the regional airliner and corporate jet markets.

Allied-Signal Automotive is the world's number one independent maker of passenger car and light truck brakes and components, turbochargers and friction materials. It also makes safety restraints, filters and sparkplugs. It supplies both air and hydraulic drum and disc brakes and related components to the medium and heavy truck markets.

Engineered Materials produces nylon and polyester carpet fibers, fluorine products, plastics, refrigerants and solvents, films, laminates and other specialty products for markets ranging from home furnishings and packaging to electronics and telecommunications.

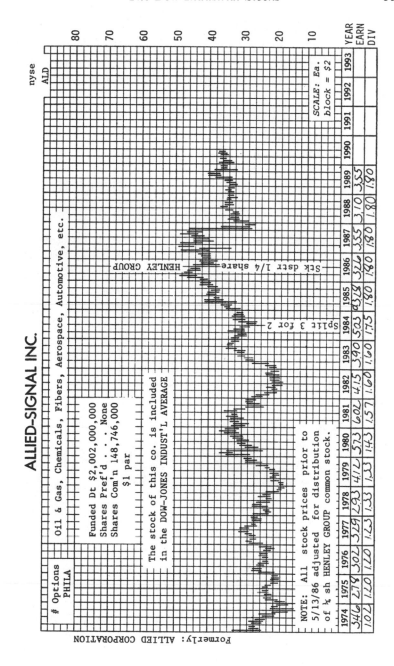

ALLIED-SIGNAL INC.

Oil & Gas, Chemicals, Fibers, Aerospace, Automotive, etc.

Options
PHILA

Funded Dt $2,002,000,000
Shares Pref'd . . : None
Shares Com'n 148,746,000
$1 par

The stock of this co. is included
in the DOW-JONES INDUST'L AVERAGE

NOTE: All stock prices prior to
5/13/86 adjusted for distribution
of ¼ sh HENLEY GROUP common stock.

nyse
ALD

SCALE: Ea.
block = $2

Split 3 for 2

Stk dstr 1/4 share

HENLEY GROUP

Formerly: ALLIED CORPORATION

	1974	1975	1976	1977	1978	1979	1980	1981	1982	1983	1984	1985	1986	1987	1988	1989	1990	1991	1992	1993
YEAR																				
EARN	3.46	2.79	3.02	3.29	2.93	4.12	5.73	6.02	4.15	3.90	5.03	2.18	3.26	3.55	3.10	3.55				
DIV	1.02	1.20	1.20	1.23	1.33	1.33	1.43	1.57	1.60	1.60	1.75	1.80	1.80	1.80	1.80	1.80				

Like some other Dow stocks we'll meet, Allied is so diversified the company really defies classifications like "cyclical" or "growth." Its 1980s performance was erratic mainly because of its diworseification activities, which are now apparently behind it.

Public relations people have a way of using words that say nothing. Here is a great example from Allied's 1989 annual report. It appears under the portentous heading Planning for Peace: "At Allied-Signal, which is involved in a number of government programs—both as a prime contractor and subcontractor—this new era will have an impact. To what extent, only time will tell."

Allied owns 40 percent of Union Texas Petroleum Holdings, Inc., a company with large oil and natural gas reserves. In May 1990 it was announced that Union Texas was for sale and that interested buyers had offered a price estimated at over $2 billion. If that happens, it will be a handsome windfall for Allied-Signal.

This stock has not performed very well over the years, but it pays a handsome yield and is interesting for both current return and future growth potential, and for the value of its assets.

ALUMINUM COMPANY OF AMERICA/ALCOA (AA)

Chances are you're either wearing, riding in, sitting on or about to drink from something made using aluminum. Maybe you're even playing with it. According to the *World Book Encyclopedia,* aluminum had its first commercial application in the form of a toy rattle made for the baby son of Napoleon III in the 1850s.

A century later, in 1959, Aluminum Company of America was added to the Dow. It replaced National Steel in the aver-

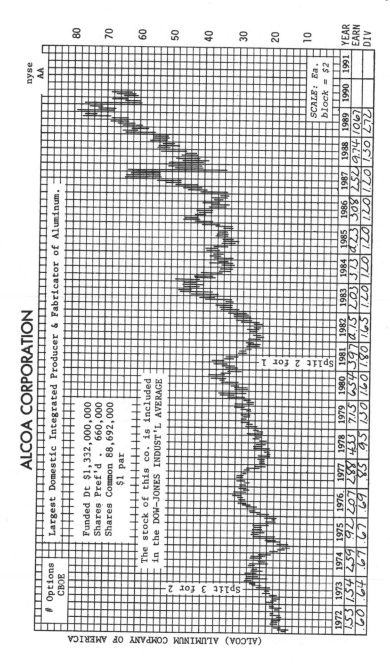

ALCOA CORPORATION

age, which continued to claim the country's two largest steel producers, United States Steel and Bethlehem Steel.

Alcoa has mining, refining, processing, fabricating and selling locations in 20 countries and is the world's largest aluminum producer, shipping some 15 percent of the free world total. Aluminum is smelted from alumina refined from bauxite. Over a third of Alcoa's sales are primary aluminum ingot and alumina. Twenty-eight percent of sales are aluminum and aluminum alloy that is fabricated into sheet, bars, wire and other forms and sold to the transportation, building, industrial and consumer products industries. End products range from various construction materials to aircraft. Alcoa's forged aluminum truck wheels lead the Australian, European, Japanese, and United States markets. About 30 percent of sales are sheet aluminum used for beverage and food cans and bottle caps.

Aluminum is a growing segment of the packaging industry primarily because it is recyclable, and Alcoa is in that business too, with 1,600 affiliated recycling centers in the United States, the United Kingdom and Australia. In one area, though— bottle caps (called closures in the trade)—plastic is overtaking aluminum in the United States. But don't worry, Alcoa is in plastics as well. Thirty percent of closure shipments in 1989 were plastic, and Alcoa's plastic closure capacity was increased at four plants in the United States and Europe.

In 1989, Alcoa had sales of $11 billion and record earnings of just under $1 billion. Aluminum is enjoying a boom period and Alcoa is taking the opportunity to absorb costs and make its plant more efficient in preparation for the next downturn.

With commercial airline fleets being replaced and increasing use of recyclable aluminum in the packaging industry, Alcoa should continue to show strong sales and earnings.

As a cyclical growth company Alcoa's stock has moved upward but in a ratchet pattern—it has more than doubled in price since 1987's crash low. Alcoa does not pay a stellar dividend, but it has growth and market-timing potential. It could fall heavily during a recession. Alcoa was made to order for the strategies we'll be discussing later on.

AMERICAN EXPRESS COMPANY (AXP)

I always get a kick out of reading annual reports. It seems the worse things are, the more grandiose their language.

"Passport to Service," American Express Company's 1989 annual report, says in its introduction: "The relationships we explore are as momentous as our performance against a backdrop of upheaval in a land of a billion people and as humble as a helping hand between two individuals."

The word "momentous" was still in Chairman James Robinson's mind when *The Wall Street Journal* interviewed him in March of 1990 and concluded an article by saying: "As for himself, 'I guess I've had to take care of some fairly momentous decisions, huh?' he says reflecting on the troubles of the past 18 months. 'I do the best I can, and I enjoy the support of a very strong board.'"

Most of us think of American Express as the credit card we can't leave home without—there are in fact some 25 million in wallets and purses around the world. This and other "travel-related services" amount to just about a third of American Express Company's $25 billion in revenues—but they accounted for almost 75 percent of net income at the end of the decade, and herein lies this company's problem.

American Express Company's nontravel revenues derive from a variety of financial services, including Shearson Lehman Hutton, acquired and expanded in the 1980s and the second largest Wall Street firm after Merrill Lynch; IDS Financial Services, a huge financial planning, insurance and mutual fund organization; and American Express Bank, Ltd., which provides a range of banking services through 100 offices in 43 countries worldwide. These activities were assembled as part of

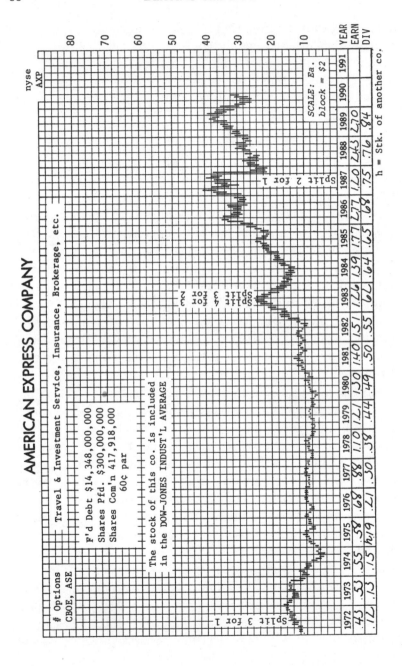

AMERICAN EXPRESS COMPANY

Travel & Investment Service, Insurance, Brokerage, etc.

nyse
AXP

Options
CBOE, ASE

F'd Debt $14,348,000,000
Shares Pfd. $300,000,000
Shares Com'n 417,918,000
60¢ par

The stock of this co. is included
in the DOW-JONES INDUST'L AVERAGE

SCALE: Ea.
block = $2

h = Stk. of another co.

YEAR	1972	1973	1974	1975	1976	1977	1978	1979	1980	1981	1982	1983	1984	1985	1986	1987	1988	1989	1990	1991
EARN	.43	.53	.55	.58	.68	.88	1.10	1.21	1.30	1.40	1.51	1.26	1.39	1.77	2.77	1.20	2.43	2.70		
DIV	.12	.13	.15	.19	.21	.30	.38	.44	.49	.50	.55	.62	.64	.65	.68	.75	.76	.84		

Split 3 for 1

Split 4 for 1

Split 3 for 1

Split 2 for 1

a grand vision that James Robinson described in the early 1980s: "By 1990 the typical consumer may have a stockbroker in California, a banker in New York, an insurance agent in Maryland, and a real estate agent jetting back and forth from Chicago to Boston. All on the American Express Card, of course."

Things haven't worked out quite that way. For many reasons synergies that looked good on paper didn't jell in practice and the Shearson unit, not alone among Wall Street firms, was beset with junk bond and bridge loan writedowns, bad loans, slow brokerage business and massive layoffs.

The good news is that American Express has enough money to take the lumps currently. A blue chip if ever there was one, the company has paid continuous dividends for 120 years, although the dividend rate is below that of the Dow Industrials on average.

As to the future, Robinson has lashed himself to the mast, saying the Shearson problem "is fixable and that's what we're going to do." He has realigned management and affirmed the corporate commitment to Shearson by purchasing the 30 percent interest held by the public. We'll see how he does.

In June 1990, Shearson Lehman Hutton was restructured as two units: one, called Lehman Brothers in a revival of one of the Street's most venerable names, is responsible for investment banking and capital markets; the other, called Shearson Lehman Brothers, is responsible for retail brokerage and money management activities. There is speculation that one purpose of the move was to facilitate the sale of one or both units.

American Express Company's annual report rhetoric is not entirely without justification. The American Express card and traveler's check represent one of the greatest business franchises in the world, and the opening of Eastern Europe, which among other things means tourism and trade, can only be a benefit.

(The value of the American Express credit card and traveler's check franchises was recognized some years back by no lesser an investor than Warren Buffett. In 1963, an American

Express subsidiary found itself potentially liable for hundreds of millions of dollars of damage claims arising from the sale of nonexistent salad oil. When American Express stock plummeted, Buffett bought a 5 percent position, representing something like 40 percent of his own capital, and watched it quintuple in the next five years. Buffett's capitalization on the famous "salad oil scandal" provides an excellent case in point of how a Dow stock in adversity can be an opportunity.)

If American Express can either get its Shearson and Lehman units on track or get rid of them, the stock, which has languished in recent years, could come up roses.

AMERICAN TELEPHONE & TELEGRAPH COMPANY/AT&T (T)

For many years AT&T, which has a record of consistent dividends dating from 1881, was considered the premier "widows and orphans" stock. Although much has changed since the court-ordered breakup of Ma Bell in 1984, to this day more people own telephone than any other American stock.

The modern chronicle of AT&T began in 1956. By then Ma Bell, or the Bell System as it was more formally known, had become an international telecommunications behemoth consisting of American Telephone & Telegraph Company (AT&T), the parent company of 22 operating subsidiaries; Bell Telephone Laboratories, engaged in research; and Western Electric, a manufacturer of equipment.

The fateful development that was to be the genesis of the new AT&T seemed relatively innocuous at the time. The Justice Department, which had been looming over Ma Bell like a tornado cloud for years, got the court in 1956 to issue a consent decree confining Western Electric's manufacturing to Bell System and government equipment and restricting AT&T from operating activities other than common carrier communications. Although this meant abandoning its promising cellular

AMERICAN TELEPHONE & TELEGRAPH CO.

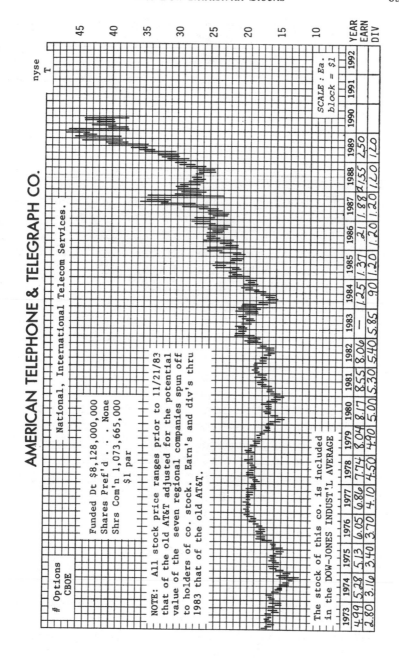

nyse
T

National, International Telecom Services.

Options
CBOE

Funded Dt $8,128,000,000
Shares Pref'd . . . None
Shrs Com'n 1,073,665,000
$1 par

NOTE: All stock price ranges prior to 11/21/83
that of the old AT&T adjusted for the potential
value of the seven regional companies spun off
to holders of co. stock. Earn's and div's thru
1983 that of the old AT&T.

The stock of this co. is included
in the DOW-JONES INDUST'L AVERAGE

SCALE : Ea.
block = $1

YEAR	1973	1974	1975	1976	1977	1978	1979	1980	1981	1982	1983	1984	1985	1986	1987	1988	1989	1990	1991	1992
EARN	4.99	5.28	5.13	6.05	6.86	7.74	8.04	8.17	8.55	8.06	–	1.25	1.37	.21	1.88	2.55	2.50			
DIV	2.80	3.16	3.40	3.70	4.10	4.50	4.90	5.00	5.30	5.40	5.85	.90	1.20	1.20	1.20	1.20	1.20			

phone activities, it was preferable to the antitrust suit hanging over Western Electric.

But in the 1960s, two things happened.

The first was the introduction by non-Bell System makers of decorative telephones that replicated antiques, bananas, Snoopy—or were otherwise novel. The second development was the emergence of competitors in the long-distance business, such as Microwave Communications, Inc. (MCI), that offered cheaper rates if you used extra code numbers.

In response to the first development, the Federal Communications Commission (FCC) opened the way for an "interconnect industry" by abolishing all rules prohibiting AT&T customers from attaching their own phones to AT&T equipment. Score one against Ma Bell. In response to the second, the FCC authorized specialized carrier operations like MCI's. Score two. But Ma Bell didn't take it sitting down.

In 1974 the Justice Department charged Ma Bell with blocking both the interconnect and specialized carrier industries and filed an antitrust suit aimed at breaking up the Bell System.

Ma Bell now had the worst of all worlds: its core businesses, the sale of phones and phone service, were being threatened by antitrust action, and the consent decree made it impossible to enter new businesses. It was regulated like a monopoly—forced, for example, to provide service where it wasn't profitable—but it lacked a monopoly's immunity from antitrust actions and competition in areas where operations were profitable.

The next development put the FCC and the Justice Department at loggerheads and left AT&T squarely between a rock and a hard place. In 1980, responding to lobbying from Ma Bell, the FCC decided that starting in 1983 the company could enter into some unregulated businesses at arm's length—that is, through an unsubsidized subsidiary. But the Justice Department sued to block even this.

In 1982, realizing it couldn't live forever under the cloud of antitrust action, Ma Bell and Justice came to the agreement that would define the AT&T we know today.

Under its terms, AT&T would divest itself of its 22 local

operating companies. It would keep Western Electric, Bell Labs and its long-distance service. And it would be given the right to enter unregulated businesses through an unsubsidized subsidiary first called American Bell and later renamed AT&T Information Systems (now making computers).

AT&T's 22 operating subsidiaries became seven regional holding companies (RHCs), familiar now as Nynex, Ameritech, Pacific Telesis, Bell Atlantic, US West, Southwestern Bell and Bell South, which are regulated monopolies providing local phone service through subsidiaries (they are the Baby Bells, or BOCs, for Bell operating companies).

The ownership of the RHCs was passed directly to the shareholders of AT&T by a distribution of one share of each RHC for every 10 shares of AT&T common-held. All those widows and orphans made out very well.

If there was ever any question that AT&T would retain its dominance as a long-distance carrier, it was eliminated in 1986 with "equal access," the abandonment of the extra digits required by MCI and other competitors. Local phone customers not already using the services of competitors were invited to choose from among AT&T and its competitors in the long-distance field.

Although it was already entrenched and in retrospect had little to worry about, AT&T didn't take any chances. Instead it mounted a half-billion-dollar advertising and marketing blitz to keep the business. Remember the almost constant and always confounding solicitations from AT&T and its competitors telling how much more efficient and economical your service would be if you switched (or stayed)?

Anyway, helped by the BOCs, which in many cases referred the bewildered and undecided to AT&T by default, AT&T walked off with 80 percent of the long-distance market. Competition continues to exist and to nibble away at its market share, but AT&T has been gaining long-distance sales every year.

AT&T had total sales of $36.1 billion and profits of $2.7 billion in 1989, with 54 percent of revenues coming from long-distance operations and 40 percent from equipment.

Its stock has had a bumpy ride up since the 1984 breakup (although it exploded upward after the '87 crash, it has lately been soft again), as the investing public read various scenarios into the developments surrounding the company. But looking at the 1990s, it's hard to imagine a company better positioned. It has a profitable and expanding business base at home that will benefit from its recent replacement of old equipment with a state-of-the-art digital communications network. It has top-notch research and development capability in the inseparable and exciting areas of telecommunications and computer technology.

Fiber-optics could revolutionize home and office communications, and AT&T is intensely involved in critical areas of that technology. It also recently introduced the AT&T Universal Card, a bank credit card, and plans to expand its role in the growing financial services sector.

Unregulated overseas, it has both the organizational (through joint ventures) and physical base to exploit opportunities both in products and services (including cellular) in Europe in 1992 and elsewhere. Even its sometimes struggling computer division will benefit for most of the 1990s from a U.S. Air Force contract valued at $5 billion.

I'm not sure I'd put a widow or orphan in any stock, but the new AT&T would be one I'd look at. Its current yield is not as high as those of the Baby Bells or the Dow average, but it has high growth potential.

BETHLEHEM STEEL CORPORATION (BS)

No industry better exemplifies "smokestack America"—and its decline—than steel. And no company has done more to reverse the decline than Bethlehem Steel.

The story goes that Charles Schwab (the steel magnate, not the discount broker) bought Bethlehem Steel in 1903 because banker J.P. Morgan tried to clip his wings as president of United States Steel after hearing he had been seen at the gaming tables in Monte Carlo.

Young Schwab's gamble with Bethlehem took guts, since he reportedly gave up an annual income of $2 million a year. That might not look like much to a Wall Street junk bond trader of the 1980s, but it was a lot of money then.

Schwab built Bethlehem into the nation's second largest steel producer, which it remained until LTV (now operating in Chapter 11 reorganization) bought out Republic Steel in 1984 and passed it. Bethlehem calls itself the second largest *integrated* steel producer, referring to activities ranging from raw material production to railroad and lake shipping operations.

The steel industry is extremely cyclical, its fortunes hinged particularly to the construction, capital goods and automotive industries. In America, the steel industry has also been badly hurt in recent years by foreign imports, most importantly from Japan and West Germany, but also from Brazil, South Korea and Third World countries. Old and technologically obsolete plants have hampered its ability to produce cost-effectively.

No exception to these misfortunes, Bethlehem, which sold at a high of $60 in 1958 and is selling at $14 as this is written, lost money from 1982 through 1986 and suspended its dividend in 1986 for the first time in 46 years. (Notably, Bethlehem was the best-performing Dow stock in 1987, the year of the crash!)

Bethlehem bit the bullet. It closed its huge and unprofitable Lackawanna, New York, mill, laying off some 7,000 workers, and it has spent nearly $1 billion modernizing its facilities since 1987. During the same period it has taken major strides in reducing its debt, which at the end of 1989 was a very comfortable 27 percent of equity.

A potential $1.6 billion pension liability hanging over the company in 1987 had been reduced to under $900 million by 1989, and Bethlehem has operating-loss carryforwards of nearly $1 billion, making future profits tax-free to that extent.

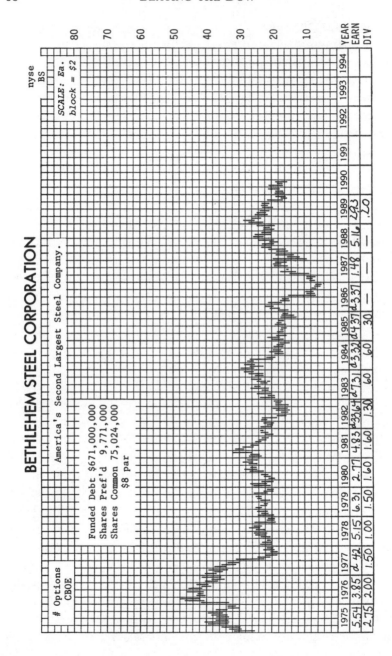

Bethlehem's 1989 sales of $5.2 billion were 93 percent basic steel operations. It is strongest in capital goods, where demand is expected to overtake consumer products in the 1990s.

With modern facilities, import quotas in place until 1992, a weakening dollar to encourage exports and discourage imports, a recently signed 50-month contract with United Steel Workers, and reduced industry capacity, Bethlehem is a turnaround situation looking better all the time.

At six times earnings and with its dividend restored, the stock is cheap. Of course, it is a cyclical stock and much depends on an uncertain near-term economic outlook, particularly as it affects automobiles. But you know how I feel about the nineties as the decade of the flowering of smokestack America.

THE BOEING COMPANY (BA)

Aerospace is one of the few industries in which the United States still leads the world, and Boeing is the undisputed leader of the industry.

Cash-rich, with a backlog of orders totaling around $90 billion, Boeing is enviably positioned to capitalize on the worldwide renewal of commercial airline fleets in the 1990s. On the down side, Boeing is also an important defense contractor and subject to the effects of cutbacks in defense spending.

Boeing was founded just before World War I by a lumber executive named William Boeing. During World War II, it was the leading producer of bombers, including the B-29 Super Fortress that dropped the atomic bomb on Hiroshima.

Although jet engine technology had been developed during the 1940s, noise and high fuel requirements had to be weighed against jets' greater speed in the commercial market. Boeing pioneered commercial jet aircraft; its 707, which could travel nonstop across the Atlantic for the first time, was used for the

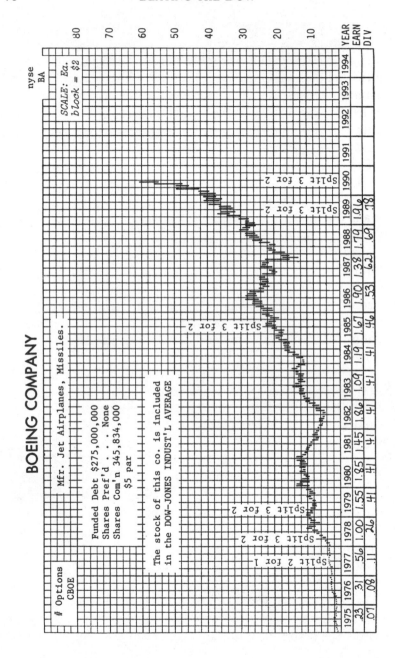

BOEING COMPANY

nyse
BA

Mfr. Jet Airplanes, Missiles.

SCALE: Ea.
block = $2

Options
CBOE

Funded Debt $275,000,000
Shares Pref'd . . . None
Shares Com'n 345,834,000
$5 par

The stock of this co. is included
in the DOW-JONES INDUST'L AVERAGE

Split 3 for 2 (1990)
Split 3 for 2 (1989)
Split 3 for 2 (1985)
Split 3 for 2 (1979)
Split 3 for 2 (1978)
Split 2 for 1 (1977)

	1975	1976	1977	1978	1979	1980	1981	1982	1983	1984	1985	1986	1987	1988	1989
YEAR															
EARN	.23	.31	.56	1.00	1.55	1.85	1.45	1.86	1.09	1.19	1.67	1.90	1.38	1.79	1.96
DIV	.07	.08	.11	.26	.41	.41	.41	.41	.41	.41	.46	.53	.62	.69	.78

first scheduled passenger jet service flight in 1958, between New York and London.

The development in the early 1960s of quieter, more fuel-efficient and far more powerful fan jet engines, inspired by the Pentagon's plans for the gargantuan C-5A cargo plane, led to the first Boeing 747 jumbo jet, built after Pan Am's Juan Trippe gambled his company on the idea of transporting 350 or more passengers at a time between continents.

The 1970s saw a shakeup and shakeout in the airframe industry as competitors like McDonnell Douglas and Lockheed entered the widebody market with their somewhat smaller DC-10 and L-1011 airbuses capable of carrying up to 250 passengers 2,100 miles and later to be introduced in extended-range versions.

But by the mid-1970s, oil prices were on the rise again and the airlines began looking to replace their aging, narrow-body Boeing 707s, 727s, and Douglas DC-8s and DC-9s, and to add more fuel-efficient widebodies to their fleets. Boeing quickly established predominance with a $3 billion commitment to develop two midsized aircraft: a narrow-body 757 and a widebody 767, each accommodating about 200 passengers on trips of 2,000 miles. Both met FAA requirements for extended-range operations and the 767 exists in a model that can fly intercontinental routes. In the mid-1980s, oil prices plummeted, putting the carriers in a financial position to go ahead with long-delayed plans to modernize their fleets.

After several delays, 1989 saw delivery of the first 747-400, which features digital electronics and other technical improvements and can fly 400 passengers more than 8,000 miles, permitting nonstop service between destinations such as New York–Seoul, Los Angeles–Sydney and London–Tokyo. The 747-400 will also be available in a transport version starting in 1993.

The 737-500, the latest addition to Boeing's short-range aircraft, will be delivered in 1990. The 737, offered in three versions, is the bestselling jetliner in commercial aviation history.

With Lockheed out of commercial production altogether and McDonnell Douglas plagued by high development costs and declining defense business, the clear beneficiary has been Boeing.

In April 1990, Boeing announced plans to finance the $4 billion development of a new 767-X that, with 300 seats, will be larger than its 767 but smaller than the four-engine 747. That announcement ended speculation that Boeing would become partners with three Japanese aerospace companies, thus aiding Japan's effort to become a world power in the industry. If it goes ahead with the new plane, Boeing expects to deliver the 767-X, which will be redesignated the 777, in 1995.

Boeing's 1989 sales were $20.3 billion, about 45 percent exports. It is a relative newcomer to the Dow, replacing Inco Ltd. in March 1987. Higher oil prices will affect the airline industry adversely and possibly cause reduced aircraft orders.

CHEVRON CORPORATION (CHV)

When I pull into an Exxon, Amoco, Mobil or Chevron station, I sometimes forget they all have a common ancestor in John D. Rockefeller's Standard Oil Company.

Chevron was the divestiture that became Standard Oil of California (Socal) and was later renamed to make peace with other Standard Oil offspring operating in the same territories.

It was also the company that, in 1984, became the white knight that saved Gulf Oil from the hands of corporate predator T. Boone Pickens. Up until then, a lot of people thought Gulf was too big to eat. At the time, it was the biggest corporate acquisition in American history.

An oil analyst I know says of the industry in general: "When business is good, the oil business is very, very good. When business is bad, the oil business is still good." (Gasoline, of course, is an oil product).

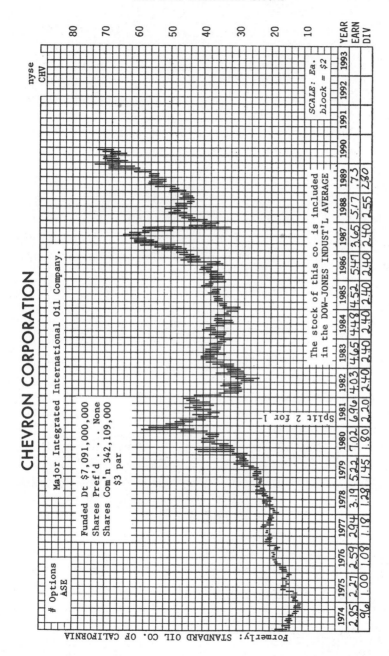

CHEVRON CORPORATION

nyse
CHV

Major Integrated International Oil Company.

Funded Dt $7,091,000,000
Shares Pref'd . . . None
Shares Com'n 342,109,000
$3 par

Options
ASE

Split 2 for 1

Formerly: STANDARD OIL CO. OF CALIFORNIA

SCALE: Ea.
block = $2

The stock of this co. is included
in the DOW-JONES INDUST'L AVERAGE

	1974	1975	1976	1977	1978	1979	1980	1981	1982	1983	1984	1985	1986	1987	1988	1989	1990	1991	1992	1993
YEAR																				
EARN	2.85	2.27	2.59	2.94	3.19	5.22	7.02	6.96	4.03	4.65	4.48	4.52	5.47	3.65	5.17	.73				
DIV	.96	1.00	1.08	1.18	1.28	1.45	1.80	2.20	2.40	2.40	2.40	2.40	2.40	2.40	2.55	2.80				

Given that everything is relative, the "oil patch" has had its high and low moments over the last 20 years and there is no lack of excitement at present. A high point (though most oil executives won't admit it) was the early seventies, when the Organization of Petroleum Exporting Companies (OPEC) cartel stopped shipping to the U.S. to protest our support of Israel in the Middle East war, then hiked prices. That drove domestic prices, and domestic oil company profits, sky-high.

Shortages in the spring and summer of 1979, prompted by the Iranian revolution, affected both prices and supply. Remember the gas lines? More than one American got punched in the nose for cutting in on somebody who had been waiting for three hours to get to a pump. Again the domestic producers had an opportunity to "replenish reserves," as they would prefer to have such windfall profits understood.

But a double whammy in a single decade was a little too much for the American public. Rarely known to do anything halfway, Americans went all out to save energy. Cars got smaller and more fuel-efficient, the highway speed limit was reduced to save gas, and we even started a new bureaucracy in the form of the quasipublic (and now defunct) Synfuels Corporation, funded by Congress to develop synthetic fuels.

All that slashed demand and, combined with a recession it helped cause, sent oil prices plunging in the early 1980s, first in the U.S., then all around the world. Down, too, went the prices of the stocks of domestic oil producers.

Enter T. Boone Pickens, who would be followed by other corporate raiders he inspired, such as Carl Icahn (see USX Corporation). These clever fellows used resourceful if sometimes questionable financing tactics to acquire companies with huge asset values at ridiculously low market prices.

Three of the majors are in the Dow group—Chevron, Exxon, and Texaco—and other Dow companies were affected, like du Pont (Conoco) and USX (Marathon Oil).

Now, as I write, oil-rich Iraq, pressured to defray debts incurred in its war with Iran, has invaded neighboring Kuwait in a move aimed at domination of Middle Eastern oil production. This aggression has so far been met with an unprecedented United Nations Security Council vote to ban trade with Iraq which is being enforced by a military interdiction in which the United States has been joined by other countries. Crude oil prices in the commodity markets have, in the days since the invasion, soared to $28 a barrel. Just weeks before the occupation, the OPEC cartel had met and established a target price of $21 a barrel.

That the situation is complex and the future unclear is summed up in a headline that more than one news organization has been unable to resist: "Between Iraq and a hard place."

Whatever eventuates from the current crisis, and whether it is OPEC or Iraq that determines prices in the future, the basic economic realities of the worldwide petroleum industry remain.

The demand is always there. Oil is the source of energy that powers our transportation, heats our homes and businesses, runs the generators that turn on our lights, and is the raw material for many of our key industries, such as chemicals, textiles, drugs and plastics.

But the supply is limited to discovered reserves and by the technology used to exploit them.

There is apparently no end to the oil in the Middle East, but even there it has to be found and then pumped out of the ground. If OPEC or whoever controls oil production there were to glut the world market, it would 1) drive prices down and reduce revenues to OPEC countries, and 2) cause OPEC producers the unwelcome expense of finding and exploiting additional reserves.

If, on the other hand, OPEC withheld oil from the world marketplace it would 1) cause non-OPEC producers (collectively called "marginal producers") to step up exploration and drilling efforts, thus bringing more capacity into the market, and 2) risk reviving the energy conservation craze we saw in the eighties.

Obviously, neither alternative is in OPEC's interest. OPEC

contrives, therefore, to keep crude oil prices just high enough. And who benefits from high enough oil prices? Who else but Chevron, Exxon, Texaco and the other domestic oil producers? Which is not to say oil prices aren't volatile. OPEC's efforts to balance greed with realism have always allowed for rather significant short-term swings, and there are many other factors in the mix—such as weather conditions and speculation, not to mention the state of the general economy.

But long-term demand for oil as an energy source is steadily growing, supply is steadily diminishing, and there is nothing on the technological horizon to change that.

I like oil. How about Chevron in particular?

When oil prices are low, companies typically cut back on exploration and drilling, which means that when prices come back, those with big reserves are in a position to prosper. Chevron has sizeable reserves and should do well when prices, recently relatively low, rebound, which they were starting to do even before the Persian Gulf crisis. But it is also committed to a major asset restructuring involving the sale of unprofitable units and the upgrading of existing exploration and production facilities. This and the debt it took on to acquire Gulf have been a drag on earnings in the last few years.

Chevron recently acquired Tenneco's natural gas properties in Mexico, which puts it in good shape to benefit from projected increases in the volume and prices of natural gas sold in North America.

Its core market continues to be southern California, where proposed environmental legislation might be a future problem.

Chevron ranks number three among U.S. oil companies with sales of $29.4 billion in 1989. It is well established in the eastern hemisphere (Calco gasoline stations). It pays a nice fat yield. Its stock took off between 1986 and 1987, crashed hard, and then reached new all-time highs even before the Iraqi invasion crisis.

As I said, I like oil.

THE COCA-COLA COMPANY (KO)

It is just possible that there is nobody in the civilized world who hasn't heard of Coca-Cola, a brand name that has become synonymous with almost anything that is popular and ubiquitous. If you don't drink Coke, you may well drink one of the company's other products, like Tab, Sprite, Minute Maid juice, or Hi-C.

The formula for Coca-Cola was invented by an Atlanta pharmacist from coca leaves and kola nuts in 1886. The original formula contained just a touch of cocaine, but that was eliminated in 1903. Code-named Merchandise 7X, the formula for Coke remains one of the world's most closely guarded secrets. When an Indian court demanded the company turn it over to its local bottlers, Coca-Cola pulled out of India.

Marketed like nothing before or since, Coca-Cola was known all over the world by World War II. Ike liked it, making it a staple on military bases, which also meant setting up plants all over the globe to put it in the familiar green bottles.

Coke's nemesis, Pepsi-Cola, had been kicking around since the 1890s, but the famous "cola wars" really didn't begin until the 1950s. As Vice President Richard Nixon was shaking his finger at Nikita Khrushchev at the exhibition of American products in Moscow in 1959, Khrushchev was sipping a Pepsi for all the television world to see. That publicity coup was staged by Don Kendall, no mean marketer himself, who would later be Chairman of Pepsico, Inc. "Lifestyle" advertising by both companies in the 1960s, built on themes like "the Pepsi generation" and "Coke is the real thing," heightened the rivalry. By the 1980s Coke's predominant market share was being seriously threatened, despite its great successes with Diet Coke and caffeine-free varieties.

In 1985 Coca-Cola decided to meet the Pepsi challenge by making the first change ever in its century-old formula and introducing the "New Coke," with a smoother, sweeter, more

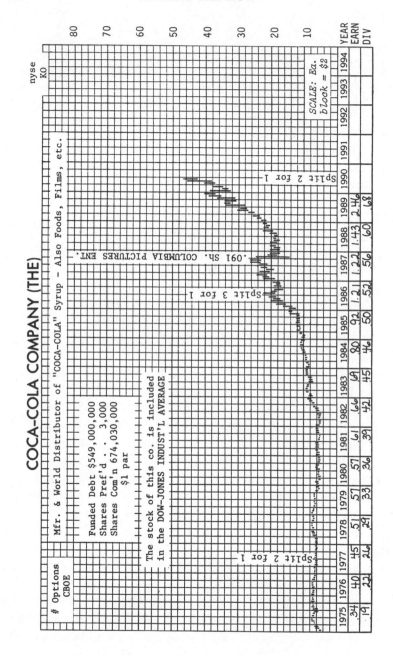

COCA-COLA COMPANY (THE)

nyse KO

Options
CBOE

Mfr. & World Distributor of "COCA-COLA" Syrup – Also Foods, Films, etc.

Funded Debt $549,000,000
Shares Pref'd . . 3,000
Shares Com'n 674,030,000
        $1 par

The stock of this co. is included
in the DOW-JONES INDUST'L AVERAGE

Split 2 for 1
Split 3 for 1
Split 2 for 1

091 Sh. COLUMBIA PICTURES ENT.

SCALE: Ea.
block = $2

	1975	1976	1977	1978	1979	1980	1981	1982	1983	1984	1985	1986	1987	1988	1989	1990	1991	1992	1993	1994
EARN	.34	.40	.45	.51	.57	.57	.61	.66	.61	.80	.92	1.21	1.22	1.43	1.79					
DIV	.19	.22	.26	.29	.33	.36	.39	.42	.45	.46	.50	.52	.56	.60	.68					

Pepsi-like taste. The New Coke flopped in a colossal way, and Coca-Cola had egg all over its corporate face. Within three months, angry loyalists were forming opposition groups, such as "Old Coke Drinkers of America," major chains like McDonald's were dropping it, and the company was reintroducing the old formula (with corn syrup instead of sugar) under the name Coca-Cola Classic.

Today, Coca-Cola, which operates in more than 160 countries, has 45 percent of the global market for soft drink sales, more than double the share of any competitor.

Some forays into diversification, such as its 1977 acquisition of Taylor Wines (sold to Seagram in 1983) and its 1982 purchase of 49 percent of Columbia Pictures (sold to Sony in 1989), were profitable investments and not serious distractions.

In 1986, the company created a new corporation, Coca-Cola Enterprises, Inc., to own its largest bottlers; CCE issued stock publicly. Coca-Cola Company owns approximately 49 percent of CCE, which is separately listed on the New York Stock Exchange. Don't confuse it with Coca-Cola common stock when you look at the newspaper listings!

CCE gives the Coca-Cola Company better control over distribution and domestic sales. Accounting rules require that $2.7 billion of goodwill carried on CCE's books (when the money paid for a company exceeds the book value of its assets, the difference is called goodwill) will have to be written off over the next 40 years. That will reduce earnings, as the bottling franchises are actually becoming worth more, so a reserve of hidden value will be steadily building up.

Coca-Cola Company's 1989 sales were $9.1 billion, of which over 80 percent was from soft drinks and the balance from food products, like Minute Maid orange juice and Hi-C powdered mixes. Almost half the company's sales are international.

Soft drink sales grow as a function of population, civilization, economic vitality and, above all, marketing. In the decade of the eighties Coca-Cola's sales, measured in gallons, increased by almost 75 percent, and earnings per share tripled. It has an unbroken record of dividends since 1893 and has increased its payout every year for the last 15 years. It paid a 200 percent stock dividend (its stock tripled) in 1986, a 100 percent stock dividend (the stock doubled) in 1987, and the stock just doubled again in 1990.

Coca-Cola's 1989 annual report says, "We are the only bona fide global force in an industry blessed with unlimited growth potential."

How can I top that? It's a fabulous company and the market knows it. The stock is now quite pricey, with a low yield and a high price to earnings ratio. Maybe they'll do something dumb again like they did with New Coke and give us a chance to buy it cheap.

E. I. DU PONT DE NEMOURS AND COMPANY (DD)

When du Pont introduced women's nylon stockings in 1940 they sold 64 million pair the first year. I haven't researched the statistics, but if there were more than 128 million female legs in America at the time, I'd be surprised.

That was the beginning of this old gunpowder maker's preeminence in artificial fibers made from petrochemicals, which dominated the textile and apparel industries until the mid-1970s, when natural fibers made a comeback.

Du Pont has a corporate legend that is rich in more ways than one. Pierre du Pont, who with his cousins bought the company from the family in 1902 with $2,100 in cash and some paper, was a numbers man (and a good one; even then the assets of the company were valued at $24 million) who revolutionized corporate finance accounting and budgeting techniques and has been called the "architect of the modern corporation." A still widely used technique for calculating return on assets is known as the du Pont formula.

He also got du Pont to buy, cheaply, 28 percent of a young

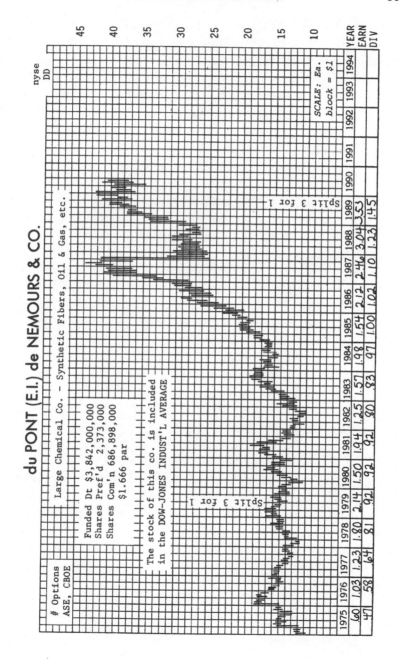

du PONT (E.I.) de NEMOURS & CO.

nyse DD

Large Chemical Co. - Synthetic Fibers, Oil & Gas, etc.

Funded Dt $3,842,000,000
Shares Pref'd 2,373,000
Shares Com'n 686,898,000
$1.666 par

The stock of this co. is included
in the DOW-JONES INDUST'L AVERAGE

Options
ASE, CBOE

SCALE: Ea.
block = $1

Split 3 for 1

Split 3 for 1

YEAR	1975	1976	1977	1978	1979	1980	1981	1982	1983	1984	1985	1986	1987	1988	1989	1990	1991	1992	1993	1994
EARN	.60	1.03	1.23	1.80	2.14	1.50	1.94	1.25	1.57	1.98	1.54	2.12	2.46	3.04	3.53					
DIV	.47	.58	.64	.81	.92	.92	.92	.80	.83	.97	1.00	1.02	1.10	1.23	1.45					

company called General Motors, and he hired Alfred P. Sloan to build it into the world's largest industrial corporation. Following an antitrust suit, du Pont's GM shares were distributed to du Pont's stockholders in 1962.

In 1981, in what was the largest transaction in business history to that date, du Pont broke up a fight for Continental Oil Company involving Seagram Distillers, Dome Petroleum and Mobil, paying $7.2 billion for the oil giant and assuring a source of raw materials. Seagram wound up holding 22 percent of du Pont, which it has to this day.

Today the company, which ranks ninth on the Fortune 500 list with sales of $35.2 billion, derives about 40 percent of its sales from oil and energy-related businesses (Conoco in the U.S., Jet and Seca in Europe); another 40 percent from industrial and consumer chemical products, fibers and polymers (Dacron, Teflon); and the balance from a group of diversified businesses ranging from agricultural products (herbicides, insecticides) to sporting goods (Remington firearms, fishing lines) and medical products and pharmaceuticals.

Du Pont has operations in 40 countries. Nearly 45 percent of its 1989 sales were generated outside the United States and the company plans to spend $1 billion in the 1990s building plants in Asian Pacific countries. One of its corporate slogans is "think globally, act locally."

It has recently increased its dividend payout (it pays an above-average yield) and has been buying back its stock, which increases share value. Although it is subject to weakness in the automotive, construction and general consumer sectors, du Pont—assuming it does not sell Conoco, as has been speculated—should profit from favorable trends in the oil industry. It also has a strong research capability, which can always produce pleasant surprises, especially in the areas of medical technology (see Merck) and genetic engineering.

Du Pont is a strongly cyclical stock. Its shares floundered from 1971 to 1982, but had quadrupled in price by 1987. It was hit hard by the crash, but has made a nice comeback.

EASTMAN KODAK COMPANY (EK)

Did you know that every time you reach for a Bayer aspirin you're contributing to the profits of the world's largest producer of photographic products? Bayer accounted for almost 15 percent of the profits of Sterling Drug Company when Kodak acquired it for $5.1 billion in early 1988.

Although film and aspirin may seem poles apart, the combination was, in theory at least, synergistic. Sterling complemented Kodak's activities in chemistry and provided a global development, registration, marketing and distribution network.

Kodak has been dogged since 1985 by a lawsuit involving instant photography patents it lost to rival Polaroid Corporation. In late 1990 there had still been neither a settlement nor an award with respect to financial damages, which were estimated to be as high as $2 billion.

George Eastman, who founded the company over a century ago and coined the name Kodak because he liked the letter K (his mother's maiden name began with it) reportedly described the company's product development as a brainstorming process that kept up until somebody in the group said, "How simple." When Eastman heard those words, he knew they were onto something. He was a man after my own heart.

The company had $18.4 billion in 1989 sales from four areas: Imaging (cameras, film, processing services, and related supplies), 38 percent; Information (office copiers, electronic equipment, and related products), 22 percent; Chemicals (solvents and other chemicals, acetate and polyester fibers, plastics), 19 percent; Health (Sterling Drugs, Lehn & Fink Products), 21 percent.

Forty-five percent of total revenues are derived from outside the United States, making Kodak global but vulnerable to weak foreign currencies. That slowed sales somewhat in 1989, when the dollar rose.

Ironically, the influx of inexpensive, simple-to-use, high-

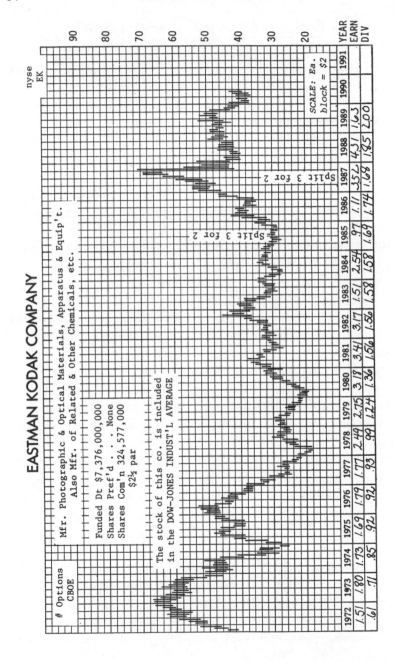

EASTMAN KODAK COMPANY

nyse
EK

Mfr. Photographic & Optical Materials, Apparatus & Equip't.
Also Mfr. of Related & Other Chemicals, etc.

Funded Dt $7,376,000,000
Shares Pref'd . . . None
Shares Com'n 324,577,000
    $2½ par

The stock of this co. is included
in the DOW-JONES INDUST'L AVERAGE

Options
CBOE

SCALE: Ea.
block = $2

Split 3 for 2

Split 3 for 2

YEAR	1972	1973	1974	1975	1976	1977	1978	1979	1980	1981	1982	1983	1984	1985	1986	1987	1988	1989	1990	1991
EARN	1.51	1.80	1.73	1.69	1.79	1.77	2.49	2.75	3.19	3.41	3.17	1.51	2.54	.97	1.11	3.52	4.31	1.63		
DIV	.61	.71	.85	.92	.92	.93	.99	1.24	1.36	1.56	1.56	1.58	1.58	1.69	1.74	1.68	1.85	2.00		

quality 35mm Japanese cameras has been a boon to Kodak. They have revived photography as a hobby and Kodak profits whenever film is bought.

The office copier and electronic printer division has been suffering from a weak office equipment market and also from internal cost and production problems.

The chemical division, last year's star performer, is off in 1990 because the industry is in a downcycle.

The Health Division, which features some leading specialized pharmaceutical products, like analgesics, and such well-known Lehn & Fink products as Lysol disinfectant, is combining Sterling Drug's strength in health products with Kodak's imaging capabilities. It sees its future coming from research and development in diagnostic imaging, cardiovascular medicine, oncology, viral diseases and central nervous system disorders.

Kodak took some medicine of its own in 1989 in the form of $875 million of restructuring costs, which included provision for special separation payments and writeoffs of inventories, capital and other assets. It is also selling or restructuring what it terms "value-consuming" assets, while implementing other cost-saving measures.

At the same time, it invested over $2 billion in capital improvements, including a new research center for Sterling to bolster the ethical drug segment. In total, it spent in 1989 $1.25 billion on research and development benefiting all four sectors of the Kodak business.

Kodak seems poised for an operational upturn. Its stock, now at around $40, is cheap, and institutional investors hold only 48 percent compared with a more typical 65 or 70 percent for Dow stocks.

That, of course, reflects the uncertainty of the Polaroid suit. Most analysts think the market has discounted the worst scenario, a $2 billion settlement, and that any amount less than that would boost the stock. Of course, the settlement could be higher, with the reverse result.

Whatever happens, financially solid Eastman Kodak will survive and eventually see better times. Yielding around 5 percent, it's a fine example of a contrarian opportunity in the Dow.

EXXON CORPORATION (XON)

Before it was renamed Exxon, this company was called Esso, the initials for Standard Oil. Esso was Standard Oil of New Jersey, called Jersey Standard, the original company of the Rockefeller family oil empire and the one the U.S. Supreme Court busted up in 1911 to create 34 separate companies (including what is now Chevron).

But Standard Oil of New Jersey remained a big, national company—so big, in fact, that the Supreme Court delivered another jolt in 1969 by ruling that the company couldn't use the trade name Esso in states where other Standard Oil companies operated.

Standard of New Jersey spent an estimated $100 million in 1969 dollars on advertising and managed almost overnight to burn the name Exxon into the national consciousness. Remember the "tiger in your tank" ads?

If there was anybody 20 years later who didn't know the name, that changed overnight when the tanker *Exxon Valdez* ran aground in Alaska's Prince William Sound in January 1989.

Horrible as that disaster was, it is a remarkable comment on the resilience of Exxon that although its stock dropped 7 percent on the news, it quickly rebounded. Today, with the cost of the cleanup estimated at over $2 billion and with legal claims potentially involving billions more, Exxon shares are higher in relation to earnings than that of most other international oils.

With $86.7 billion in annual sales, Exxon is the world's largest oil company and third largest industrial corporation. It is a totally integrated producer of oil and natural gas, with activities ranging from exploration to transportation and marketing.

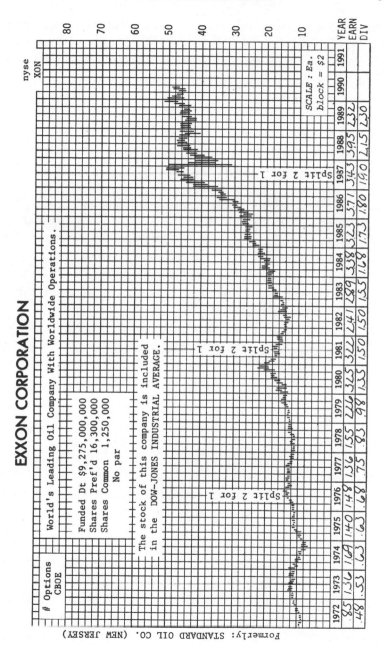

EXXON CORPORATION

nyse
XON

World's Leading Oil Company With Worldwide Operations.

Funded Dt $9,275,000,000
Shares Pref'd 16,300,000
Shares Common 1,250,000
No par

The stock of this company is included
in the DOW-JONES INDUSTRIAL AVERAGE.

Options
CBOE

SCALE : Ea.
block = $2

Split 2 for 1.

Split 2 for 1.

Split 2 for 1.

Formerly: STANDARD OIL CO. (NEW JERSEY)

	1972	1973	1974	1975	1976	1977	1978	1979	1980	1981	1982	1983	1984	1985	1986	1987	1988	1989	1990	1991	YEAR
	.85	1.36	1.69	1.40	1.48	1.36	1.55	2.16	3.25	3.22	2.41	2.89	3.38	3.23	3.71	3.43	3.95	2.32			EARN
	.48	.53	.63	.63	.68	.75	.83	.98	1.35	1.50	1.50	1.55	1.68	1.73	1.80	1.90	2.15	2.30			DIV

It is a major producer of coal and manufacturer and marketer of petrochemicals.

Since 1882 Exxon has paid generous portions of its immense profits ($3.4 billion last year) in dividends.

Except for an ill-fated but relatively inexpensive ($1.2 billion) acquisition of Reliance Electric in 1979, Exxon used its prosperity in the 1980s to improve its position in the energy field rather than diversify. Smart management. In recent years, it has been using profits after dividends to buy back its own stock, adding a boost to the market value of the remaining public holdings.

In 1989, through its 70 percent-owned Canadian subsidiary, Imperial Oil, Exxon bought Texaco Canada for approximately $4.1 billion. That adds significantly to its already vast reserves of oil and natural gas.

Exxon has also been working on modernizing facilities and is in an excellent position to capitalize on energy shortages expected by the mid-nineties.

Exxon is not simply a great oil company. Despite its public relations fiasco, it is one of the greatest companies in the world of any kind. Let us hope that its clever management learned a lesson from the black eye of the *Valdez*.

As I said before, I like oil!

GENERAL ELECTRIC COMPANY (GE)

This company's 12-year-old corporate slogan is "We bring good things to life." Toward that end, it recently spent half a billion dollars to revive the sagging fortunes of its Kidder Peabody Group, the venerable broker-dealer it acquired in 1986, which has been suffering junk bond and other woes common to Wall Street firms these days.

Still, GE is a fortress among corporations. With sales of $55.3 billion, accounting for over 1 percent of the entire U.S. gross national product, GE enjoyed profitable growth for 40 consecu-

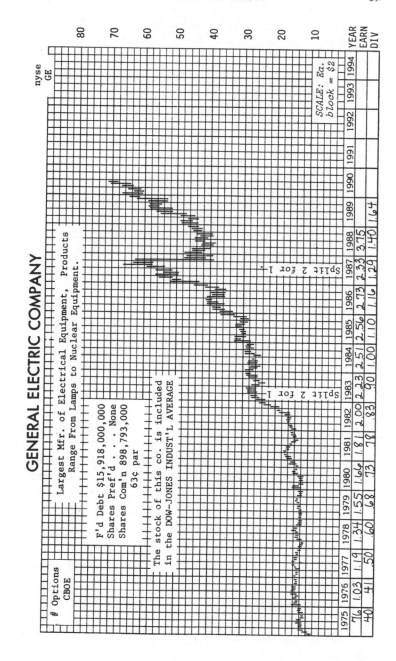

GENERAL ELECTRIC COMPANY

nyse
GE

Largest Mfr. of Electrical Equipment, Products
Range From Lamps to Nuclear Equipment.

F'd Debt $15,918,000,000
Shares Pref'd . . . None
Shares Com'n 898,793,000
63¢ par

The stock of this co. is included
in the DOW-JONES INDUST'L AVERAGE

Options
CBOE

SCALE: Ea.
block = $2

Split 2 for 1

Split 2 for 1

	1975	1976	1977	1978	1979	1980	1981	1982	1983	1984	1985	1986	1987	1988	1989	1990	1991	1992	1993	1994	YEAR
	76	1.03	1.19	1.34	1.55	1.66	1.81	2.00	2.23	2.51	2.56	2.73	2.33	3.75	1.64						EARN
	40	41	50	60	68	73	78	83	90	1.00	1.10	1.16	1.29	1.40							DIV

tive quarters in the 1980s. With Exxon and IBM, it ranks among the top three American corporations in terms of total market value.

In a recent letter to shareholders the company says, "People sometimes grapple with what to call GE. An electrical equipment manufacturer? Sure. But that ignores two thirds of our earnings. Are we a conglomerate? No . . . we are an integrated, diversified company." In GE's case, it's true.

It goes on to cite a corporate philosophy that for diversity to represent strength, each separate business must rank number one or number two in terms of its market share. In keeping with that policy, GE sold businesses that made up 25 percent of its 1980 earnings and spent $17 billion on acquisitions in the 1980s.

GE enters the 1990s in the following sectors, shown with their contributions to revenues: Financial Services (GEFS) (GE Capital Group, Employee Reinsurance Group and Kidder Peabody), 24 percent; Plastics (Borg-Warner Chemicals, Lexan and other plastics used in the automotive, packaging, and construction industries), 9 percent; Aircraft Engines (sold to Boeing and other commercial and military aerospace manufacturers), 14 percent; Aerospace (satellites et al.), 10 percent; Broadcasting (NBC, CNBC Cable TV), 6 percent; Appliances (GE, Hotpoint, RCA, Monogram), 10 percent; Lighting/Industrial Electrical Products/Motors/Transportation Systems (lightbulbs, circuitbreakers, motors for BMW windows, locomotives and mining vehicles), 12 percent; Medical Systems/Communications and Services (X-ray and ultrasound systems, computer and communications systems and services), 7 percent; Power Systems (generating systems), 8 percent.

Despite its problems with Kidder Peabody, GE is in excellent shape. Its annual report promises increased dividends, and the company plans to repurchase some $10 billion of its common stock over the next five years.

GE will benefit from aircraft orders, from expected growth in nuclear power generation, and from anticipated deregulation of the TV networks. The major networks have been losing market share to cable and are at an increasing disadvantage to international entertainment conglomerates that have been buying American film libraries to satisfy an insatiable demand for program product in Europe and the Pacific Rim. A lifting of the regulation prohibiting networks from owning film studios could be major good news.

Although its yield is relatively low, GE is a growth company par excellence—and its assets are very valuable.

GENERAL MOTORS CORPORATION (GM)

GM has just entered into an agreement with NBC to spend between $500 million and $750 million on advertising, the largest commitment in the history of television. It pleased me that such a tidy sum would be passed between two Dow companies (NBC is owned by General Electric), but it also seemed to be a measure of GM's resolve to regain North American market share lost during the 1980s.

GM is the world's largest corporation. Its annual sales of $127 billion in 1989 are approximately 3 percent of the United States gross national product. But that doesn't make it the world's smartest corporation—at least not lately.

For most of the 1980s until his replacement as chairman by Robert C. Stempel in April 1990, it was open season on Roger Smith, who, after taking office in 1981, presided over an unprecedented 10 percent plunge in North American market share to under 35 percent last year. Smith's seeming obliviousness to public sensibilities was even the subject of a satirical movie called *Roger & Me.*

Not everybody blames Roger Smith for GM's lackluster performance in the 1980s. GM's preeminence fifteen years earlier was achieved via a weak Ford, an unhealthy Chrysler, and an absence of serious competition from Japanese producers.

But a strong Ford, a healthy Chrysler, and abundant compe-

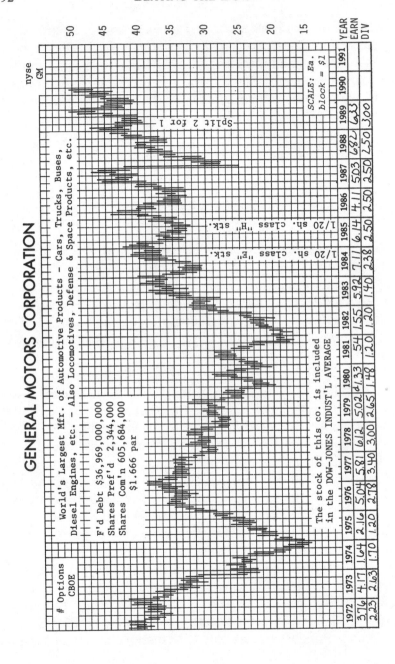

GENERAL MOTORS CORPORATION

nyse
GM

World's Largest Mfr. of Automotive Products – Cars, Trucks, Buses,
Diesel Engines, etc. – Also Locomotives, Defense & Space Products, etc.

F'd Debt $36,969,000,000
Shares Pref'd 2,344,000
Shares Com'n 605,684,000
$1.666 par

Options
CBOE

Split 2 for 1

1/20 sh. class "H" stk.

1/20 sh. class "E" stk.

The stock of this co. is included
in the DOW-JONES INDUST'L AVERAGE

SCALE: Ea.
block = $1

	1972	1973	1974	1975	1976	1977	1978	1979	1980	1981	1982	1983	1984	1985	1986	1987	1988	1989	1990	1991	YEAR
EARN	3.76	4.17	1.64	2.16	5.04	5.81	6.12	5.02	d1.33	.54	1.55	5.92	7.11	6.14	4.11	5.03	6.82	6.33			
DIV	2.25	2.63	1.70	1.20	2.78	3.40	3.00	2.65	1.48	1.20	1.20	1.40	2.38	2.50	2.50	2.50	2.50	3.00			

tition from the Far East are realities challenging Robert Stempel, who is the first "car man" (an engineer, not a financial man) since "Engine Charlie" Wilson retired in 1953. It was Wilson, you may recall, who as President Dwight Eisenhower's Secretary of Defense said, "What's good for General Motors is good for the country."

Of course, GM has done much right. Just being the leading automaker since 1920 is no mean accomplishment, but there are other examples of responsive and farsighted management.

When gas got scarce in the 1970s, GM was the first auto company to come out with smaller, more fuel-efficient cars. At the same time, they committed billions to create a state-of-the-art line of cars called Saturn, using advanced technology (for example, both automatic and stick shift models will be assembled on the same production line—a first) and an innovative approach to labor relations. The first Saturns are scheduled for the 1991 model year and will compete with high-volume imports. The Saturn is billed as GM's answer to such Japanese competition as the Honda Civic.

The establishment of a joint venture with Toyota in California to produce the Chevy Nova, since renamed the GEO Prism, was another forward-looking move.

And despite its loss of North American market share, GM is strongly positioned internationally, particularly in Europe. There are six serious contenders in the low- and middle-end markets in Europe, and three of them tend to concentrate on one market—Fiat in Italy, and Peugeot and Renault in France. The three that are broad-based, and can benefit from recent events in Eastern Europe as well, are Volkswagen, Ford and GM. GM has also recently agreed to buy a 50 percent stake in Sweden's Saab-Scandia, giving it a piece of Europe 1992's luxury market.

Although it is best known as an automaker, GM is much more than that. General Motors Acceptance Corporation (GMAC) is the world's largest finance company, and GM makes trucks, giant locomotives, military vehicles, radar and weapons systems, as well as computer chips, satellite communications networks and information systems and services.

In 1984 GM paid $2.6 billion for Ross Perot's Electronic Data Systems (EDS), the biggest company in the fast-growing business of running other companies' data processing systems. Half its work is done for GM, but the non-GM portion is growing rapidly, and EDS has been a profitable acquisition. GM also has a class of common shares, called Series E, which are separately traded and receive an earmarked flow of dividends, based on a specified percentage (currently 30 percent) of EDS' profits.

In 1984, GM acquired Hughes Aircraft Corporation, a defense electronics company, for $5 billion, combined it with the existing operations of Delco Electronics under a newly formed GM Hughes Electronics Corporation (GMHE) and created another separate class of common shares, called Series H. Like Series E shares, Series H shares are separately listed and receive dividends approximately equal to 35 percent of the income of GMHE. (The investment firm First Boston represented the seller in the Hughes–GM acquisition, and based on the size of its fee—something like $15 million—*First Boston's* stock jumped 5 percent on the New York Stock Exchange.)

Series E and H shares are not common stock in the strict sense. They have inferior voting rights and are not the GM shares we will be discussing in this book. The Dow stock is the straight GM common (symbol GM).

GM's stock is cheap these days because of the company's mixed performance over the last decade and the economy's effect on auto sales. But its capital spending is behind it. It has new top management. It is embarked on a strenuous cost-cutting campaign, including plant closings and staff cuts. It has exciting new models coming out and seems determined to regain its lost market share.

The often-cited worry about Japanese manufacturers having plants in the United States is probably exaggerated. It's getting cheaper to produce here than in Japan, and already much of the

U.S. production is being exported back. Besides, GM is itself a participant with its California joint venture with Toyota.

A recent *Wall Street Journal* article began with the question: "Will the real Robert Stempel please stand up?" and questioned whether GM's new top management was up to the task. Particularly, it speculated whether GM's new CEO was still the "car man" he once was or whether his stodgy financial colleagues had made a convert out of him.

Now that GM's got Saab, maybe they should submit him to the oil stick test. If he passes that, my bet is GM will turn around. And in the meantime, GM pays the Dow's highest yield. GM had more in cash at the end of 1989 than 80 percent of the Fortune 500 had in sales. You probably won't go too far wrong if you get stuck with General Motors.

GM's 1989 annual report makes a big boast of the fact that "The seven percent average yield on GM $1⅔ common stock [that's the regular common stock] was the highest among the top ten American companies." That's a curious thing to crow about because, as we will discuss later in considerable detail, it means the stock is a bargain.

GOODYEAR TIRE & RUBBER COMPANY (GT)

If you're into puns, the name of this company may strike you as propitious, but don't get carried away. Goodyear, with sales of $11 billion, is the world's largest producer of rubber and this country's biggest tire maker, but its road has not been without potholes.

Tires are dependent to a large extent on new car sales, and with the economy sluggish, sales have been off.

Worldwide industry capacity, meanwhile, has been expanding, and virtually all the important American tire manufacturers except Goodyear have been bought up by foreign firms.

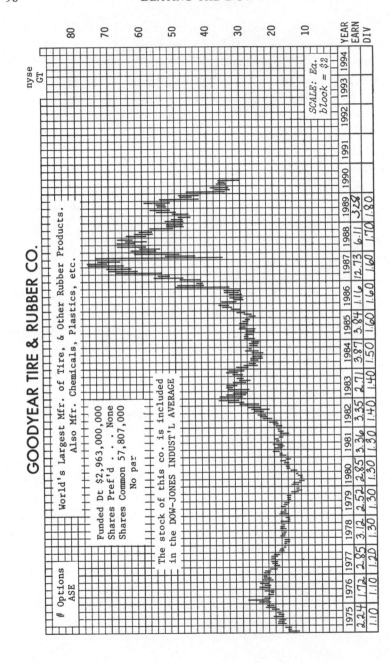

GOODYEAR TIRE & RUBBER CO.

nyse
GT

World's Largest Mfr. of Tire, & Other Rubber Products.
Also Mfr. Chemicals, Plastics, etc.

Funded Dt $2,963,000,000
Shares Pref'd . . . None
Shares Common 57,807,000
No par

The stock of this co. is included
in the DOW-JONES INDUST'L AVERAGE

Options
ASE

SCALE: Ea.
block = $2

	1975	1976	1977	1978	1979	1980	1981	1982	1983	1984	1985	1986	1987	1988	1989	1990	1991	1992	1993	1994
YEAR																				
EARN	2.24	1.72	2.85	3.12	2.52	2.85	3.36	3.35	2.71	3.87	3.84	1.16	12.73	6.11	3.28					
DIV	1.10	1.10	1.20	1.30	1.30	1.30	1.30	1.40	1.40	1.50	1.60	1.60	1.60	1.70	1.80					

Pirelli bought Armstrong, Continental AG bought General Tire, and Michelin is close to a deal on Uniroyal Goodrich. Goodyear itself was hit upon by international raider Sir James Goldsmith in 1986; they fended him off but paid him greenmail and weakened their balance sheet in the process.

Forced to fight hard to preserve its market share, the company's annual report bravely proclaims: "The lone survivor among American tire giants of the past, Goodyear enters the new competitive arena fully equipped for battle under the flags of quality, leadership and profitability."

Profitability has been further hampered by a regrettable foray into the oil business in the 1980s. Although the company sold Celeron Oil in 1987, it has been unsuccessful in its efforts to sell a $1.4 billion California to Texas crude oil pipeline that has been a drain on earnings. Although Goodyear reported a $207 million profit in 1989, earnings were off 41 percent from the prior year.

About 85 percent of Goodyear's sales derive from automotive products, mainly tires, but also hoses, belts, tubes, foam cushioning accessories and repair services. Most of the balance is from the manufacture of chemicals, plastics, shoe products, roofing materials and industrial products.

Traditionally a higher-priced brand, Goodyear is introducing two lower-priced tires to expand its low-end market position, previously served through its subsidiary, Kelly Springfield Tire Company. The company expects this to enhance its competitive position.

Goodyear is another Dow stock that has taken its lumps and is accordingly relatively cheap. At around $35 as this is written, it is selling a hair below its book value, in fact. Its yield in mid-1990 is generous.

Goodyear is a cyclical stock that has been hammered by recession fears. But it has invested in modern plants, has restructured itself organizationally, and has largely rid itself of the distraction of the oil business so it can concentrate on making tires.

A surge in new car sales would help the company, although replacement tires are still a big part of its business.

And if you happen to be in the market for an oil pipeline, Goodyear would be happy to talk with you.

INTERNATIONAL BUSINESS MACHINES CORPORATION (IBM)

If you're long enough in the tooth, you'll no doubt remember IBM's original (early 1920s) corporate slogan, THINK, which became ubiquitous almost overnight and was used for several decades. Today you see THINK signs everywhere, either hanging upside down or with the last two letters squished together in a horrendous failure of forethought. And just about everybody's forgotten where it all began.

"Big Blue," as stock traders call IBM (after the color of its corporate logo), led America into the computer age and for many years *was* the computer industry.

But, as somebody said, when other computer companies started being called "the next IBM," it was a clear sign Big Blue was in for a bumpy ride. And bumpy it has been.

It's interesting, the kind of problems a company has when an industry comes of age in a relatively few years. For instance, one of the biggest problems IBM's top management has these days is mediating internal squabbling among managers—those whose careers were made on traditional proprietary products and those who see the future in "open systems."

The latter refers to a free-for-all competitive environment characterized by inexpensive open-system work stations that run on industry-standard software, and that is where IBM is putting its money in the 1990s.

Because computers are now such a part of everybody's life, it's hard to believe that before the mid-fifties they were virtually nonexistent. But that all changed when Thomas Watson founded IBM and IBM developed the first computer, right?

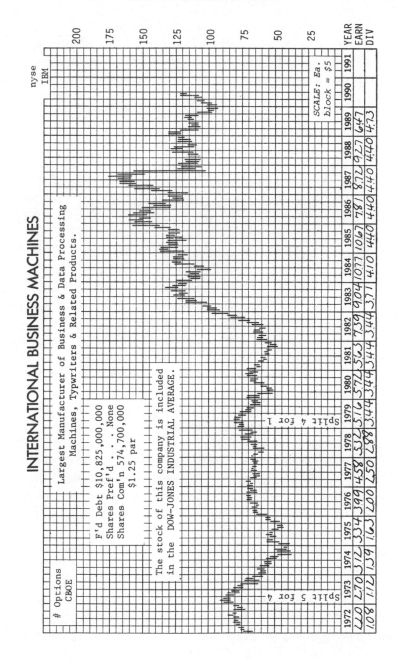

INTERNATIONAL BUSINESS MACHINES

nyse
IBM

Largest Manufacturer of Business & Data Processing
Machines, Typewriters & Related Products.

F'd Debt $10,825,000,000
Shares Pref'd . . . None
Shares Com'n 574,700,000
$1.25 par

The stock of this company is included
in the DOW-JONES INDUSTRIAL AVERAGE.

Options
CBOE

SCALE: Ea.
block = $5

Split 4 for 1

Split 5 for 4

	1972	1973	1974	1975	1976	1977	1978	1979	1980	1981	1982	1983	1984	1985	1986	1987	1988	1989	1990	1991
YEAR	770	270	312	334	399	458	532	516	572	523	739	904	1077	1067	781	872	922	647		
EARN			312	1.63	200	250	288	344	344	344	344	371	410	440	440	440	440	473		
DIV	1.08	1.12	1.39																	

Wrong.

The company that became IBM started when Charles Randall Flint combined a group of small businesses making grocery scales, slicers, time clocks and tabulating machines into a company called Computing-Tabulating-Recording Company. He hired a young marketing whiz named Tom Watson away from National Cash Register Company. Watson emphasized the tabulating part of the business and, by stressing what is now called corporate culture, which included the slogan THINK, built a superbly managed business that fed off the insatiable accounting needs of Social Security and other New Deal programs. In 1924, Watson changed the name to International Business Machines.

Meanwhile, research was being done on electronic computing devices at such places as Bell Labs, Harvard, and the University of Pennsylvania. At Penn, two eggheads named John Mauchly and J. Presper Eckert assembled a Rube Goldberg-type contraption using electronic vacuum tubes that they called the Electronic Numerical Integrator and Computer, which was demonstrated publicly in 1946.

The two men recognized the commercial potential of their invention and, to keep the patent, quit Penn and started a company to market their computers, which they now named UNIVAC. But they weren't businessmen and they lacked capital, so they went looking for a buyer.

They first approached IBM, but Watson turned thumbs down. Computing devices using electronics, he felt, had no future. They had better luck at Remington-Rand, IBM's chief competitor in the office supply field. Remington-Rand bought the UNIVAC business in 1950.

Remington-Rand could have used UNIVAC to walk away with the computer revolution. Almost immediately they struck a deal with CBS to use UNIVAC to predict the results of the 1952 presidential election. By 9:00 P.M. UNIVAC forecast the Eisenhower landslide. Although CBS wasn't quite ready to trust a computer and waited for confirming ballot counts, mil-

lions heard Walter Cronkite tout this electronic miracle, helping to make the name UNIVAC as synonymous with computers as Frigidaire was with refrigerators. But Remington-Rand,
which became Sperry-Rand in 1955, hesitated to expend the
capital to exploit the full market potential of UNIVAC.

In the meantime, Thomas Watson was succeeded as president of IBM by his son, Thomas Watson, Jr. Young Tom
Watson clearly saw that the future belonged to computers, and
in 1952 introduced the 701, the first of several generations of
IBM computers that would dominate the marketplace for two
decades.

In the 1960s, IBM undertook the most massive privately
financed corporate project in history with its $5 billion develop-
ment of the IBM 360 series of computers. Designed for any
kind of commercial data processing need, these huge "mainframes," which cost $1 million or more, were aimed at large
organizations such as corporations and government agencies.

Soon after its April 1964 debut in 62 U.S. cities and 14
foreign countries, the 360 had so established IBM's market
dominance that analysts referred to the industry as "IBM and
the Seven Dwarfs," the dwarfs being Sperry-Rand, Control
Data, Honeywell, RCA, NCR, General Electric and Burroughs.

Unfortunately for IBM, its dominance and power to set industry standards and compete for new business (there was a
saying that IBM may not be the best, but nobody ever got fired
for buying it) was not lost on the Department of Justice. An
antitrust suit, filed in 1968, haunted IBM until it was dropped
in January 1982.

The 1970s were a rocky period for IBM. Independent firms
began undermining IBM's mainframe leasing business by offering lower rental rates, while others started selling IBM-compat-
ible peripheral equipment ("clones") at prices cheaper than
IBM's.

IBM's efforts to counter this competition resulted in a series
of small but nettlesome lawsuits. The Seven Dwarfs, now down

to five and renamed the BUNCH (Burroughs, Univac, NCR, Control Data and Honeywell), continued to nibble away at IBM's market share.

But the biggest development was the blossoming of the mini-computer industry, featuring smaller, more flexible systems that companies could adapt more easily to their particular needs. Digital Equipment had been first with an inexpensive $120,000 system. They grew like crazy, and were joined by Data General, Hewlett-Packard and others.

IBM had missed the boat on mini-computers and saw its overall market share drop from 60 percent to 40 percent by the end of 1979.

The 1980s were the era of the home microcomputer for data processing and entertainment. Steve Jobs started in the early 1970s "phonephreaking" (making little electronic boxes that beat the phone company out of the cost of calls) with his pal Steve Wozniak. He worked for Atari, then he rejoined Wozniak in a now-famous garage. Jobs had already built Apple Computer into an organization with sales of $117 million when IBM introduced the PC (for personal computer) by 1981.

Determined not to miss out in microcomputers as it had in minicomputers in the 1970s, IBM took advantage of Apple's early growing pains and by 1983 was the dominant producer of microcomputers in a crowded field that included Commodore, Texas Instruments, Tandy, Osborne, Atari, Coleco and others, most of which have since fallen by the wayside.

By the middle 1980s, Apple had successfully launched its Macintosh, and many IBM "clones" were on the market, but despite heightened competition and price wars, IBM continued to dominate, albeit with reduced market share.

On the commercial mainframe front, IBM introduced a medium-scale entry called the 4300 at the outset of the decade that met heavy demand early on but got bogged down in production delays and other problems. These affected earnings, sent the stock price south, and opened the way for increased competition from makers of compatible equipment. The company also brought out new generations of high-end mainframes with mixed success.

The mid-1980s was a time of slackened growth in the computer industry generally. IBM, having the most to lose in terms of market share, was the biggest loser.

Referring to the company's stubborn adherence to a strategy emphasizing proprietary products, especially its giant mainframe computers, *Business Week* quoted an "IBM insider" as saying, "We took our eye off the ball."

But that strategy has been turned upside-down for the 1990s. In February, CEO John Akers announced a line of open-system workstations known as AIX and a policy of encouraging links between these smaller computers and IBM's big models. It thereby aims for a major share of the booming open-systems market while also boosting sales of mainframes.

Much depends on timely delivery of IBM's new software programs, designated SSA by the company, designed to smooth over differences between the company's various computer lines, and the lining up of software developers to design programs compatible with AIX.

With restructuring costs and technology investment write-downs behind it, IBM seems ready to focus again on growth. It seems strange to view IBM, a name synonymous in the American business vocabulary with technology and growth, as a yield stock. But that's what it is. (In 1990, it was yielding nearly 5 percent.)

IBM's goal is to capture a third of the world workstation market by 1992, which was worth $6.1 billion in 1989 and is growing at the rate of 30 percent annually. Sun Microsystems leads, with a 29 percent market share, followed by Hewlett-Packard/Apollo, with 26 percent, and Digital Equipment, with 16 percent. IBM starts with a meager 1.8 percent.

IBM ended the decade with sales of $63.4 billion. Says *Business Week:* "Big Blue is so big that if at first it doesn't succeed, it can try, try again."

I couldn't have said it better myself, and it gives resonance to the point of this book. With IBM, as with other companies of immense resources, the opportunity is greater than the risk if you buy when it's out of favor.

INTERNATIONAL PAPER COMPANY (IP)

There's a very good chance International Paper made the page you're reading, and that the tree was cut from one of 6.5 million acres of southern real estate the company owns. That's almost half the area of the state of West Virginia. International Paper has the distinction of being America's largest private landowner.

International Paper Company is the world's largest producer of packaging, printing and writing papers, as well as corrugated boxes, photographic papers and films, lumber and wood products. Through more than 170 outlets, it distributes paper and building materials mainly manufactured by others. It is also involved in oil and gas exploration and drilling through royalty arrangements with oil companies, and is engaged in real estate activities.

Approximately two-thirds of IP's sales are equally divided between pulp and paper, on one hand, and paperboard and packaging, on the other. About 20 percent of revenues come from distribution activities and the balance from wood products, timber and specialty products.

Paper is a cyclical business, waxing and waning with the economy generally and the construction sector specifically. But it is also a growth business, tied to growing worldwide literacy and also to economic activity. Environmental concerns currently favor paper packaging over nonbiodegradable plastics.

It is an industry in which technology plays an important role, and International Paper has invested nearly $7 billion in the last decade to make itself one of the lowest-cost producers in each of its market sectors.

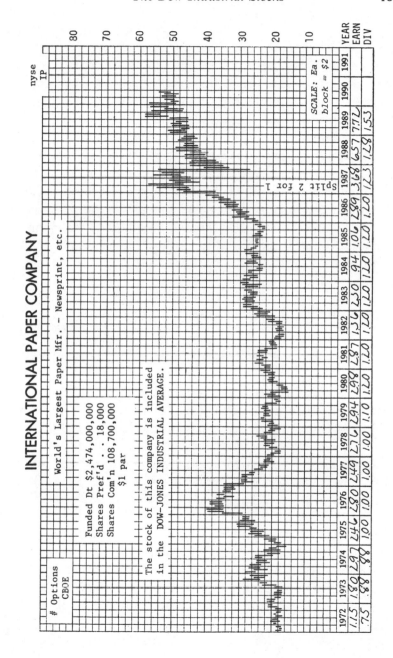

INTERNATIONAL PAPER COMPANY

nyse
IP

World's Largest Paper Mfr. – Newsprint, etc.

Funded Dt $2,474,000,000
Shares Pref'd . . 18,000
Shares Com'n 108,700,000
$1 par

The stock of this company is included
in the DOW-JONES INDUSTRIAL AVERAGE.

Options
CBOE

SCALE: Ea.
block = $2

Split 2 for 1.

YEAR	EARN	DIV
1991		
1990		
1989	7.72	1.53
1988	6.57	1.28
1987	3.68	1.13
1986	2.89	1.07
1985	1.06	1.07
1984	.94	1.07
1983	2.30	1.20
1982	1.36	1.20
1981	2.87	1.20
1980	2.98	1.20
1979	2.94	1.10
1978	2.76	1.00
1977	2.49	1.00
1976	2.80	1.00
1975	2.46	1.00
1974	2.97	.88
1973	1.80	.88
1972	1.15	.75

The company has manufacturing operations in 22 countries, and it exports to more than 70 countries. In 1986, IP acquired Hammermill Paper and in 1988, Masonite. In 1989, it acquired two leading European paper producers, Aussedat Rey S.A., a leading manufacturer of reprographic paper and uncoated specialty paper in France, and Zanders Feinpapiere AG of West Germany, an important supplier of coated papers to the European Community. From 1978 through 1988 average consumption of paper products in Europe grew at a rate more than four times that of the United States, according to the company. So IP is well positioned for Europe 1992.

International Paper has the technology and the market position to continue to dominate an industry that should enjoy strong global growth in the 1990s.

MCDONALD'S CORPORATION (MCD)

McDonald's has been described as "the world's largest small business."

When it opened a restaurant on Red Square in Moscow in early 1990, nothing better symbolized glasnost and perestroika—the hamburger, an American tradition named after a West German city, served with an order of French fries.

McDonald's is a great source of impressive statistics. I don't know how many billion hamburgers they have sold to date (they know, though; look at their sign the next time you drive by), but here are a few others:

McDonald's claims to be the most advertised single brand in the world. At the end of 1989, it reported its 99th consecutive quarter of record sales, revenues, and operating results; it had opened its 11,000th restaurant, in Hong Kong; and it added, in that year alone, a record 649 restaurants to the world landscape.

McDonald's operates, licenses and services the world's larg-

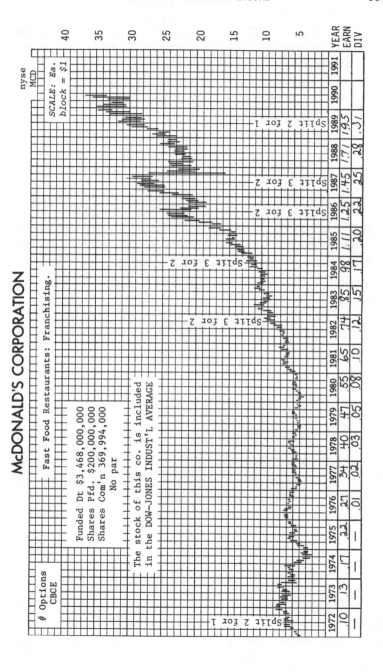

McDONALD'S CORPORATION

Fast Food Restaurants: Franchising.

Options
CBOE

nyse
MCD

SCALE: Ea.
block = $1

Funded Dt $3,468,000,000
Shares Pfd. $200,000,000
Shares Com'n 369,994,000
No par

The stock of this co. is included
in the DOW-JONES INDUST'L AVERAGE

Split 2 for 1

Split 3 for 2

Split 3 for 2

Split 3 for 2

Split 3 for 2

Split 2 for 1

	1972	1973	1974	1975	1976	1977	1978	1979	1980	1981	1982	1983	1984	1985	1986	1987	1988	1989	1990	1991
YEAR																				
EARN	.10	.13	.17	.22	.27	.34	.40	.47	.55	.65	.74	.85	.98	1.11	1.25	1.45	1.71	1.95		
DIV	—	—	—	—	.01	.02	.03	.05	.08	.10	.12	.15	.17	.20	.22	.25	.28	.31		

est chain of fast food restaurants. According to Standard & Poor's, at December 31, 1989, there were 8,270 units in the U.S. and 2,892 units in foreign countries, mostly in Japan, Canada, West Germany, the United Kingdom and Australia. Sixty-eight percent of their restaurants were owned by franchisees, 24 percent by the company, and the rest by affiliates.

McDonald's is also a real estate company, owning some 60 percent of its locations and long-term leases on virtually all the others. Real estate and restaurant decisions are kept separate financially.

With the free world expanding, there seems to be almost no limit to the growth potential of McDonald's. And new locations are not its only means of increasing sales.

Even where they have saturated their markets—where there is seemingly not an empty belly left in which to stuff a Big Mac—they have shown themselves to be remarkably resourceful marketers, coming up with innovations like drive-in windows, a breakfast menu, salad bars, and chicken sandwiches. Under pressure from health-conscious consumers, they've recently found a new way to cook fries without beef fat and whip up lower-fat shakes.

They're starting to do their bit for the environment, too. Despite continued use of styrofoam, in April 1990 they announced "McRecycle USA," soon to be extended abroad; in addition to using recycled paper napkins and containers, they will give preference to recycled materials when building, remodeling, or reequipping their restaurants.

Sad to say, all of this has not gone on with the investing public in the dark. McDonald's is selling at a relatively typically high PE (growth stocks have higher PEs) of 16 and has a low yield of 1 percent.

As an example of the popularity of McDonald's stock, an organization called the National Association of Investment Clubs publishes an excellent magazine, *Better Investing,* which keeps book on what investment clubs around the country are holding. McDonald's ranks number one, with 2,535 clubs owning shares.

Is the stock overpriced? "McDonald's has broken the 'can't go much higher barrier' year after year," says no lesser a prophet than Peter Lynch.

McDonald's, a relative newcomer to the Dow, replaced American Brands in 1985.

MERCK & CO., INC. (MRK)

In *Dow 3000,* Thomas Blamer & Richard Shulman quote George Merck II on the role serendipity played in this venerable company's rise to preeminence in medical research. Recalling the Three Princes of Serendip in their quest for treasure, Merck said "they didn't find what they were looking for, but they kept finding other things just as valuable. That's serendipity and our business is full of it."

The choice of anecdote is apt for a company whose latest annual report is titled "Health Challenges for the 1990s" and whose cover pictures DNA molecule/enzyme diagrams for 17 afflictions ranging from AIDS to stroke and the common cold to cancer.

Merck is the premier prescription pharmaceutical company in the world, with a total market share of almost 5 percent.

Unlike many pharmaceutical companies, Merck has emphasized massive investment in basic research, averaging on the order of $500 million annually in recent years ($751 million in 1989). The result has been such widely used products as Aldomet and Vasotec (hypertensives), Meloxin and Primaxin (antibiotics), Timopic (for glaucoma), Mevacor (for lowering cholesterol), Pepcid (for ulcers), and Clinoril and Indocin (anti-inflammatory medicines).

The company's Human and Animal Health Products area, which contributes 92 percent of sales, produces drugs that are

MERCK & COMPANY

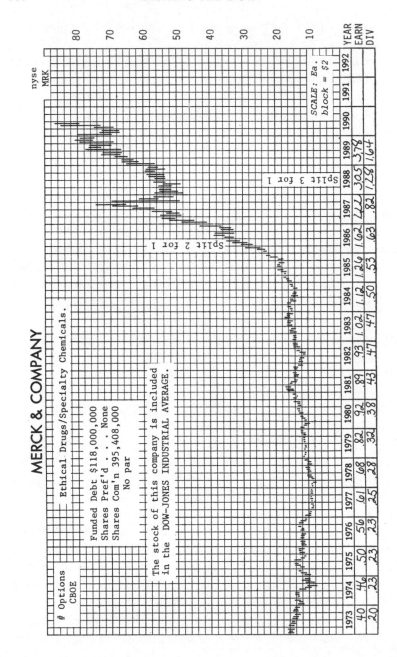

nyse
MRK

Ethical Drugs/Specialty Chemicals.

Funded Debt $118,000,000
Shares Pref'd . . . None
Shares Com'n 395,408,000
No par

The stock of this company is included
in the DOW-JONES INDUSTRIAL AVERAGE.

Options
CBOE

SCALE: Ea.
block = $2

Split 3 for 1

Split 2 for 1

YEAR	1973	1974	1975	1976	1977	1978	1979	1980	1981	1982	1983	1984	1985	1986	1987	1988	1989	1990	1991	1992
EARN	40	46	50	56	61	68	82	92	89	93	1.02	1.12	1.24	1.62	2.22	3.05	3.78			
DIV	20	23	23	23	25	28	32	38	43	47	47	50	53	63	82	1.28	1.64			

important in treating livestock. Its Heartgard-30 for the prevention of heartworm in dogs is the leading pharmaceutical product for small animals.

Merck also has a Specialty Chemicals Division, which includes Calgon Corporation, known best for water purification but also a producer of wound dressings, and Kelco Division, which makes alginates and xanthan gum used in processed foods, oil field applications, and other industrial and consumer products.

Merck has also entered joint ventures with Johnson & Johnson, which will establish it in the rapidly growing over-the-counter drug business, and with du Pont, which will advance the development, regulatory approval, and marketing of medicines important in high blood pressure, heart disease, and Parkinson's disease.

Among Merck's promising research developments is a drug called Proscar, which reduces the size of enlarged prostates in older men.

Merck had sales of $6.5 billion in 1989, about 50 percent coming from foreign operations. It plans to spend $855 million on R&D in 1990. Although it's not a high-yield stock, Merck increased its dividend twice in 1989, for a total payout that was up 28 percent from the 1988 level.

The inside front cover of Merck's 1989 annual report is wholly devoted to a listing of the awards and distinctions this superb company earned in 1989: most admired, best managed, product of the year, top sales force, best in service, best for equal opportunity—the list goes on.

The report notes elsewhere that over the last five years, Merck stock provided investors with a total return of 427 percent. Over that period Merck repurchased 11 percent of its shares and is currently in the second year of a multiyear, billion-dollar stock repurchase program.

Not surprisingly, this darling of institutional portfolios is no bargain at the moment. But it's one hell of a company, another sterling example of a growth company par excellence.

MINNESOTA MINING AND
MANUFACTURING COMPANY (MMM)

When the relics of capitalist society are studied a million years from now, one artifact that might cause archeologists some head-scratching will be the ubiquitous "suggestion box." It sends a double message. On one hand, it acknowledges that fresh ideas are needed and welcomed. Yet by promising anonymity, it implies that the employee who ventures a new idea might otherwise do so at some risk of job security.

Of course we all know that is exactly what does happen, however subtly, in corporations. The people who get promoted are usually those who play the game and don't challenge the accepted way of doing things. The down side, unfortunately, is that the really creative people all too frequently pack up and leave.

At 3M, which for my money is the world's most interesting corporation, there's no suggestion box because none is needed.

This remarkable organization has been built on a steady stream of new products, some 60,000 in all, that are largely the inventions of 87,500 employees who work in 52 countries. Scotch tape and Post-it notes are among the most familiar examples.

How 3M managed to create this entrepreneurial environment is a fascinating tale.

To begin with, the word "mining" in the corporate name is a misnomer stemming from a mistake. In 1902 a bunch of Minnesota boys, thinking they had found a corundum mine, established a quarrying plant and formed a company called Minnesota Mining and Manufacturing. What they really had, they were to discover, was nothing but a sand bank, so they got some financing and started making sandpaper. That's how it all started.

The first major success occurred in the 1920s with a product called Wetordry, a sandpaper that could be used with water and represented a breakthrough in sanding automobiles.

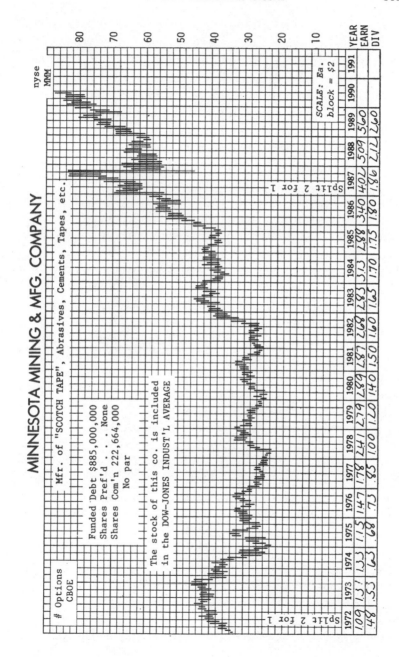

MINNESOTA MINING & MFG. COMPANY

nyse
MMM

Mfr. of "SCOTCH TAPE", Abrasives, Cements, Tapes, etc.

Funded Debt $885,000,000
Shares Pref'd . . . None
Shares Com'n 222,664,000
No par

The stock of this co. is included
in the DOW-JONES INDUST'L AVERAGE

Options
CBOE

SCALE: Ea.
block = $2

Split 2 for 1.

Split 2 for 1.

	1972	1973	1974	1975	1976	1977	1978	1979	1980	1981	1982	1983	1984	1985	1986	1987	1988	1989	1990	1991
YEAR	1972	1973	1974	1975	1976	1977	1978	1979	1980	1981	1982	1983	1984	1985	1986	1987	1988	1989	1990	1991
EARN	1.09	1.31	1.33	1.15	1.47	1.78	2.41	2.79	2.89	2.87	2.68	2.93	3.13	2.88	3.40	4.02	5.09	5.60		
DIV	.48	.53	.63	.68	.73	.85	1.00	1.20	1.40	1.50	1.60	1.63	1.70	1.75	1.80	1.86	2.12	2.60		

Today 3M coats adhesives to film (Scotch brand tapes), abrasive granules to paper (sandpaper), low-tack adhesives to paper (Post-it brand notes), iron oxide to plastic backing (magnetic recording tape), glass beads to plastic backing (reflective sign materials), light-sensitive materials to metal (printing plates), nutrients to film (bacteria culture dishes), ceramics to granules (roofing granules), and dozens of others.

But coatings are just one product category. Others include nonwoven fibers, fluorochemistry, industrial abrasives and hardware ranging from hand-held tape dispensers to sophisticated equipment for open-heart surgery.

The 3M system that so uniquely rewards creativity and, just as important, rewards sharing ideas with other people is really rather formalized.

According to Blamer and Shulman, 3M's tradition of innovation and problem solving began with a bookkeeper-turned-salesman named William McKnight, who joined the company in 1907 and later headed it for several decades.

Lacking formal sales training, McKnight tried an unusual tack. Instead of presenting his card at a potential customer's front office, he went directly to the production areas, where he would ask the workers what they liked or didn't like about the products they worked with. To this day, 3M gets 50 percent of its new product ideas from soliciting customers' suggestions.

Internally, entrepreneurship is encouraged with a "15 percent rule" that permits employees to spend 15 percent of their time pursuing their own ideas. Once an idea is born, the Genesis and Alpha programs provide time and funding.

If employees with ideas can't persuade their own divisions to fund them, they are encouraged to shop the idea around the company's other 40 or so divisions or certain special sources. Division managers, though, aren't quick to reject ideas, since they are expected to meet a requirement that 25 percent of divisional sales come from new products developed in the last five years.

Once funding has been lined up, the employee has to recruit

and organize a project team. This helps separate the ideas with market potential from those that are simply ingenious. And once the project team is put together it stays together as long as the project meets the company's financial and marketing criteria.

Post-it brand notes were invented by a 3M scientist who sang in his church choir and got frustrated every time the page marker fell out of his hymnal. Remembering a colleague's discovery of a barely sticky adhesive, he brushed some on a piece of paper and it worked perfectly. He was able to sing without interruption thereafter, and the success of Post-it is now legendary.

In 1989 3M had sales of just under $12 billion, about 46 percent from abroad (the percentage from international sales is increasing, which makes 3M more susceptible than many companies to currency fluctuations). About 50 percent of sales are to service-related businesses, 40 percent to industry and 10 percent to consumers. Thirty percent of sales came from new products introduced in the last five years, beating the 25 percent goal.

During 1989 3M increased stockholder dividends 22.6 percent, and it raised the quarterly dividend in February 1990, marking the thirty-second consecutive year when dividends have been increased. It is a growth company, though, so yields have recently been less than generous.

If only they'd do something wrong, and give us contrarians a break!

NAVISTAR INTERNATIONAL CORPORATION (NAV)

As they say out in farm country, this one's been "rode hard and put to bed wet." And to add insult to injury, you're probably saying "what the hell *is* Navistar, anyway?"

Navistar is the truck part of the old International Harvester Company, and it's the most beaten-down stock in the Dow. This is a pure case of Murphy's Law in action: whatever could go wrong has gone wrong with Navistar.

Needless to say, it has a big place in my contrarian heart.

In a way, no company better illustrates my theory about major companies. Navistar, at this writing, is a $3 stock that's got $2.00 a share in cash, 28 percent of the truck market, $4 billion in sales, a huge loss carryforward to shelter it from future taxes, a modern factory system, some 15,000 trained employees, a solid dealer network and a few other things to boot. Whatever happens to the truck business, sooner or later a company with these advantages is going to do something right. Navistar is an example of a company that has turned around but whose stock hasn't yet.

The old International Harvester Company was started around the turn of the century and for many decades was the nation's leader in the manufacture of farm equipment, trucks and tractors.

The farm equipment industry, however, is dependent on agricultural economics and government farm policy. The huge grain sale to the Soviet Union in the early 1970s created high farm prices and benefited allied industries. But by the 1980s, the farm sector was in crisis. High interest rates, President Carter's embargo on grain sales to the Soviet Union, and growing levels of food imports all contributed to sinking commodity prices.

International Harvester, not helped by a six-month strike in 1979–80, began showing losses in 1980 and at one point came close to declaring bankruptcy. In 1985, the company sold its agricultural equipment division and the name International Harvester to J.I. Case, a subsidiary of Tenneco, Inc.

Renamed Navistar, the company began to focus on the truck business and now leads the North American market for medium and heavy trucks and the world market for midrange diesel engines. It has four operating divisions: Trucks, including school buses; Parts; Engine and Foundry; and Financial Ser-

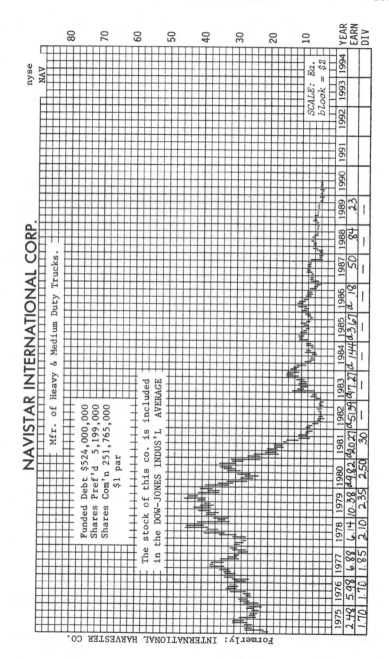

NAVISTAR INTERNATIONAL CORP.

Mfr. of Heavy & Medium Duty Trucks.

nyse
NAV

Funded Debt $524,000,000
Shares Pref'd 5,199,000
Shares Com'n 251,765,000
$1 par

The stock of this co. is included
in the DOW-JONES INDUS'L AVERAGE

SCALE: Ea.
block = $2

Formerly: INTERNATIONAL HARVESTER CO.

	YEAR	1975	1976	1977	1978	1979	1980	1981	1982	1983	1984	1985	1986	1987	1988	1989
EARN		2.48	5.48	6.88	6.14	10.38	d4.82	d2.027	d5.39	d7.27	d1.44	d3.67	d.18	.50	.84	.23
DIV		1.70	1.70	1.85	2.10	2.35	2.50	.30	—	—	—	—	—	—	—	—

vices, which exists essentially to insure and finance the lease and purchase of trucks at the wholesale and retail levels.

Operations turned profitable in 1987, although sales and profits have been negatively affected by the softened economy. In an improved economy, Navistar should profit from its cost-cutting programs and new product lines. And capital goods businesses should thrive in the smokestack economy I am predicting.

Navistar's stock price has not reflected its brightening prospects because in 1985 it issued over a hundred million new shares, causing dilution, which means earnings have to be distributed over that many more shares, with consequently lower earnings per share.

To offset that dilution and the potential dilutive effect of outstanding warrants, options, and convertible preferred shares, the company announced in 1988 it would use a portion of its improving cash flow for a major five-year stock repurchase program.

Navistar is as beat up as a Dow stock is likely to get, and for my money there's nowhere to go but up, in the long run. It's just possible you could make a *whole* lot of money in this stock.

PHILIP MORRIS COMPANIES (MO)

The April 1990 *Forbes* cover showed Philip Morris Chairman Hamish Maxwell tucking a napkin under his chin beside a caption asking, "Who's Next?" It was a reference to PM's appetite for acquisitions, which, together with internal growth, made it one of the hot growth stocks of the 1980s.

Citing the rises in this stock even after lackluster results with the acquisitions of Miller Brewing, General Foods, and Seven-Up, Peter Lynch observed that at Philip Morris even diworse-ification couldn't hurt the stockholders.

Philip Morris, as everyone knows, is an old-line tobacco

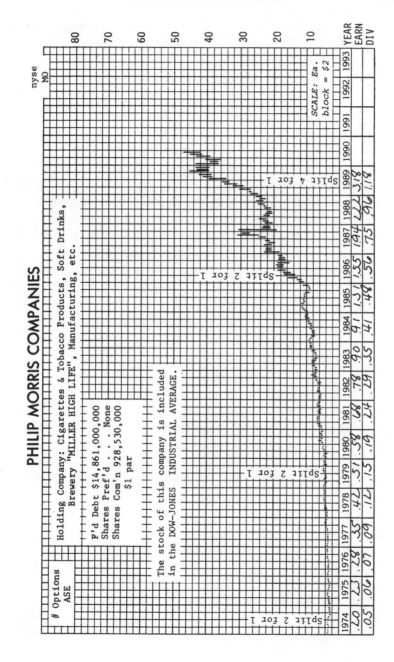

PHILIP MORRIS COMPANIES

nyse
MO

Holding Company: Cigarettes & Tobacco Products, Soft Drinks,
Brewery "MILLER HIGH LIFE", Manufacturing, etc.

F'd Debt $14,861,000,000
Shares Pref'd . . . None
Shares Com'n 928,530,000
$1 par

The stock of this company is included
in the DOW-JONES INDUSTRIAL AVERAGE.

Options
ASE

SCALE: Ea.
block = $2

Split 4 for 1.
Split 2 for 1.
Split 2 for 1.
Split 2 for 1.

YEAR	EARN	DIV
1993		
1992		
1991		
1990		
1989	3.18	1.18
1988	2.22	.96
1987	1.94	.75
1986	1.55	.56
1985	1.31	.48
1984	.91	.41
1983	.90	.35
1982	.78	.29
1981	.68	.24
1980	.51	.19
1979	.51	.15
1978	.42	.12
1977	.35	.09
1976	.28	.07
1975	.23	.06
1974	.20	.05

company, famous originally for its own brand name ("Call Fooooor Phil-ip Maaaaar-ace") then later for Parliament, Virginia Slim, and Marlboro, the world's bestselling cigarette.

Of course, when you are an oligopsony of sorts and have folks addicted to your product, profitability comes easy. At the end of 1989, 40 percent of PM's revenues and 64 percent of earnings came from cigarette sales. The company is marketing aggressively overseas to offset steadily declining tobacco use in the United States, although its market share here has been growing.

But Philip Morris is not only the most successful and profitable cigarette company in the world. With the acquisition of Kraft, Inc., in 1988, it became the largest and most diversified food and beverage company in the United States. With sales of $39 billion, it is number ten on the Fortune 500 list.

The company's diversification began in 1970 with Miller Brewing Company, which had a big success with the introduction of Lite beer in the 1970s. During the 1980s, though, its flagship Miller High Life lost significant market share to competitors. Its newest beer, Miller Genuine Draft, is the fastest growing premium beer on the market. Beer now accounts for about 10 percent of MO's sales.

Philip Morris acquired Seven-Up in 1978, and following an unsuccessful effort to market a caffeine-free lemon-lime drink called Like, it sold Seven-Up's domestic operations in 1986.

The $5.7 billion purchase of General Foods in 1986 brought such well-known products as Maxwell House Coffee, JELL-O, Birds Eye frozen foods and Oscar Meyer, but lacked product lines with real growth potential.

Hence the record-breaking—until the RJR Nabisco leveraged buyout (LBO)—$13 billion acquisition in December 1988 of Kraft, Inc., with Kraft cheeses, Breyers ice cream, Parkay margarine, Light n' Lively and a range of popular brands that gave the combined Kraft General Foods Division 10 percent of the U.S. brand-food market.

Although PM's acquisitions were financed to a large extent with debt, so copious is its cash flow that it had $1.3 billion left over last year after interest payments and even after capital expenditures and a dividend increase. The stock has an average yield.

Philip Morris is one of the richest and best-run companies in the world. But long run, tobacco revenues have a poor projection and the industry has been lucky so far in having product liability suits ruled in its favor. That could change anytime. The threat of adverse litigation hangs over the cigarette industry like a sword of Damocles.

Philip Morris has been called Wall Street's most popular stock, which of course is anathema to a contrarian like me. But it is nonetheless interesting. Mr. Maxwell's licking of chops is financially logical—something must be done to further reduce the company's dependence on cigarettes, and the obvious solution is another acquisition. Companies like Campbell Soup, PepsiCo, and troubled RJR Nabisco are frequently mentioned as possibilities.

Although I see the coming decade belonging more to traditional manufacturing stocks than to consumer stocks like this company, Philip Morris has both vulnerability and survivability, the ingredients of contrarian opportunity.

PRIMERICA CORPORATION (PA)

In her bestselling book about the junk bond era, *The Predator's Ball*, Connie Bruck describes a 1985 cocktail party encounter at the Beverly Hills Hotel between Gerald Tsai, then vice-chairman of American Can Company, and Nelson Peltz of Triangle Industries. Raising his voice over the music, Peltz, a client of host Michael Milken of Drexel Burnham Lambert, told Tsai: "Someday I'd like to talk to you about buying your cans."

American Can has become Primerica, now a financial services conglomerate. An original Dow stock that got turned

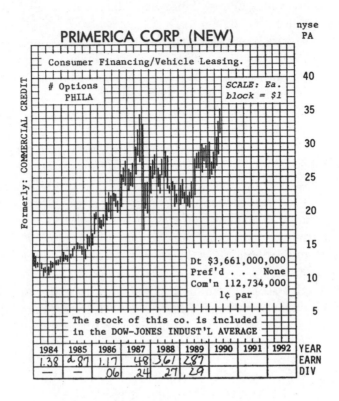

PRIMERICA CORP. (NEW)

nyse
PA

Formerly: COMMERCIAL CREDIT

Consumer Financing/Vehicle Leasing.

\# Options
PHILA

*SCALE: Ea.
block = $1*

Dt $3,661,000,000
Pref'd . . . None
Com'n 112,734,000
1¢ par

The stock of this co. is included
in the DOW-JONES INDUST'L AVERAGE

	1984	1985	1986	1987	1988	1989	1990	1991	1992	YEAR
EARN	1.38	2.87	1.17	48	3.61	2.87				EARN
DIV	—	—	.06	.24	.27	.29				DIV

completely on its head, it's a case where the shift from manufacturing to service happened all in one company.

American Can was a leading container and packaging company, which had brought us such Americana as the Dixie Cup and the beer can along with heavy industrial cans. Then it underwent a series of corporate convolutions that took it in and out of several businesses, including aluminum recycling and phonograph records (Sam Goody).

Its rebirth as a financial services company had its genesis in Shanghai-born Wall Street wunderkind Gerald Tsai, Jr., who started his career in the sixties as a fund manager for Fidelity Investments. Tsai left Fidelity to form his own Manhattan Fund, a glamour growth stock fund whose rapid expansion and briefly spectacular performance made him one of the more celebrated of the "go-go" fund managers of that era of Wall Street history.

But the market selloff in 1969–70 almost wiped out the Manhattan Fund (it's made a great comeback under Neuberger and Berman), and Tsai spent the next ten years dabbling in financial ventures of dubious distinction and mixed success. The last of these ventures was a tiny insurance holding company named Associated Madison, which he expanded into a direct-mail insurance operation, later to be renamed Mutual Benefit Life.

In 1981, having read press reports that American Can was thinking of shifting from manufacturing to the faster-growing service sector, Tsai went to American Can's president William Woodside and proposed a joint venture that would use the mailing list of American Can's direct-mail general merchandise retailer, Fingerhut Cos., to market Associated Madison's insurance policies.

Although the proposed venture didn't work out, the two executives hit it off, American Can acquired the struggling Associated Madison for $127 million, and Tsai became the resident financial services expert at American Can. He was soon calling the shots, spending nearly a billion dollars in less than three years on different financial services acquisitions and selling off the company's paper and Canadian packaging operations.

In 1986 Tsai, at age 56, succeeded Woodside as CEO of American Can. Three months later, he sold American Can's domestic packaging operations to Triangle Industries' National Can subsidiary for $580 million (which Nelson Peltz raised from Drexel to complete the courtship begun at the Beverly Hills cocktail party) and laid off more than half the headquarters staff in Greenwich, Connecticut.

On April 29, 1987, American Can, now stripped of its manufacturing activities, changed its name to Primerica Corporation. The same year, Primerica acquired broker-dealer Smith Barney for $750 million. That was a few months before the October 1987 market crash, and Smith Barney ended up that year with a $93 million loss. What timing! Primerica was now faltering.

When Gerry Tsai's star was falling in the 1970s following the collapse of his Manhattan Fund, a new star had begun rising in the person of Brooklyn-born former messenger boy Sanford I. Weill.

While Tsai was struggling to get his bearings, Weill was stringing together a group of small brokerage firms that by the end of the seventies had become Shearson Loeb Rhodes, a formidable fusion of Our Crowd veneration and New Crowd aggressiveness. Weill had become one of the foremost powers in the financial community.

In 1981, the same year Tsai joined American Can, Weill sold out to American Express for 21.3 million shares of the company. Weill became president (but not CEO) of that illustrious Dow giant. But the brash and entrepreneurial Weill was a fish out of water at Amex, whose patrician chairman, James Robinson III, left no question who was in charge. Rich but unfulfilled, Sandy Weill quit American Express in 1985. A year later, eager for activity, he acquired Baltimore-based Commercial Credit Corporation, a depressed consumer finance company with assets of about $4 billion. Keeping his home in New York, Weill saw Commercial Credit as a base from which to make it back to the big time—the same way Gerry Tsai had looked at American Can.

Weill and Tsai knew each other. Prior to Tsai's second divorce and remarriage, they had lived near each other in Greenwich. Some preliminary discussions about Weill's taking over Primerica got nowhere because Tsai wanted too much money.

But Primerica's problems were serious enough and Commercial Credit a serious enough prospect that Tsai sought the advice of Felix Rohatyn and Ira Harris of Lazard Freres. They called Sanford Weill and a deal was struck whereby Commercial Credit Group, Inc., which Weill had restored to a robust cash cow, would acquire Primerica for $1.7 billion in stock and cash. The deal was consummated in December 1988.

Weill was back. The former Brooklyn messenger boy, by acquiring what a *Barron's* article punned "The House that Gerry Built," was now head of a true financial supermarket with assets of over $17 billion—albeit with a few headaches.

I should clarify that although Commercial Credit was the acquiring company and the merged entity would logically be called Commercial Credit, the latter changed its legal name to Primerica Corporation. That's why in discussions of the company's history, you'll find references to the "old" Primerica, which succeeded American Can but preceded Commercial Credit, and the "new" Primerica, which is the combined entity.

As a footnote to the saga just told, the April 18, 1990, *Wall Street Journal* reported that Gerald Tsai had sold 85 percent of his holdings—1 million shares for $26.43 apiece—in March. The price in mid-April had risen to $31. I can't feel *too* sorry for him, but Gerald Tsai's luck has been mixed.

What's ahead for Primerica?

Sanford Weill is a team builder and motivator. Profiles written of him suggest a curious blend of grandiosity and humility. He had a chimney put through the roof of the World Trade Center so his office could have a working fireplace. Yet he is known as a hands-on, shirtsleeves manager whose door is as widely open to the lowest clerk as to the highest vice president. This style of personality has worked well for him. It's how he built Shearson and turned around Commercial Credit. His challenge at Primerica is to sort out a jumble of activities and clearly define its direction. He may be just the guy to do it.

Primerica's 1989 annual report, the first combining the old and new Primericas, is a sober, dignified document that embodies the message Weill has expressed publicly elsewhere: "We do not want to be all things to all people. We want to be the efficient deliverer of financial products to different demographic segments of the financial consumer." Instead of size, he aims for businesses that are "more focused, more disciplined, and better positioned for profitability."

In 1989 total revenue was $5.7 billion. Consumer Services (small loans, direct-mail activities) contributed 32 percent of revenue and 35 percent of earnings; Insurance Services (including only two months of A.L. Williams, the largest term life insurance company, plus credit, accident and health, and property and casualty insurance operations) provided 37 percent of revenues and 48 percent of profits; and Investment Services (Smith Barney, plus mutual funds, asset management and mortgage banking activities) contributed 31 percent of revenues and 17 percent of earnings.

Weill is restructuring and trying to sell low-profit activities, such as medical insurance and direct marketing. Smith Barney has been somewhat under the weather like the brokerage industry in general, but it has a fine image, it has acquired 17 branches and 400 top-notch brokers from Drexel Burnham, and it should prosper when industry conditions improve.

The stock has taken a beating because of Smith Barney, because Wall Street isn't sure Primerica has its act together, and for reasons as far out as rumors the company's insurance operations might be particularly vulnerable to the AIDS epidemic. But Primerica has some mighty powerful assets, and Sandy Weill has been a winner before.

PROCTER & GAMBLE COMPANY (PG)

Try to guess what happened the year one company said the following in its Letter to Shareholders: "We are reasonably pleased with the results of the past year. And yet, as we have stated in previous letters, the long-term development of the business is more important than the results of a single year."

In most annual reports words like "reasonably" and "long-term" mean things weren't so hot. But don't underestimate the modest self-confidence of Procter & Gamble. Its 1989 annual report, from which that quote was taken, highlighted an 18 percent increase in earnings and a dividend increase for the thirty-third consecutive year. That's pretty good going.

Procter & Gamble began in 1837 making soap and candles out of pig fat in Cincinnati, then jokingly called "Porkopolis." The company's identification with such household staples as Ivory soap, Mr. Clean, Head & Shoulders, Crest, Pampers, Charmin, Bounty and Tide makes it one of the most visible consumer products companies in the world. Not to mention the "soaps" sponsored by P&G, like *Search for Tomorrow* and *As the World Turns*, that have fulfilled more than a few fantasies over many years. Although personal care and household products amount to some 80 percent of sales, the company's food products are equally familiar: Folgers coffee, Crisco, Pringles potato chips and Duncan Hines cake mixes. The company estimates that 98 percent of American households contain at least one P&G product.

Recent acquisitions have included Blandax, used to brush more German teeth than any other toothpaste, and the proprietary drug companies Richardson Vicks, Inc. and G.D. Searles.

In fiscal 1989, P&G had sales of $21.4 billion and net earnings of over $1 billion. Nearly 40 percent of sales came from its expanding international activities.

It is one of the world's great companies. It has superb domestic and international marketing and a diverse product base not

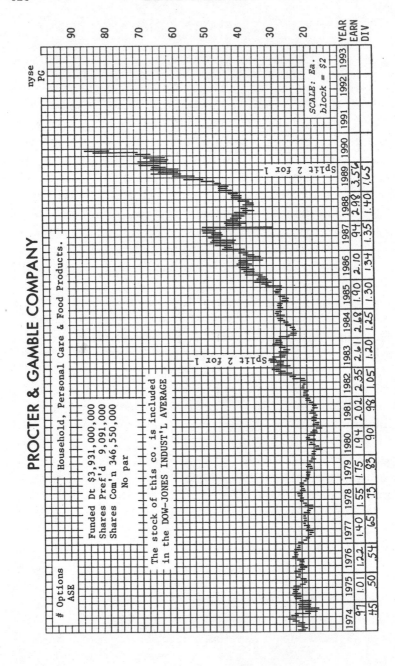

PROCTER & GAMBLE COMPANY

Household, Personal Care & Food Products.

nyse
PG

Funded Dt $3,931,000,000
Shares Pref'd　9,091,000
Shares Com'n 346,550,000
No par

The stock of this co. is included
in the DOW-JONES INDUST'L AVERAGE

Options
ASE

SCALE: Ea.
block = $2

Split 2 for 1

Split 2 for 1

YEAR	1974	1975	1976	1977	1978	1979	1980	1981	1982	1983	1984	1985	1986	1987	1988	1989	1990	1991	1992	1993
EARN	.97	1.01	1.22	1.40	1.55	1.75	1.94	2.02	2.35	2.61	2.68	1.90	2.10	.94	2.98	3.56				
DIV	.45	.50	.54	.65	.73	.83	.90	.98	1.05	1.20	1.25	1.30	1.34	1.35	1.40	1.65				

really prone to economic cyclicality. It is active in research and development, even in the potentially dramatic area of pharmaceuticals. It is rock-solid financially and will probably continue its steady and profitable growth in the 1990s.

Earlier this year, the company announced the development of a new product, Olestra, which could have revolutionary implications in the food industry. Olestra, which is made from sugar and vegetable oils, is a calorie-free fat substitute. If approved by the FDA, Olestra could replace up to 75 percent of the fat in cooking oils and shortenings.

Of course, the world also loves Procter & Gamble, and with its recent P/E of 18, the market has discounted future earnings growth for now. Its yield is average.

One thing about companies this good is that there's not much excitement on the up side, and should something happen to the down side there's plenty of room to drop. Needless to say, that's when I get interested.

SEARS, ROEBUCK & COMPANY (S)

If P&G's soap operas fulfill fantasies, so has the Sears, Roebuck catalog over the decades. Measuring three to four inches thick in its heyday, it displayed everything from ladies' lingerie to light bulbs and log-splitters and was a staple in houses (the out variety included) throughout the country.

Sears started as a mail order operation. When the automobile made America mobile, Sears began opening retail stores, eventually becoming America's largest retailer. In 1972 Sears' sales amounted to 1 percent of the United States gross national product.

Today, Sears is neck and neck with K-Mart for honors as the world's largest retailer in a field that includes other giants like Wal-Mart and Penney. But it is also a financial services giant. It acquired Allstate Insurance, a provider of property and lia-

SEARS, ROEBUCK & COMPANY

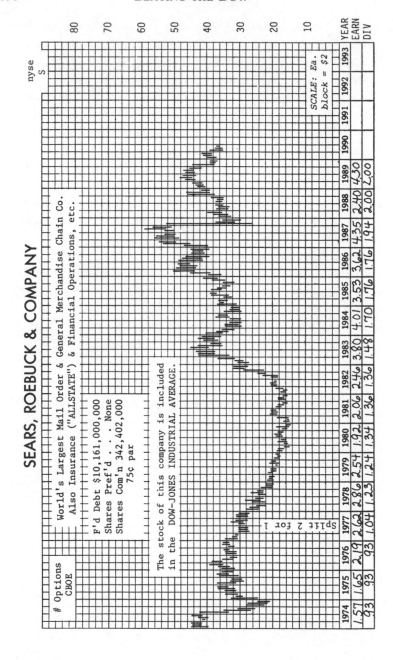

World's Largest Mail Order & General Merchandise Chain Co.
Also Insurance ("ALLSTATE") & Financial Operations, etc.

F'd Debt $10,161,000,000
Shares Pref'd . . . None
Shares Com'n 342,402,000
75¢ par

The stock of this company is included in the DOW-JONES INDUSTRIAL AVERAGE.

Options
CBOE

nyse
S

SCALE: Ea.
block = $2

Split 2 for 1

	1974	1975	1976	1977	1978	1979	1980	1981	1982	1983	1984	1985	1986	1987	1988	1989	1990	1991	1992	1993	YEAR
	1.57	1.65	2.19	2.62	2.86	2.54	1.92	2.06	2.46	3.80	4.01	3.53	3.62	4.35	2.40	4.30					EARN
	.93	.93	.93	1.04	1.23	1.24	1.34	1.36	1.36	1.48	1.70	1.76	1.76	1.94	2.00	2.00					DIV

bility insurance, way back in 1921. It has been a Dow stock since 1924 and it was the first to diversify into unrelated financial services. (Sears and other Dow companies have always had "captive" finance companies primarily to finance product purchases.)

In the 1980s, Sears caught the financial supermarket bug. It acquired Dean Witter Financial Services, engaged in brokerage, investment banking, consumer finance and mortgage banking; Coldwell Banker Real Estate, a developer, manager and broker of real estate (since divested of its commercial division); and introduced the Discover credit card.

In 1989, sales were $53.8 billion from Sears Merchandise (59 percent); Allstate (31 percent); Dean Witter (7 percent); and Coldwell Banker (3 percent).

Sears goes into the 1990s with some interesting challenges. As a retailer it has stores wherever locations are desirable in the U.S., virtually ruling out new stores as an avenue of growth. To try to improve its competitive position, it has spent money making existing stores "stores of the future;" has embarked on a new "everyday low pricing" strategy affecting some 50,000-plus items to replace its weekly sale days; and has started to sell national brand appliances and consumer electronics in addition to its own brands (Kenmore, Craftsman et al.) An interesting renaissance in the mail order catalog business in the 1980s has benefited Sears to some extent but has tended mainly to be a specialty market.

Allstate is profitable but not exciting because it is a big auto liability writer and states are giving insurers trouble on rate hikes. Dean Witter, whose results include the now-profitable Discover card, seems to be having fewer problems than many of its competitors, and the soft real estate market isn't helping Coldwell.

Something's got to happen at Sears in its retail operations to breathe some life into its stock performance, which has been lackluster in recent years. Some help will come from the recent refinancing of Sears Tower, its headquarters building and Chicago's tallest skyscraper; proceeds from that transaction were earmarked to reduce debt and finance a continuation of the company's stock buy-back program. The yield is currently high.

President Franklin Roosevelt once said the best way to teach the USSR the attractions of capitalism would be to drop Sears, Roebuck catalogs all over the nation. Sears never acted on the suggestion, but maybe when perestroika gets a little further along they should look at the idea again. They could sell a lot of fur hats there.

TEXACO, INC. (TX)

Texaco was rechristened in 1959 when the Texas Company decided to adopt its cable address as its corporate name.

The company was founded at the turn of the century by an oil prospector and ex-Standard Oil employee named Joseph Cullinan and a high-rolling gambler and entrepreneur named John Gates after oil was discovered at Spindletop near Beaumont on the Texas coast. Standard Oil had a virtual nationwide monopoly at the time, but Texas, having passed antitrust legislation, was one state the Rockefellers had to stay out of.

Texas Company had a knack for marketing and for making money. In the 1930s it struck a deal with Standard Oil of California whereby it traded capital and marketing knowhow for a half-share in Socal's vast Saudi Arabian oil concession. By the end of World War II Texas Company was America's most profitable large oil company, with stations in every state.

In the 1970s, however, when crude oil began rising in price, Texaco missed the boat, lapsing into inefficient marketing and failing to take advantage of the opportunity to invest in exploration and replenish its reserves. When its top management changed in the early 1980s, Texaco began to face up to its problems.

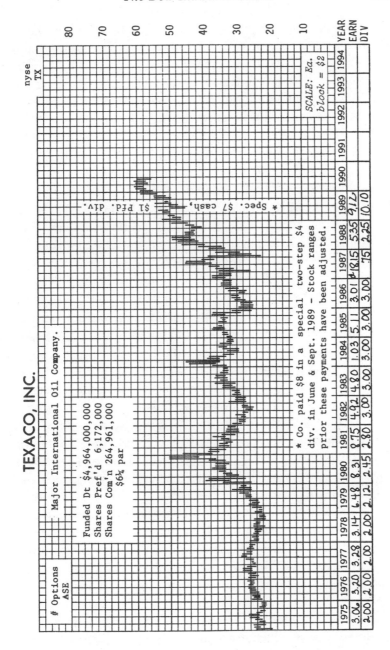

TEXACO, INC.

nyse TX

Options
ASE

Major International Oil Company.

Funded Dt $4,964,000,000
Shares Pref'd 6,172,000
Shares Com'n 264,961,000
$6¼ par

* Co. paid $8 in a special two-step $4
div. in June & Sept. 1989 - Stock ranges
prior these payments have been adjusted.

SCALE: Ea.
block = $2

* Spec. $7 cash, $1 Pfd. div.

YEAR	1975	1976	1977	1978	1979	1980	1981	1982	1983	1984	1985	1986	1987	1988	1989	1990	1991	1992	1993	1994
EARN	3.06	3.20	3.28	3.14	6.48	8.31	8.75	4.92	4.80	1.03	5.11	3.01	4.15	5.35	9.12					
DIV	2.00	2.00	2.00	2.00	2.12	2.45	2.80	3.00	3.00	3.00	3.00	3.00	.75	2.25	10.10					

Texaco's modern saga began just after New Year's Day of 1984. Getty Oil Company, a relatively obscure giant rich in reserves, was racked by internecine warfare involving Gordon Getty, son of the legendary J. Paul Getty; Sid Peterson, the CEO of Getty Oil; and the Getty Trust, which owned 12 percent of the stock and was represented by now-famous takeover lawyer Martin Lipton.

After vigorous negotiations lasting late into the night and following day, dealmaker Lipton seemed to have found a solution. Gordon Getty and a relative upstart oil producer named Pennzoil, Inc., led by Hugh Liedtke, would buy Getty Oil. By January 3 the deal seemed done. The Getty board approved the offer by a 15–1 vote and a joint press release by Pennzoil and Getty announced that an agreement in principle had been reached.

But then trouble erupted. Word got out from Wall Street, notably from Goldman Sach's mergers and acquisitions department, that Getty would listen to offers higher than the $110 a share offered by Pennzoil. They even called a few prospects, one of them being Texaco.

Texaco needed Getty's reserves and was interested. At first reluctant to horn in on what looked like a done deal, it hired First Boston and its M&A demon Bruce Wasserstein, who assured Texaco's chairman, John McKinley, that Getty was still up for grabs. Further assurance was obtained from Skadden, Arps, Slate, Meagher & Flom, a big law firm specializing in takeovers.

So McKinley decided to buy Getty and was soon presented with a contract for sale at $125 a share from Martin Lipton, representing the Getty Trust. Part of the paperwork was a document indemnifying the Getty Trust and everyone connected with Getty Oil from any litigation, a formality made necessary by Getty family squabbling, Lipton said.

The deal was done, but Pennzoil's Liedtke was madder than a junkyard dog. He sued, a not uncommon development following any takeover, and Texaco's counsel, Skadden, Arps, took it in stride.

So routinely did Skadden view the matter that it neglected what seemed like a minor thing. It failed to respond to a claim filed in Delaware by Pennzoil against Texaco for tortious interference with a contract. That procedural failure was a big mistake. It allowed Pennzoil to sue, not in Delaware, where corporations are treated with tender, loving care, but in Texas where juries think real big.

The rest is history. Pennzoil hired a talented lawyer named Joe Jamail, who got the biggest jury verdict in history. Texaco was ordered to pay over $10 billion in actual and punitive damages. Texaco appealed and lost. It then declared bankruptcy to avoid having to post a bond to cover the award. That also meant suspending its dividend.

Enter corporate raider and TWA Chairman Carl Icahn, also of USX fame, who obtained a 12 percent voting interest in Texaco from the late Australian wheeler-dealer Robert Holmes à Court.

The arrival of Carl Icahn anywhere is rarely cause for celebration, but here he proved to be just what the doctor ordered. Shuttling between Pennzoil's Liedtke and Texaco's new CEO James Kinnear, and knowing that a settlement would make his own holdings worth a fortune, Icahn used his considerable persuasive powers to convince both sides a settlement was the only way to go. Texaco was determined to take the case to the U.S. Supreme Court and little Pennzoil had to weigh losing everything or gaining something.

The case was finally settled for $3 billion, and Texaco emerged from bankruptcy in April of 1988.

A restructuring followed in which Texaco sold its interests in a West German subsidiary and Texaco, Canada, Inc. (to Exxon), and got Icahn out of its hair through various agreements, including the declaration of two special dividends in cash and preferred stock totaling $8 a share.

Texaco had sales of $35 billion in 1989 deriving 51 percent

from the United States, 19 percent from other Western Hemisphere markets, and 29 percent from the Eastern Hemisphere. Its legal problems and restructuring are behind it, and its new management has a stated determination "to make the '90s and beyond a new era for Texaco. We have a good plan to get where we want to be as an industry leader."

As I said earlier, I'm writing just as a major crisis unfolds in the Middle East. Whether short-term it will mean more oil on the world market or less is a question I can't answer any better than anybody else. But I'm optimistic about the oil stocks in general and Texaco should be no exception.

UNION CARBIDE CORPORATION (UK)

Union Carbide has been realigned into a holding company and three separate operating companies, Union Carbide Chemicals and Plastics, Inc., UCAR Carbon Company, Inc., and Union Carbide Industrial Gases, Inc. Each reports its financial results directly to shareholders in its own summary annual report while the holding company reports overall results.

The expressed purpose of the realignment was to replace bureaucracy with entrepreneurship. More cynical observers believe the purpose was to create stand-alone entities that would be easier to spin off into a joint venture or to shareholders. To understand what's going on at UK, you need a little background.

For 60-odd years, through the 1970s, Union Carbide was a stolid producer of chemicals, ranking second only to du Pont, and rolling with the punches of a cyclical industry. Then came the recession of the early 1980s, which hammered the industry in general and Union Carbide in particular.

After attempting unsuccessfully to sell some of its commodity operations, Carbide shut down marginal facilities, laid off employees and began to emphasize commercial research and

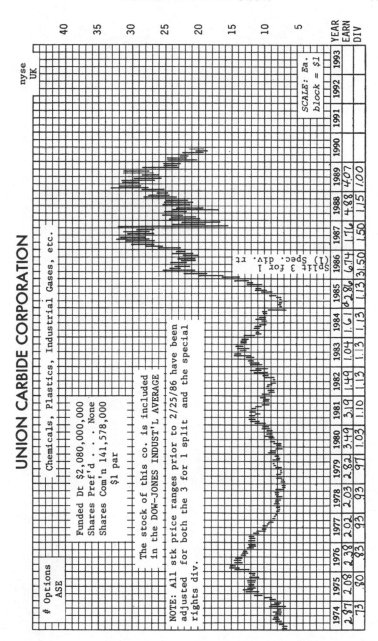

UNION CARBIDE CORPORATION

Chemicals, Plastics, Industrial Gases, etc.

nyse
UK

Options
ASE

Funded Dt $2,080,000,000
Shares Pref'd . . . None
Shares Com'n 141,578,000
$1 par

The stock of this co. is included
in the DOW-JONES INDUST'L AVERAGE

NOTE: All stk price ranges prior to 2/25/86 have been
adjusted for both the 3 for 1 split and the special
rights div.

SCALE: Ea.
block = $1

Split 3 for 1
(1) Spec. div. rt

YEAR	1974	1975	1976	1977	1978	1979	1980	1981	1982	1983	1984	1985	1986	1987	1988	1989	1990	1991	1992	1993
EARN	2.97	2.08	2.38	2.01	2.03	2.82	3.49	3.19	1.49	1.04	1.61	2.86	6.74	1.76	4.88	4.07				
DIV	.73	.80	.93	.93	.93	.97	1.03	1.10	1.13	1.13	1.13	1.13	31.50	1.50	1.15	1.00				

move into consumer businesses that would provide a hedge against the cyclicality of commodity chemicals.

Using cost advantages from its strength in basic chemicals, it gained significant market share in such consumer products as antifreeze, batteries, and plastic wrappings, like Glad Bags.

Then came the infamous Bhopal disaster in 1984, when deadly gas leaked from a 51 percent-owned pesticide plant, killing over 3,000 people. Arriving in India, UK Chairman Warren Anderson was held for six hours on criminal conspiracy and homicide-related charges before being freed and expelled from the country. Litigation on behalf of Bhopal victims exceeded $3 billion. The case was finally settled in 1989, but individual lawsuits are still pending. That was followed a year later by a hostile takeover attempt led by Samuel Heyman, head of GAF Corporation.

To fend off the takeover, Carbide frantically sought for a white knight, but with the ignominy of Bhopal, none was to be found. To placate shareholders, Carbide sold its consumer products division, its agricultural division, and its sybaritic suburban Connecticut headquarters for $3.5 billion and paid shareholders $4.5 billion in special dividends and other payments. It had preserved its independence, but at the price of heavy debt and the loss of its most promising activities.

Carbide faces the 1990s essentially back to basics, a cyclical business sitting in a down cycle and relying on entrepreneurship to stir what one analyst described as "a sleeping giant that no one ever seems able to goose."

But some observers see the beginning of progress. According to a summer 1989 *New York Times* article titled "Is Union Carbide Heading for Good Times?", the Chemicals and Plastics operation, which ended that year with 66 percent of total sales and 76 percent of profits, is closing its highest-cost domestic plants and looking abroad for opportunities to build or acquire assets, an acknowledged shortcoming of Carbide, whose operations are largely domestic in a global marketplace. It is also providing seed money to employees with ideas for new businesses and has already come up with a substitute for environmentally offensive solvents used to spray-paint cars.

The Industrial Gases company, which contributed 27 percent of sales and 17 percent of profits, has already found some new applications for old gases, using oxygen to incinerate solid waste and nitrogen to freeze vegetables.

The UCAR Carbon Company supplies products to the steel industry, which is in its own slump and has little opportunity for innovation, except in new processes.

The overall company has made significant reductions in its debt and in 1989 regained the investment-grade credit rating it lost in 1985.

Wall Street loves to hate this company, so I'm watching it carefully. With almost $9 billion in sales and 50,000 employees being rewarded for new ideas, they'll find a way to come back. UK, which currently yields over 5 percent, is a case study in resilience and adaptability.

UNITED TECHNOLOGIES CORPORATION
(UTX)

This is one of those companies better known for its parts than its whole. The "United" comes originally from United Aircraft and Transport, a company formed in the twenties and split up in 1934, creating United Airlines, Boeing, and United Aircraft. The latter was the predecessor of United Technologies.

United Aircraft and its subsidiaries, Hamilton Standard and Pratt & Whitney, were synonymous with aircraft propellers and engines during World War II. Today Pratt & Whitney vies with General Electric and Rolls Royce for dominance of the world market for jet engines.

Another subsidiary, Sikorski, was the main supplier of helicopters during the Vietnam War and continues as a major

UNITED TECHNOLOGIES CORP.

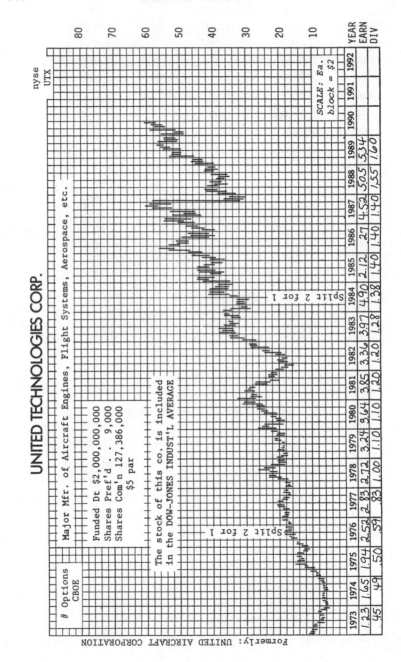

Formerly: UNITED AIRCRAFT CORPORATION

nyse
UTX

Major Mfr. of Aircraft Engines, Flight Systems, Aerospace, etc.

Options
CBOE

Funded Dt $2,000,000,000
Shares Pref'd . . 9,000
Shares Com'n 127,386,000
       $5 par

The stock of this co. is included
in the DOW-JONES INDUST'L AVERAGE

Split 2 for 1

Split 2 for 1

SCALE: Ea.
block = $2

YEAR	1973	1974	1975	1976	1977	1978	1979	1980	1981	1982	1983	1984	1985	1986	1987	1988	1989	1990	1991	1992
EARN	1.23	1.65	1.94	2.52	2.83	2.72	3.24	3.64	3.85	3.36	3.97	4.90	2.12	.27	4.52	5.05	5.34			
DIV	.45	.49	.50	.59	.83	1.00	1.10	1.10	1.20	1.20	1.28	1.38	1.40	1.40	1.40	1.55	1.60			

producer of rotary-wing aircraft for government and commercial use.

Like other major aerospace and defense contractors in the early 1970s, United Aircraft began a diversification program aimed at reducing its dependence on those sectors.

Under the leadership of Harry Gray, who was recruited from the conglomerate Litton Industries, United made some major commercial acquisitions, including Otis Elevator, Carrier Corporation (heating, ventilating and air conditioning equipment) and several other businesses that were later sold.

Today United Technologies, which was renamed in 1975, has sales of just under $20 billion from four categories of activities it puts under two umbrellas. Aerospace and Defense, which provides about half the revenues, is comprised of Power (Pratt & Whitney), 35 percent; and Flight Systems (Sikorski, Hamilton Standard, Missiles and Space Systems), 18 percent. Commercial and Industrial is comprised of Building Systems (Carrier and Otis), 37 percent; and Industrial Systems (electronic, electromechanical, hydraulic systems and components for the automotive industry), 10 percent.

Although military and space-related work represented less than 25 percent of revenues in 1989, the company remains vulnerable to reduced government spending in those areas. It supplied 75 percent of the 1989 engine orders for the midsize Boeing 757 and will be competing for a major share of the fleet replacement market in the 1990s.

Otis, according to the current annual report, had 24 percent of the global new-equipment market in 1989, twice the market share of its nearest competitor. Service and modernization activities account for half its revenue, so it is only partly hostage to the commercial construction industry.

Carrier is also the world's market share leader and has particular strength in Europe and the Far East, with the exception of Japan, where local competition is formidable and where Carrier is trying to improve its competitive position.

UT Automotive had record sales in 1989 for the seventh

consecutive year despite sluggish domestic car sales because of increased North American market penetration and strong car sales in Europe. It supplies the "Big Three" in various ways (electrical systems, door trim, keyless entry systems and the like), and its wire systems and engine-cooling business enjoys growing demand in the European auto market. It owns Sheller-Globe Corporation, a leading supplier of steering wheels, instrument panels and other automotive components.

United Technologies has a lot of potential, especially in the jet engine market, but its heavy involvement with the recession-sensitive automotive and construction industries and with the military procurement sector somewhat counterweights the present outlook.

The company defies classification, not unlike Allied-Signal, with which, coincidentally, it skirmished and lost as a would-be white knight in the Bendix/Martin-Marietta affair of 1982.

UTX is a solid, not terribly exciting stock with a normal P/E and an average yield. It had a backlog at the end of 1989 of $20 billion and will probably enjoy earnings growth, pay increased dividends and show steady gains into the nineties.

If they get some more big engine orders, and if the economy really picks up, the stock could get interesting.

USX CORPORATION (X)

USX is the nation's largest integrated producer of a variety of semifinished and finished steel products. The untelling name was inspired in 1986 by the company's biggest shareholder, Carl Icahn, to reflect a change in the corporation's activities. Icahn's plan was to split the traditional steel business off from the company's recently acquired oil and gas activities and rename it United States Steel, the name it had used for 85 years.

The Icahn plan was voted down in a proxy fight in May 1990, but the plan forced USX management to focus on its share

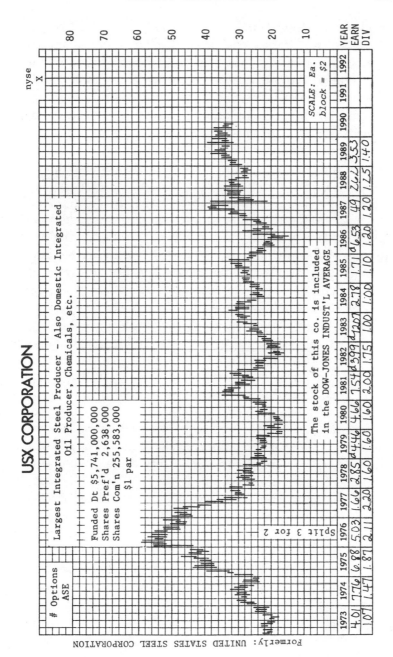

USX CORPORATION

Largest Integrated Steel Producer – Also Domestic Integrated
Oil Producer, Chemicals, etc.

Funded Dt $5,741,000,000
Shares Pref'd 2,638,000
Shares Com'n 255,583,000
$1 par

Options
ASE

nyse
X

Split 3 for 2

Formerly: UNITED STATES STEEL CORPORATION

The stock of this co. is included
in the DOW-JONES INDUST'L AVERAGE

SCALE: Ea.
block = $2

	1973	1974	1975	1976	1977	1978	1979	1980	1981	1982	1983	1984	1985	1986	1987	1988	1989	1990	1991	1992
YEAR																				
EARN	4.01	7.76	6.88	5.03	1.66	2.85	4.46	4.66	15.4d	d3.99	d2.07	2.78	1.71	d6.53	49	2.62	3.53			
DIV	1.07	1.47	1.87	2.11	2.20	1.60	1.60	1.60	2.00	1.75	1.00	1.00	1.10	1.20	1.20	1.25	1.40			

price, which is lower now than it was in 1975. In late 1990, speculation had it that something similar to the Icahn plan might yet take place on the initiative of management.

I'm reminded of the early 1960s, when Roger Blough, CEO of Big Steel, as it was then nicknamed, raised prices in defiance of an anti-inflation understanding between President John F. Kennedy and industry leaders. An angry Kennedy quoted an observation of his father, no mean capitalist himself, that "businessmen are sons of bitches." The young president summoned Blough to the White House and got him to back down.

The original United States Steel was founded in 1901 by banker J.P. Morgan, who bought out Carnegie Steel and put it together with a group of other companies to form what at the time was the world's largest corporation, capitalized at over a billion dollars. To run it, he hired Andrew Carnegie's protégé, Charles Schwab. While he accomplished much in the three years he stayed, Schwab, as we have seen, went on by way of Monte Carlo to buy and build Bethlehem Steel.

We talked about the beleaguered steel industry in our earlier discussion of Bethlehem Steel. USX's steel operations have been no exception, but its story has some wrinkles of its own.

The recent history of USX began in 1982, when United States Steel paid $5.8 billion to buy Marathon Oil, a fully integrated, medium-sized oil and gas company with international activities and extensive North Sea holdings. The idea was to use Marathon's strength to counter the cyclicality of the steel business. In 1986 U.S. Steel augmented its energy holdings, especially in natural gas, by paying $4 billion plus for Texas Oil & Gas.

Low crude oil prices and poor steel conditions, however, conspired to depress the stock, which caught the predatory eye of Mr. Icahn. First attempting a $7 billion takeover of the whole company in October 1986, Icahn was rebuffed by a poison pill defense, but he wound up with 13.3 percent interest and things haven't been the same since.

Although the steel segment has greatly improved as a result of closing unprofitable plants and laying off tens of thousands of steelworkers, Mr. Icahn has persistently pressed the argument that the profits and cash flow of the energy operations were propping up the capital- and labor-intensive steel activities, that the two divisions would be worth more to existing shareholders as separate entities and that the energy company would be attractive to an outside buyer if its wings weren't freighted with steel.

Although his own wings were clipped by the proxy defeat and the poison pill, Icahn can be expected to remain a gadfly until his own shares are worth more. USX management admits it must pursue measures aimed at giving USX shares a higher market value.

Management's restructuring plan, in addition to plant closings and the modernization of facilities, includes selling off the reserves of its Texas Oil and Gas subsidiary. Cash realized from that will be used to further reduce debt and to repurchase USX stock.

There is also talk that USX will consider the public sale of a 20 percent interest in the steel business once the industry recovers from its downcycle.

In 1989, USX had sales of $17.7 billion from energy (65 percent), steel (31 percent), and diversified activities (4 percent), with earnings in approximately the same proportions.

USX's stock chart since 1979 looks like a monogram for the MMM company. While its stock has declined in value since its 1976 high, it has fluctuated rather widely in response to industry conditions and news developments. Using strategies discussed in later chapters, we could have made money with USX.

As I have said before, I see a future in the 1990s for both steel and energy. USX management is under great pressure to do what's good for its stock, and given that it has already taken some meaningful steps and has others on its agenda, I think we'll see significant future gains. Its juicy current yield makes me happy at the present time.

WESTINGHOUSE ELECTRIC
CORPORATION (WX)

Anybody who was in New York when the lights went out back in the 1960s got a stunning revelation of the extent to which we take electricity for granted. Forget that you couldn't see. There were no subways, no traffic lights, no elevators, no door bells, no air conditioning, no cash registers (when you went to buy candles), and when you finally decided to stop fighting it there was no cold beer. It's a documented fact that more babies than usual were conceived that lightless night. Thank goodness some things have been left untouched by electricity.

The patent application for Thomas Edison's long-lasting incandescent light bulb was rejected in 1894 because it was poorly written. The rights to a refined version of the bulb, a breakthrough in technology, were scooped up by another aggressive young inventor and entrepreneur named George Westinghouse.

The Westinghouse Company had been formed eight years earlier, in 1866, to manufacture and promote alternating current (AC) electrical equipment. Unless you're technically inclined, AC might not mean much, but it is one of the truly revolutionary technological developments.

The direct-current (DC) generators existing at the time couldn't economically provide power more than a mile from the generator. Alternating current, which was invented by English and French engineers, permitted greatly increased voltage that would carry far greater distances and could be reduced to safe levels at the point of use.

Westinghouse bought the rights to AC and satisfied skeptics of its safety by illuminating the entire 1893 Columbian Exhibition in Chicago. One anti-AC crusader attempted to prove its dangers by purchasing Westinghouse equipment, wiring up a chair and installing it in a prison. That's how the electric chair got created.

Before the turn of the century, Westinghouse had a contract

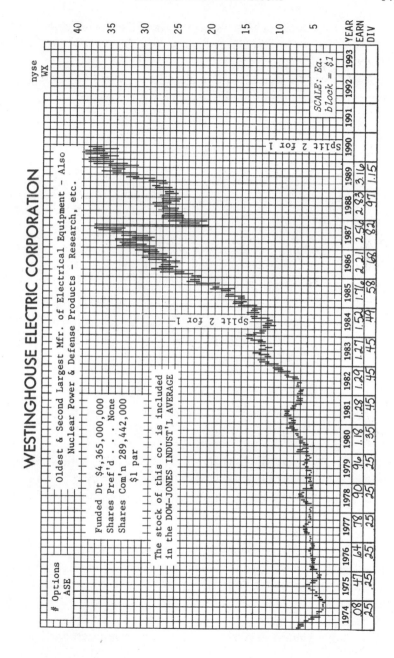

WESTINGHOUSE ELECTRIC CORPORATION

nyse
WX

Oldest & Second Largest Mfr. of Electrical Equipment – Also
Nuclear Power & Defense Products – Research, etc.

Funded Dt $4,365,000,000
Shares Pref'd . . . None
Shares Com'n 289,442,000
$1 par

The stock of this co. is included
in the DOW-JONES INDUST'L AVERAGE

Options
ASE

Split 2 for 1

Split 2 for 1

SCALE: Ea.
block = $1

	1974	1975	1976	1977	1978	1979	1980	1981	1982	1983	1984	1985	1986	1987	1988	1989	1990	1991	1992	1993
YEAR EARN	.08	.47	.64	.78	.90	.96	1.18	1.28	1.29	1.27	1.52	1.76	2.21	2.56	2.83	3.16				
DIV	.25	.25	.25	.25	.25	.25	.35	.45	.45	.45	.49	.58	.68	.82	.97	1.15				

to install three AC generators at Niagara Falls, which became the nation's first big hydroelectric project and made AC the industry standard.

In 1957, Westinghouse designed and developed the first nuclear power plant, in Shippingport, Pennsylvania, and has since designed and built reactors and nuclear generators throughout the United States and around the world. The U.S. Navy's nuclear submarines and warships are mainly powered by Westinghouse reactors.

Westinghouse, second only to GE in electrical equipment, leads the world in nuclear reactors. But of course it is much more than even that.

Group W is now the nation's largest non–network radio group, and is a major factor otherwise in broadcasting through its television stations, satellite communications, and expanding global activities in program production and syndication.

Westinghouse's Commercial Group operates a diverse group of businesses including Longines, known as "the jeweler's watch company," and a large office furniture business that includes such names as Shaw-Walker in the U.S. and Reff, Inc., in Canada.

The company is also into financial services, including community land development, and has important activities in the area of environmental systems, including resource recovery plants and hazardous waste management.

Overall sales and revenues in 1989 were $12.8 billion, contributed as follows: Industrial, 37 percent; Energy and Utility Systems, 21 percent; Electronic Systems, 21 percent; Financial Services, 6 percent; Broadcasting, 5 percent; and Other Commercial, 10 percent.

Nuclear power has, of course, been the focus of much controversy, before and since the famous Three Mile Island disaster—that was a Babcock & Wilcox reactor operated by a General Public Utilities Corporation subsidiary.

Westinghouse was embarrassed in the late 1980s when the Aquino government in the Philippines cited faulty construction as a reason for refusing to turn on a $2.2-billion reactor project. It didn't help that Westinghouse was accused of having bribed the Marcos government to get the contract or that it located the reactor next to a volcano.

Beginning in the mid-1970s, a series of events brought Westinghouse close to financial disaster. In order to sell reactors to utilities in the 1960s, the company had entered into contracts to supply millions of pounds of uranium. But in 1972 the uranium producers formed a secret cartel and around the same time the Nixon administration took measures to shift the government's enrichment activities to the private sector. The effect of both was to more than triple uranium prices.

Faced with crippling losses, Westinghouse reneged on its contracts to supply uranium and brought an antitrust suit against the uranium cartel. The case was finally settled in 1981 with Westinghouse receiving a small ($100 million) settlement. The company began a comeback.

Recent sluggish earnings and concerns about defense business (various agencies of the U.S. government account for 22 percent of sales) have inhibited stock performance in recent months, but Westinghouse, which has restructured and cut costs, has a big stake in major megatrends of the 1990s and should perform strongly when the economy improves. Westinghouse is no General Electric, but it's interesting nonetheless.

WOOLWORTH CORPORATION (Z)

The 1990 O'Higgins Award (dubious though the honor may be) for the most imaginative annual report cover goes—envelope, please—to Woolworth Corporation.

It's a drawing of a modern two-tiered shopping mall, complete with fountains, skylight, potted trees, and loveseat benches, except that every shop in it is a Woolworth enterprise—Kinney Shoes, Lady Foot Locker, Woolworth Express,

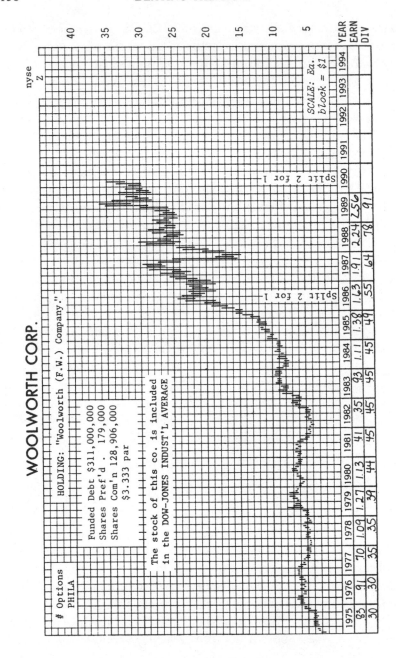

WOOLWORTH CORP.

nyse
Z

HOLDING: "Woolworth (F.W.) Company."

Funded Debt $311,000,000
Shares Pref'd . 179,000
Shares Com'n 128,906,000
       $3.333 par

Options
PHILA

The stock of this co. is included
in the DOW-JONES INDUST'L AVERAGE

Split 2 for 1

Split 2 for 1

SCALE: Ea.
block = $1

YEAR	1975	1976	1977	1978	1979	1980	1981	1982	1983	1984	1985	1986	1987	1988	1989	1990	1991	1992	1993	1994
EARN	.85	.91	.70	1.09	1.27	1.13	.41	.35	.93	1.11	1.38	1.63	1.91	2.24	2.56					
DIV	.30	.30	.35	.35	.39	.44	.45	.45	.45	.45	.49	.55	.64	.78	.91					

Herald Square Party Shop, Foot Locker, Rubin, Woolco, Susie's, Afterthoughts, Northern Reflections, Sportelle, Champs Sports, Anderson-Little, Richman's, Athletic-X, and Kids Mart. That's not all of them, either. And you thought Woolworth's was still the old Five & Dime out of a Norman Rockwell print?

Woolworth Corporation, which goes all the way back to 1879, currently has stores and related support operations in fifteen countries on four continents—North America, Europe, Australia, and Asia. Headquartered in the landmark Woolworth Building in New York, it operates more than 8,000 stores in the United States, Canada, West Germany, Australia, Belgium, and the Netherlands—including some 6,400 specialty units and more than 1,600 general merchandise stores. Woolworth's global presence is enhanced by 11 buying offices located throughout Asia and Mexico and by 9 overseas manufacturing facilities producing footwear and apparel for certain of its stores.

Following World War II major retailing, which had been dominated first by huge mail order firms serving rural America and then by chains and inner-city department stores, changed its principal venue to the suburban malls. The fifties saw the emergence of the discounter, best symbolized at the time by E.J. Korvette, an acronym for eight Jewish Korean War veterans. The discounters used the time-honored retail maxim that a quick nickel beats a slow dollar; they kept overhead low and offset lower profit margins with higher volume. Korvette's eventually went bankrupt, but discounting became entrenched and other retailers either joined the discount movement, like Woolworth competitor S.S. Kresge, with its highly successful K-Mart stores, or responded to the challenge in other ways. Sears shifted its orientation to a somewhat more upscale market, with mixed results, as we have seen.

A rash of newcomers, deciding that the automobile was causing more inconvenience than convenience, revived a catalog mail order industry that had the additional advantage of avoiding state sales taxes.

Woolworth, after attempting unsuccessfully with Woolco Stores to follow Kresge into large-scale discounting, finally threw in the towel. In 1982 it restructured and has since been following a three-part strategy of revitalizing its domestic variety stores, expanding its shoe and specialty stores, and acquiring new specialty retail businesses.

So far, so good. 1989 marked its sixth consecutive year of dividend increases from seven consecutive years of increased earnings.

In 1927, F.W. Woolworth opened a 25 & 50 pfennig store in Bremen, Germany. The development was in keeping with a pronouncement made by Mr. Woolworth and his fellow directors ten years earlier during World War I, in which they advocated "the future expansion of business in foreign lands when conditions permit" and recognized "the advisability of having [associates] trained in foreign languages."

Woolworth plans to capitalize heavily on trends toward global unification, especially in the European Community and in Eastern Europe. It already has nearly 400 stores in Germany alone.

Woolworth's stock has been recovering from extreme undervaluation in the early through mid-80s. The company is financially strong and getting stronger, and given an upturn in the economy should continue to show improvement.

With the stock symbol "Z," and the last on an alphabetical list of Dow stocks, Woolworth is an appropriate note to end on. Old, once illustrious, then down in the dumps, now back and moving forward, Woolworth exemplifies the character of a Dow stock and the essential ingredients of a potential contrarian opportunity: strength, adaptability, resilience.

THE DOW COMPANIES' OFFICES

Allied-Signal Inc.
Columbia Road & Park Avenue
Morristown, NJ 07962
(201) 455-2000

Aluminum Company of America
1501 Alcoa Building, 425 6th Avenue
Pittsburgh, PA 15219
(412) 553-4545

American Express Company
American Express Tower
World Financial Center
New York, NY 10285
(212) 640-2000

American Telephone & Telegraph Company
550 Madison Avenue
New York, NY 10022
(212) 605-5500

Bethlehem Steel Corporation
701 East Third Street
Bethlehem, PA 18016
(215) 694-2424

The Boeing Company
7755 East Marginal Way South
Seattle, WA 98108
(206) 655-2121

Chevron Corporation
225 Bush Street
San Francisco, CA 94104
(415) 894-7700

The Coca-Cola Company
310 North Avenue N.W.
Atlanta, GA 30313
(404) 676-2121

E.I. du Pont de Nemours and Company
1007 Market Street
Wilmington, DE 19898
(302) 774-1000

Eastman Kodak Company
343 State Street
Rochester, NY 14650
(716) 724-4000

Exxon Corporation
1251 Avenue of the Americas
New York, NY 10020
(212) 333-1000

General Electric Company
3135 Easton Turnpike
Fairfield, CT 06431
(203) 373-2211

General Motors Corporation
3044 West Grand Boulevard
Detroit, MI 48202
(313) 556-5000

Goodyear Tire & Rubber Company
1144 East Market Street
Akron, OH 44316
(216) 796-2121

International Business
Machines Corporation
Old Orchard Road
Armonk, NY 10504
(914) 765-1900

International Paper Company
2 Manhattanville Road
Purchase, NY 10577
(914) 397-1500

McDonald's Corporation
McDonald's Plaza
Oak Brook, IL 60521
(312) 575-3000

Merck & Co., Inc.
126 East Lincoln Avenue
Rahway, NJ 07065
(201) 574-4000

Minnesota Mining and
Manufacturing Company
3M Center Building
St. Paul, MN 55144
(612) 733-1110

Navistar International
Corporation
401 West Michigan Avenue
Chicago, IL 60611
(312) 836-2000

Philip Morris Companies
120 Park Avenue
New York, NY 10017
(212) 880-5000

Primerica Corporation
65 East 55th Street
New York, NY 10022
(212) 891-8900

Procter & Gamble Company
1 Procter & Gamble Plaza
Cincinnati, OH 45202
(513) 983-1100

Sears, Roebuck & Company
Sears Tower
Chicago, IL 60684
(312) 875-2500

Texaco, Inc.
2000 Westchester Avenue
White Plains, NY 10650
(914) 253-4000

Union Carbide Corporation
39 Old Ridgebury Road
Danbury, CT 06817
(203) 794-2000

United Technologies
Corporation
United Technologies Building
Hartford, CT 06101
(203) 728-7000

USX Corporation
600 Grant Street
Pittsburgh, PA 15230
(412) 433-1121

Westinghouse Electric
Corporation
Westinghouse Building
Gateway Center
Pittsburgh, PA 15222
(412) 244-2000

Woolworth Corporation
233 Broadway
New York, NY 10279
(212) 553-2000

PART III

MARKETS
AND
CYCLES

BEFORE WE get to the strategy section, I think it's important that we talk a bit about the inevitable ups and downs of the market that occur over time.

Market cycles may be as inevitable as the tides, but that doesn't mean their timing can be predicted with the same exactitude. Not that people will ever stop trying. Part of the fun of being a contrarian has been to keep a file on just how wrong experts can be. I'll share some of my favorite examples in a minute.

When it comes to soothsaying, I'm no better than anybody else, which is to say that I don't know now, never have known, and never will know in advance what the market is going to do. Nobody does.

Beating the Dow is about buying good stocks when they are cheap, and how that can make you money regardless of what the market does.

But to look at the way stocks, big and small, have behaved in relation to each other, to fixed-income investments and to inflation over the years will help us understand why money management will never be an exact science and why no market strategy—even mine—works perfectly each and every year.

Which we should be glad for. Markets being what they are, a strategy that worked without exception would put itself out of business. It's the occasional off-year that allows anomalies, like the strategies we'll be discussing, to exist.

It's popularly observed that historical market comparisons going back prior to 1970 aren't really relevant today. Institutional domination, deregulation of brokerage commissions, persistent inflation, computerized markets, derivative instruments like index futures and index options that make possible index investing and give rise to program trading, the domination of OPEC, floating foreign exchange rates—these, and a host of other developments affecting the financial markets in important ways, all happened after 1970.

In general, prior to 1970 the stock market was supported by wealthy personal investors who bought stock primarily for income and switched to bonds when interest rates exceeded the dividends and expected growth of stocks.

Today the market is supported by mutual funds, pension trusts, and other institutional investors who invest for total returns, looking for capital gains plus dividends (in the case of stocks) or capital gains plus interest (in the case of bonds). As observed earlier, competitive pressures force a short-term focus.

It's probably true that enough has changed to make most such comparisons dubious. But I also know that the human forces of fear and greed, the basic determinants of market psychology, have been with us since day one, causing the extremes of euphoria and pessimism that have defined market tops and bottoms over the years. The best line to use when the cocktail party talk turns to the stock market is still, "The more things change the more they remain the same."

Market psychology, which is measured by a wide variety of "sentiment indicators," determines share prices and the market's direction along with other "real" factors, the most important of which are corporate earnings, interest rates, inflation rates, and actions of the Federal Reserve Board.

The relationship between interest and stock prices has become more complicated but is still quite simple to explain:

1. Interest is a cost of doing business, so higher interest causes lower earnings and lower stock prices.
2. Higher interest rates reflect a monetary supply imbalance—more demand for money than supply—which is bad for companies that depend on borrowings to finance expansion.
3. Higher interest rates reflect Federal Reserve policy, indicating that in the Fed's opinion the economy needs slowing down. A slower economy is bad for business.
4. Higher interest rates draw investment capital away from stocks and into bonds, Treasury bills and money market funds.
5. Interest rates are a price of sorts, so higher interest implies increased inflation.

Inflation is both good and bad for the stock market. Let's look at it.

As recently as the fifties and early sixties, inflation, which had been averaging under 2 percent, was simply not a major problem. To the extent that it did erode purchasing power, the popular wisdom had it that stocks were a hedge against inflation. Stocks represented ownership in companies that had a large percentage of their assets in real estate and machinery, the value of which would rise with the inflation rate and bring share prices with it. Companies, within limits, could also raise prices to customers, increasing sales and profits.

Then came the 1970s and a phenomenon labeled "stagflation," a combination of soaring inflation rates and stagnant economic growth brought about primarily by OPEC-driven oil prices that drove up the consumer price index while they slowed spending and business output. (Sound familiar?)

With depressed corporate profits came a bear market. Precipitous declines in the Dow in 1970 and 1974 were matched by new peaks in the inflation rate, first to over 6 percent, then to over 12 percent.

So much, it seemed, for common stocks as an inflation hedge. Indeed, until 1978 stocks ticked down whenever inflation ticked up and vice versa.

But then a crazy thing happened: Inflation soared, reaching a peak in 1980 of over 14 percent, and stock prices, led by small growth issues in energy and energy-related technology, soared with it. At the same time interest rates went into orbit as well (to put it mildly; this was when the prime rate got over 20 percent).

What to make of all this and what's happened since?

First, 63-year comparisons such as those cited at the outset of this chapter and shown in Figure 1 on page 11 clearly show that stocks outperform inflation over the long run, and there is no reason to believe that won't be the case in the future.

The experience of recent years, however, would indicate that hyperinflation is bad for stocks because it affects *real* corporate profitability (for reasons having to do with depreciation and inventory accounting); because it means higher interest rates; and because it raises the specter of Federal Reserve action to slow the economy down by tightening credit.

The fact that stocks have risen throughout the late 1980s despite relatively high interest rates is a comment on the respect we've gained for "controlling inflation" as the hallmark of a healthy economy.

When interest rates rise moderately, the market is inclined to see the increase as an indication that the Fed is heading off dangerous inflation and to treat it, if not as a positive, at least not as a negative.

We have also come to see relatively high rates as necessary to keep foreign capital invested in America, thus financing our deficit and contributing to what is generally perceived as economic stability.

A sharp rise in rates, however, is still enough to give the market the jitters. Any drop in rates will have the market feeling its oats. People believe what they want to believe, and are more apt to view a rate drop as good for profits rather than as a relaxation of the Fed's prudence with respect to inflation. If all this confuses you somewhat, join the club. The economic outlook or, more accurately, the question of whether the government really can control the economy and prevent both recession and inflation is the basis for a conflicted investment community.

The way the investment community appears to be dealing with the confusion is to give blue chips with demonstrated earning power higher than normal multiples and, temporarily at least, to leave the bargains alone. It is reminiscent of the early 1960s when the Kennedy administration was engaged in "fine tuning" the economy, just as the Bush administration is trying to engineer its "soft landing."

THE MARKET'S reaction to economic events and business cycles over the years has produced interesting investment cycles:

THE 1960S

Prior to the 1960s, a traditional rule prevailed that stocks should sell at 10 or 15 times earnings (P/E). With the "Soaring Sixties," also known as the "tronics boom," that old saw became history. This was the decade when man set foot on the moon, and if a stock, especially an initial public offering, had the words space or electronics in its name (never mind what the company actually did), P/Es of 100 were not unusual. Some— Control Data in 1961, for example—sold briefly at twice that multiple.

In 1962, it all came tumbling down. The scapegoats varied. Some blamed President Kennedy's facing down of the steel industry. Others admitted that the market had excessively valued companies based on naïve speculation rather than demonstrated earning power.

Soon another craze had taken hold, this time in the name of "synergism." The theory was that the whole of an intelligently diversified company is worth more than the sum of its parts because divisions complement each other in various operational ways and benefit from a common source of financial support.

"Leisure time" was a big thing. Technology meant we were all going to be working short weeks and retiring early. A company that made surfboards and sold books somehow had synergy because both were "leisure-related."

"Conglomerates"—which included names like Litton, Ling-Temco-Vought, Gulf & Western, ITT, Textron, City Investing and Avco—also represented a management philosophy: by making divisions responsible in terms of the parent company's return on investment, divisions would be relatively autonomous and the entrepreneurial spirit would enjoy a revival in big companies. Mainly, though, the acquisition of companies added earnings per share, thus increasing the conglomerate's market value. That became the basis of new borrowing power with which to make further acquisitions, and so on.

But synergy was fool's gold, and the heads of the conglomerates, often financial men, proved largely incapable of managing the complex and still essentially vertical organizations under them.

When Litton Industries announced its first quarterly earnings disappointment in January 1968, following nearly ten years of 20 percent annual earnings increases, conglomerates as a group slipped 40 percent in market value.

The conglomerates continued to decline and never really recovered. Being generally highly leveraged, high interest rates compounded their profit problems. Tight money in the early 1970s put them at the mercy of frightened bankers who didn't really understand the companies they were lending to. Efforts to restructure organizationally in ways that made them seem less complex didn't fool an investing public that had become somewhat phobic about what Wall Street called "conglomeritis." "Deconglomeration" eventually became the "in" thing, ironically feeding the merger mania and leveraged buyout craze of the 1980s.

IN THE mid-sixties "concept stocks" hit the boards. By now, mutual funds had become important, performance was a big word, and names like Gerald Tsai of the Manhattan Fund had star quality.

By the latter part of the decade, the action was in names like National Student Marketing, Four Seasons Nursing Centers of America (bankrupt by 1970) and Performance Systems, the first two selling at multiples of over 100 times earnings, the third, a franchiser of fast-food chickens, believe it or not, having an infinite multiple because it had no earnings.

Run by promoters rather than real managers, overextended, too rapidly expanded and, in some cases, fraudulent in their accounting practices, the concept stocks joined the high-tech growth companies and the conglomerates in leading the steep market declines of 1969 and 1970, taking a good many of the "go-go" fund managers down with them.

THE 1970S AND THE NIFTY FIFTY

Wall Street entered the seventies like a bear with a bad hangover, pledging never to drink such heady stuff again. Only top shelf from now on—the solid, blue chip stocks with good growth records that could be relied upon not to come crashing down and that, because they would continue their steady growth, could be bought at any price without fear of loss, provided you held on.

By now mutual funds and institutional investors had become dominant. Such "one-decision" stocks appealed to the big guys for another reason: they were large-capitalization companies and the institutions could buy huge positions without upsetting the market.

There weren't all that many stocks around fitting such standards, and the four dozen or so that did became institutional favorites known as the nifty fifty, including IBM, Kodak, McDonald's, du Pont, General Electric, Westinghouse and other Dow stocks, plus names like Xerox, Avon Products, Polaroid and Disney.

Again the institutional managers proved that expertise plus power does not equal sanity. As a general rule, the P/E of a company should equal its annual rate of growth; if the P/E of McDonald's is 18 earnings should be growing at the rate of 18 percent a year. But the pros ignored this rule of thumb and, by the end of 1972, *despite a general market decline*, had driven many of the nifty fifty to multiples nearing 100 times earnings, a far cry from any company's ability to sustain growth.

For a while there was a two-tier market, with the institutional favorites, benefiting from what today would be called a "greater fool" theory, going up while the market in general went down.

When the bear market of 1973–74 settled in, however, the growth stocks, small and large, had their comeuppance, or I should say come-downance; 27 of the nifty fifty dropped an average of 84 percent from their 1971–72 highs. The money managers looking best in those years were those holding cash, the "market timers."

When the market resumed an upward trend in 1975, growth issues lagged and cyclical stocks came into favor. Profiting from what analysts saw as a new era of "pricing power," the basic industries like steel, chemicals, aluminum, paper and copper had a glorious, if short-lived, revival.

By the end of the seventies, the cyclicals were back in a

slump, the market was neither here nor there, and the market leaders were the energy issues, because of shortages and higher oil prices stemming from the Arab embargo in 1973; technology, including energy-related technology and small "biotech" issues; and defense/aerospace issues, reacting to the Iranian hostage crisis and anticipating a Republican administration.

THE 1980S

The 1979 market continued through 1980, but in 1981, anticipating recession, the market dropped, with energy and technology stocks the hardest hit.

Emerging from the recession, 1983 saw the height of the small-capitalization (often high-tech) stock craze and a flock of money to new issues that was reminiscent of the 1960s, all at the expense of high-capitalization stocks. At the peak, the price/earnings ratio of small stocks as a group enjoyed a premium of two and a half times the Dow's. But the small-stock boom was a flash in the pan, and lots of investors lost lots of money again. While the cyclicals enjoyed a brief rebound in 1983, the star performers in the early eighties were big companies whose "private market values" were low in relation to their market values—in other words, companies with understated book values, which became targets of a wave of hostile takeovers financed by the junk bonds made infamous by Michael Milken of Drexel Burnham Lambert. The buyout craze carried throughout most of the decade, finally winding down and then symbolically ending with Drexel Burnham's bankruptcy filing in early 1990.

Otherwise, the market from 1984 on has been characterized by a blue chip rally led by noncyclical, consumer stocks like McDonald's, Coca-Cola, and Philip Morris. Up until midsummer 1990, the Dow continued to reach record levels within flirting distance of the magical 3000 mark. This was true even as the broader market was distinctly lackluster and some of the small-stock indexes were actually showing declines.

Nineteen eighty-nine was a freakish year. The institutions, not totally persuaded a "soft landing" could be pulled off, eschewed the bargains in the Dow, preferring to bid the blue chip growth stocks even higher.

Some market watchers saw in the two-tiered market that prevailed in midsummer 1990 a parallel to the early 1970s and the nifty fifty.

In August 1990, the United States was faced with crisis in the Middle East. The Dow dropped 150 points in two business days as the specter of gas lines and stagflation, if not war with Iraq, loomed as serious possibilities. As this is written, the oil stocks, rising on the prospect of higher prices, are an exception in a nervous market where transportation stocks, vulnerable to higher oil prices, and financial stocks, sensitive to higher interest rates, are especially under selling pressure.

What will happen as a result of the Middle East crisis is anybody's guess at this moment. In any event, it would appear we can't rule out a period of stagflation caused by higher oil prices essentially similar to that which led to the bear market of 1974 and 1975.

Are the big institutions likely to repeat their mistake of the seventies, overpricing a nifty fifty only to watch them fall in a bear market? I don't think so.

The economic uncertainty to which investors are reacting so conservatively cannot go on much longer. Either we're going to see a recession or we're not.

Either way, you should make out following the strategies in *Beating the Dow.* In fact, it has been in lackluster markets that my methods have really shined. From 1972 to 1984, when the Dow went virtually sideways with a total return of just 120 percent, my Basic Method (five-stock) portfolio returned 853 percent.

While we may see a resurgence of the long-neglected small-capitalization stocks, there's no reason that has to be at the expense of the blue chips, which the institutions have to hold because their liquidity needs can only be met with high-capitalization stocks.

For these reasons, and because it simply has to happen sooner or later, I see the cheap Dow cyclicals leading the next major market move.

HOW DOES a contrarian like me look back at the years just discussed? With sweet nostalgia.

Some time back, I prepared for my clients, mainly for their information but also for fun, a piece based on my collection of headlines. The following will give you the idea:

In August 1982 the Dow Jones Industrial Average was at 780. Here were some of the headlines in the financial press:

Dark Days on Wall Street
Managers Skittish on Stocks
Wary Outlook for Stock Rise
A Time to Stay on the Sidelines
Running Scared from Stocks
An Analyst's Bearish View

In June 1983 the Dow had risen to 1250. Here were the headlines then:

Time Is Now for Playing Stock Market
Year of the Bull
Happy Birthday, Bull Market
Return of the Mutual Funds
Money Managers Still See Gains Ahead
Pension Funds Loading up on Stocks

In June 1984 the Dow was down to 1079. The headlines:

Correction Expected to Continue
Wall Street Firms Retrench

What Happened to the Stock Market?
Few Stocks Pierce the Gloom
A Downtrend Seen for Prices
Bull Dead in a Gloomy Market

Within months the Dow began a record-breaking six-year advance that would ultimately take it to the brink of 3000.

PART IV

BEATING THE DOW

INTRODUCTION

ENGINE CHARLIE Wilson was only partly right when he said that what's good for General Motors is good for the country.

Competition, employment, productivity, quality—in these respects the business world and the world at large have the same agenda. Corporations try to analyze and anticipate how people will think and behave, and to varying degrees they succeed. But they will always fall short, have setbacks affecting their share prices and finances, and require some time to adjust.

At those junctures, the majority of investors overreact. A few, recognizing the difference between real and perceived risk, have the opportunity to profit.

Change is inevitable. Problems are inevitable. Companies are vulnerable, but the biggest and best of them also have survivability. The best stocks to invest in are of companies that know how to survive.

In the following chapters of *Beating the Dow,* I'll show you how to structure your own Dow stock portfolio.

The inevitability of individual stock price fluctuations and of market cycles raises two obvious questions: If companies are essentially sound and growing, isn't one way to beat the market simply to buy stocks and hold them? And since the stock market is cyclical, aren't there times when one should be in stocks and other times when one should be out? The answer to both questions is yes, but.

Buying and holding has the attraction of no ongoing commission expense, no management fees, no capital gains taxes, no risk of losing out on a stock dividend or a split, and no demands on your time.

But there are several problems with a buy and hold strategy. The first is your own possible need for liquidity. Although it would, of course, be unwise in the extreme to put your reserve for emergencies in common stocks, conceivably some circumstance could develop where you'd need to convert your stocks to cash. You might then find yourself faced with the choice of selling your best performers or taking a loss on stocks that are temporarily underperforming. A buy and hold strategy is an option only if you are prepared to do just that—to buy and hold and not to sell until some point fairly far in the future.

The second and more important problem is that even the most well-selected stocks would probably produce returns inferior to those possible with an actively managed portfolio.

Common sense would dictate that your buy and hold portfolio be chosen from quality stocks having the best earnings prospects. Earnings prospects are evaluated by those people having the greatest expertise and access to corporate information selection, namely Wall Street security analysts.

A fixed portfolio requires inhuman prescience to structure initially and is, by definition, unresponsive to changing market conditions. It is therefore vulnerable to significant deterioration of company prospects, a problem active portfolio management can avoid.

The following report in the May/June 1987 *Financial Analysts Journal* by Michelle Clayman of New Amsterdam Partners speaks of the futility of predicting earnings:

> The bestseller *In Search of Excellence* by Thomas J. Peters and Robert H. Waterman, Jr. profiled companies that had been identified as "excellent" on the basis of outstanding financial

performance as ranked by several measures of profitability and growth. This article examines 29 of the companies and finds that their financial health—as measured by the same ratios—began to decline virtually across the board starting right from the date on which they were selected as "excellent." Furthermore, 39 companies ranked at the bottom by the same ratios showed widespread improvement over the next five years.

Over the next five years, a portfolio of 29 "excellent" companies wound up with 18 underperformers and 11 outperformers. It beat the S&P by 1% per year. A portfolio of the "unexcellent" companies ended up with 25 outperformers and 14 underperformers. It beat the S&P by over 12% per year.

So the "worst" companies did a whole lot better than the "best" companies! It's a comment on the value of Wall Street earnings forecasting, which somebody described as "a science that makes astrology look respectable."

Beating the Dow—Basic Method outlines the simplest method of outperforming the Dow. It uses a combination of the highest-yielding and least expensive stocks to structure a five-stock portfolio. Its portfolio has done almost five times better than the unmanaged Dow over the last 17 years, a period that included a bear market, a sideways market, and a bull market. Also described is a one-stock strategy that did over eight times better than the Dow over the same period.

For more conservative investors, the Basic Method also includes a ten-stock high-yield portfolio that did better than three times the Dow over the same period. *Each of these three strategies involves reviewing and updating your portfolio once a year and fastidiously and deliberately ignoring it in between.*

Out-of-favor stocks in the Dow universe have produced superior returns. You can get these returns because you have two advantages over the pros. One is the freedom to operate in a universe as small as the Dow stocks. And you also have the freedom to take a truly disciplined approach. Discipline does not mean long-term. It means buying and selling on your timetable, not one dictated by clients.

Beating the Dow—Advanced Method is for those of you with a taste for thickening the plot. It should also fascinate stock followers with an interest in the research I have done on the Dow stocks, since it shows how contrarian strategies that have been applied successfully to other universes work out when applied to the the Dow. Each of the advanced strategies produces superior returns and outperforms the Dow. Several reduce risk and variability of returns. But be prepared for some surprises. Complexity is *not* necessarily better; when dealing with the Dow stocks, the best strategy is simplicity itself.

CHAPTER 6

Beating the Dow—Basic Method

TEN SIMPLE STEPS TO SUPER RETURNS

HERE ARE ten simple steps to extraordinary returns:

Step 1: Determine Your Equity Fund

The very first order of business is deciding how much money you can set aside for investing in common stocks. Remember, stocks fluctuate even if they generally grow with time, so we're not talking about the food money, the cash set aside for emergencies, or even the money you plan to use for a child's college education if the need is short term (three years or less).

This is not a book about financial planning, critical though that subject is. You should be prepared either by yourself or with the help of a financial planning expert to:

1) analyze your circumstances—what you own, what you owe, what you have coming in, and what you spend;
2) determine your major financial goals—buying a home, financing education, starting a business, providing for vacations, your retirement;
3) prepare a budget—a *realistic* projection of income and expenses that provides for *essential* needs, such as medical

and life insurance, a reserve for emergencies (one rule of thumb is two months' income), for savings toward your financial goals and—important, and the reason why most budgets are unrealistic—for the day-to-day *luxuries* you allow yourself.

When you have determined the amount of money that is *not* essential to the maintenance of your lifestyle, you have identified the amount of money appropriate for equity investments.

There is another, more subjective, consideration, which is your *emotional* ability to take risks. The fancy term for this is your "risk comfort level"; investment professionals like to measure it in terms of how "risk-averse" you are.

It's a very important concept, but like most things, it doesn't have to be as complicated as it sounds. I like to think of it as simply the sleep factor. You know yourself whether or not you tend to be a worrier. If you wear a belt and suspenders and still worry about your pants falling down, you'd be better off in government bonds or a money market fund. If you're a compulsive gambler, you'd be happier at the racetrack (but much better off getting help). If, like most of us, you're somewhere in the middle range, all it involves is deciding whether you are more comfortable with a one-stock, five-stock, or ten-stock Dow portfolio; greater diversification means more safety and somewhat lower returns.

Step 2: Open a Discount Brokerage Account

One of the beauties of the strategies we'll be using is that all the investment advice you need is in *Beating the Dow.* That means you can avoid the relatively high commission rates charged by "full-service" brokerage firms by opening an account with a discounter.

Discount brokers offer no investment advice. Basically, they are computerized operations that use salaried personnel to give quotes over the phone and to execute orders.

They vary in the range of products they sell and in the extent of their basic service; some, for example, sell mutual funds, others do not; some accept telephone orders and provide quotes 24 hours a day, seven days a week, others do so only during regular business hours. Some allow you to request a specific account representative (unless you're a member of a lonely hearts club, you can probably do without this); others put you through to the next available representative.

Because of such differences in basic service, however, the rate structures of discount brokers vary widely. Since our strategies require only the most basic of service, you can choose from among the least expensive discount brokers.

There are approximately 200 independent and bank discount brokers in the United States. An annual survey is available for $27 from Mercer, Inc., 80 Fifth Avenue, New York, NY 10011 (212-807-6800). They identify the least expensive independent discounters in the United States for 25 typical benchmark stock transactions and tell you how much each charges.

For example, the difference between what it would cost to buy or sell 1 to 100 shares of a $40 stock varies from $23 to $45 on a list of 50 "least expensive discount brokers." The Mercer survey might very well pay for itself.

Most discounters have minimum commissions ($25 or more). Ironically, if you plan to spend less than $1,000 on a particular stock, you may be better off at a full-service broker! They generally don't have minimums and their higher commission rate plus the usual extra charge for odd-lot trades (under 100 shares) may actually amount to less than the discount broker's minimum charge.

It pays to shop!

Commissions decline as volume increases. The cost of transacting 5,000 shares of a $50 stock would cost from $150 to $750 at firms on the list of the least expensive discount brokers. That's quite a difference, but the typical full-service broker would charge much more—close to $2,000 for that $250,000 trade.

Another thing to note is that the cheapest broker in one transaction category (number of shares at a particular price level) is not necessarily the same firm as the cheapest broker in another transaction category.

You should figure out in advance how much money you expect to spend on how many shares and shop a list of discounters to see who's cheapest in that category.

The annual turnover (number of stocks bought and sold) will vary with the different strategies we'll be discussing. But you can figure that if you are spending a total of $5,000 on five stocks, you should be able to keep your annual transaction cost down around 3 percent, or $150.

When you get under $5,000, commission costs become a higher percentage of the value because of the minimums that apply. You might consider getting a group of friends or relatives together and pooling your funds to get the benefit of lower transaction costs.

A few other tips on discount brokerage accounts:

• Verify that the broker is SIPC-insured. That stands for Securities Investor Protection Corporation, an organization funded by member broker-dealers that insures customer accounts up to $500,000 (there's a limit of $100,000 on cash) against loss due to failure of the discount broker. The law requires that brokers have this insurance; it's a good way to verify that the broker is legitimate.

• Most discount brokers prefer that securities left with them be registered in "street name"—that is, in the name of the firm as opposed to your own name. This is simply a practical procedure to facilitate buying and selling and presents no problem, assuming the broker has SIPC insurance.

• You may be asked to choose between a cash account and a margin account. The latter, which typically requires a deposit of $5,000 in cash or securities, enables you to borrow up to 100 percent of the value of your stock to buy additional stock.

The cost of borrowing on margin is as little as ½ percent to 1 percent above the "broker call loan rate" listed in the financial pages. Moreover, it is fully tax-deductible. There is a risk, since if the market value of your collateral declines more than 25 percent, you will be forced to come in with more cash or sell enough stock to bring the margin to the minimum maintenance level (which can be higher than 25 percent, depending on the firm's policy). This is the dreaded margin call.

Buying on margin can make a lot of sense if you know what you're doing but can be a real trap if you don't. You can make twice as much or lose twice as much. If you already know about margin buying, you probably don't need any caveats from me. If it's coming as news to you, do yourself a favor and wait a while before you get into margin buying.

You may have no choice but to open a margin account, since many brokers won't accept cash accounts. That doesn't mean, however, that you have to use it to borrow. There may be times when you will want to use the privilege just as a convenience, to facilitate a transaction that you are planning to settle in cash.

Margin borrowing privileges are also available for general borrowing needs as a feature of *asset management accounts* offered by some firms. Such accounts, which usually require minimum account balances, also typically provide credit card and checking privileges as well as automatic crediting of income and sales proceeds to an interest-paying money market account.

• Find out what the firm does with cash that flows into your account, either from the sale of stock or from dividends. Discounters will usually pay interest on credit balances, but they may require minimum balances before they do so. Ask.

Our investment return calculations assume full investment of principal and reinvestment of dividends, but in practice you may have the option of being paid out cash on request, having dividends paid to you according to some weekly or monthly payment arrangement, reinvesting cash, or keeping a cash balance in a cash management account of some sort. You should decide what you want done and make sure the firm is equipped to accommodate you.

To open an account just dial the 800 number of the broker and ask for the forms.

Discount Brokerage Firms

Below is a sampling of discount brokers and their rates. All are SIPC-insured. They were selected at random among several hundred discount brokerage companies around the country. It is quite possible your local bank offers discount brokerage services. Each broker has its own commission structure and range of services. Rates and services are subject to change and should always be confirmed. As I said, it is quite possible that the broker least expensive for a transaction of a given number of shares and dollar amount would not be the least expensive for a transaction involving different quantities and dollars. The brokers below were asked three questions: What would be your commission to buy or sell 25 shares of a $40 stock? How about 5000 shares of a $40 stock? What is your minimum charge?

Broker	Price per Share: $40.00		
	25 Shares	5000 Shares	Minimum
Bidwell & Company 209 S.W. Oak St. Portland, Oregon 97204 800-547-6337	$21.70	$403.75	$20.00
Burke, Christensen & Lewis Securities, Inc. 303 West Madison St. Chicago, Il. 60606 800-621-0392	30.00	405.00	30.00
Fidelity Brokerage Services, Inc. 161 Devonshire St. Boston, MA 02110 800-225-1799	41.75	340.75	36.00

| Broker | Price per Share: $40.00 | | |
	25 Shares	5000 Shares	Minimum
First National Brokerage Services 1822 Douglas Street Omaha, Nebraska 68102 800-228-3011	31.00	560.00	31.00
Norstar Securities 2 North Riverside Plaza Suite 1717 Chicago, IL 60606 800-621-0662	34.00	342.00	34.00
Pacific Brokerage Services 5757 Wilshire Boulevard Beverly Hills, CA 90211 800-421-8395	27.00	197.00	27.00
Quick & Reilly, Inc. 120 Wall Street New York, NY 10005 800-221-5220	37.50	290.00	37.50
Charles Schwab & Co., Inc. 101 Montgomery Street San Francisco, CA 94104 800-648-5300	42.00	341.00	39.00
Muriel Siebert & Co. Inc. 444 Madison Avenue New York, NY 10022 800-872-0711	34.00	150.00	34.00
York Securities 11 Wall Street 160 Broadway (East Bldg.) New York, NY 10038 800-221-3154	35.00	200.00	35.00

Step 3: Prepare a Portfolio Planning Worksheet

For this you'll want to buy a pad of accounting paper at your stationery store.

As pictured in Figure 2, list the Dow stocks alphabetically next to their symbols in the lefthand columns numbered (1) and (2). The symbols will help you make sure you're looking at the right stock when you turn to the newspaper stock tables. We'll also be using them as shorthand from time to time as we discuss the different stocks.

Following the form used in Figure 2, label column (3) "closing prices," column (4) "yield," column (5) "rank," column (6) "lowest price," and column (7) "execution price."

This worksheet is your annual overhead equivalent of Merrill Lynch Pierce Fenner & Smith's brokerage, research, and economics departments, so keep it away from the dog and kids.

Step 4: List the Closing Prices

Open *The Wall Street Journal, The New York Times,* or another paper with a comprehensive business and financial section and turn to the New York Stock Exchange Composite listings. All the Dow industrials are listed on the New York Stock Exchange.

Figure 3 shows *The Wall Street Journal* listings in its January 2, 1990, edition, which reported closing prices as of the last trading day of 1989. The research material we will be reviewing in the next chapter that documents total returns for Beating the Dow—Basic Method is based on year-end to year-end closing prices.

(The calendar year-end cutoff needn't be used unless it happens to satisfy your sense of organization. As we will see in our later discussion of market timing, there may be an advantage to buying late in December and selling early in January. The important thing, as we'll see, is the discipline of buying stocks that meet certain criteria at a given point in time, and replacing them 12 months later (give or take a few days) with whatever

Symbol	Dow Stock	Closing Prices	Yield	Rank	Lowest Price	Execution Price	Closing Price - End	Dividends	Total Return
1 ALD	Allied-Signal	34 7/8	5.2	(2)	✓				
2 AA	Aluminum Co. of America	76	2.1		.				
3 AXP	American Express	34 7/8	2.4						
4 T	American Tel. & Tel.	45 1/2	2.6						
5 BS	Bethlehem Steel	18 1/2	.5						
6 BA	Boeing	59 1/8	2.0						
7 CHV	Chevron	67 3/4	4.1	(9)					
8 KO	Coca-Cola	77 1/4	1.8						
9 DD	du Pont	123	3.9						
10 EK	Eastman Kodak	41 1/4	4.9	(6)	✓				
11 XON	Exxon	50	4.8	(7)					
12 GE	General Electric	64 1/2	2.9						
13 GM	General Motors	42 1/4	7.1	(1)					
14 GT	Goodyear Tire & Rubber	43 1/2	4.1						
15 IBM	Int'l Business Machines	94 1/8	5.1	(5)					
16 IP	International Paper	54 1/2	3.0						
17 MCD	McDonald's	34 1/2	.9						
18 MRK	Merck	77 1/2	2.2						
19 MMM	Minnesota Mining & Mfg.	79 3/8	3.2						
20 NAV	Navistar	3 7/8	--						
21 MO	Philip Morris	41 5/8	3.2						
22 PA	Primerica Corp.	28 1/2	1.1						
23 PG	Procter & Gamble	70 1/4	2.6						
24 S	Sears, Roebuck	38 1/8	5.2	(3)	✓				
25 TX	Texaco, Inc.	58 7/8	5.1						
26 X	USX Corporation	23 3/4	3.9	(4)					
27 UK	Union Carbide	30 3/4	4.3	(10)	✓				
28 UTX	United Technologies	54 1/4	2.9	(8)	✓				
29 WX	Westinghouse Electric	74	3.2						
30 Z	Woolworth	26 3/4	2.9						

FIGURE 2

BEATING THE DOW

FIGURE 3

stocks meet the criteria then, ignoring anything that happens in the interim. This discipline explains the outperforming returns. It doesn't matter what 12-month period is used as long as it is used consistently over time).

With a highlighter, underline or circle each of the Dow stocks (using the stock symbol to be sure you're not confusing Coca-Cola Enterprises with Coca-Cola Company or that sort of thing) so you can easily find them for later reference.

Now transfer the closing prices (those in the newspaper column headed "last") to column (3) of the worksheet next to the appropriate stock.

These are the prices you will use as the basis for your portfolio selection after we have performed the next few steps.

Step 5: List the Yields

Transfer the numbers in the newspaper column under the heading "Yld" (5.2 for Allied-Signal, 2.1 for Alcoa, and so on) to column (4) of the worksheet.

Step 6: Rank the Yields

Now circle the ten highest yields in column (4) (if there's a tie, take the alternative with the lower closing price) and in column (5) rank the circled stocks from 1 (the highest yield) to 10 (the lowest). You have now identified the ten highest yielders in the Dow.

Step 7: Identify the Lowest-Priced High Yielders

In column (6), put a checkmark next to the five circled stocks with the lowest closing prices. You have now identified the five stocks combining the highest yield with the lowest price.

Put a second checkmark next to the second lowest-priced high yielder. You have now identified the Penultimate Profit Prospect, or PPP (penultimate means next to last), which I'll get more into later.

Step 8: Select Your Portfolio

You now have your choice of three strategies.

1. *Ten highest-yielding stock portfolio* This portfolio of the ten stocks identified with circles is the most conservative alternative since it provides the most diversification. The more stocks there are, the less vulnerable the portfolio is to a decline in one or more individual stocks.

2. *Five high-yield/lowest-priced stock portfolio* Identified by single checkmarks, this portfolio offers five- rather than ten-stock diversification. It has the incidental advantage of requiring less capital because of fewer stocks and lower prices.

3. *Penultimate Profit Prospect (PPP)* This is not, strictly speaking, a portfolio, but rather a single stock, the second lowest-priced high yielder. There is method in this seeming madness, but you'll have to wait until the next chapter to see it.

Step 9: Place Your Order

Once you have decided which of the above suits your wallet and temperament, placing your order is as simple as picking up the phone and dialing your discount broker's 800 number, giving the account person your account number, and telling him or her to place an order to buy the stock. Most brokers will accept payment on purchases by check between the trade date and the "settlement date," which is five days later. Some firms, however, require that sufficient funds be in your account at the time your order is executed. You should check into this.

However many stocks you buy, you should buy an equal dollar amount of each. This is conventional practice in portfolio management and is the assumption underlying the returns we'll be looking at, but it also enhances returns, since lower-priced stocks, which tend to register greater gains, are bought in greater quantity.

The simplest and easiest way to order stock is to place a

market order, in effect instructing the broker to make the transaction at the prevailing market price—the best price the broker
can get for you at that time.

You may, however, want to consider placing a limit order.
This can protect you against the order being executed (actually
transacted on the floor of the stock exchange) at an unfavorable
price (as could happen in a volatile market), but you run the
risk that the order will go unexecuted if the market price fails
to hit the price specified in your order.

For example, if you look at the sample worksheet (Figure 2),
Allied-Signal turns up in the five high-yield/lowest-priced portfolio at a closing price of 34⅞. You decide to go with that
portfolio and thus will be buying Allied-Signal, or ALD. But
already a few days have passed since ALD closed at that price,
and who knows what will happen to its price today?

There are two things you can do. In both cases, you would
ask the broker for a quote on ALD. If it's currently still trading
at around 35 or so or at a price that is acceptable to you, you
can place a market order and be pretty well assured that in the
few minutes it normally takes to execute a Dow stock trade it
will be executed at or near that price.

If, however, the price has risen or you have reason to think
you'll get a poor execution (if the market is going haywire when
you call), you can place a limit order instructing the broker to
execute the order only if the price dips to 35 or better. Limit
orders can be placed for a day, a week, a month or can be placed
on a "good till canceled" basis. They can be used on the sell side
as well, in which case you tell the broker to execute only if the
price rises to the limit price or better.

My feeling is that the degree of protection against volatility
afforded by limit orders is not significant enough, and our returns are significant enough, that the risk of a market order is
preferable to the risk of having the order not executed.

You may be tempted to place a *stop-loss* order, but I strongly
advise against doing so. A stop-loss order, which becomes a
market order to sell when a stock's price declines to a level

specified by you, is designed to protect against losses, but you may find yourself selling out a stock that is merely fluctuating and that will have a net gain for the period over which returns are being measured. The dramatic returns we will soon be reviewing were achieved using discipline and no such tampering. Let's keep it simple.

Whatever type of order you place, you should request that it be read back to you to ensure there is no misunderstanding.

Normally, a broker will confirm the price while you are still on the telephone or call you back in a matter of minutes. The execution price should be entered in column (7) of your worksheet. That will be your basis for calculating price changes a year later.

Step 10: Take Stock and Revamp

Here's where we fast-forward to a year later, reach again for the worksheet, take the newspaper and list the closing price at period's end in column (8). The difference between the prices at which the order was originally executed and the closing prices at the end of the period (the selling prices of stocks replaced) plus dividends received during the year equals your total return for each stock.

To get the portfolio return, the totals for each stock are then added and the sum divided by the number of stocks.

How have the three Beating the Dow—Basic Method strategies performed historically?

For the 17 years from 1973 through 1989 the three strategies produced the following cumulative total return, excluding commissions and taxes:

1. Ten highest-yielding stocks:	1553.71%
2. Five high-yield/lowest-priced stocks:	2401.35%
3. Penultimate Profit Prospect	4210.10%
Cumulative total return of the Dow Jones Industrial Average for the same 17-year period:	499.35%

No magic was performed here. These are the actual cumulative total returns assuming annual review and replacement with stocks meeting the high-yield criteria.

The key to these remarkable returns is discipline—putting the 30 Dow stocks to the same tests year in and year out, selling stocks when they fail to measure up, buying those that do. Come hell or high water.

The low incidence of negative returns is remarkable.

On average, between three and four stocks were replaced each year in the ten-stock portfolio and the turnover in the five-stock portfolio averaged 50 percent—i.e., an average of 2½ stocks had to be replaced annually to maintain the high-yield portfolio. The PPP turnover was 100 percent, with the exception of one zero turnover year. As mentioned earlier, transaction costs at a well-selected discount broker would not be expected to exceed 3 percent and would decline as portfolio value increased.

I don't know about you, but for my money that kind of return from a bunch of stuffy old dividend-paying blue chips ain't bad.

CHAPTER 7

Why High Yield and Low Price Work

BEFORE WE consider why high-yield stocks outperform the Dow—and why adding the element of low price enhances your portfolio even more—let's look at a breakdown of our three Basic Method strategies:

TOTAL RETURN* COMPARISONS

Year	PPP	Five High-Yield/ Low-Priced	Ten Highest-Yield	DJIA
1973	73.41%	19.64%	3.94%	−13.12%
1974	−41.70	−3.75	−1.28	−23.14
1975	157.24	70.07	55.87	44.40
1976	55.08	40.79	34.81	22.72
1977	4.29	4.47	0.93	−12.71
1978	1.01	1.65	−0.13	2.69
1979	−10.08	9.91	12.37	10.52
1980	50.57	40.53	27.23	21.41
1981	27.25	.01	5.02	−3.40
1982	95.26	37.36	23.58	25.79
1983	36.05	36.11	38.73	25.65
1984	−2.82	12.64	7.64	1.08
1985	26.35	37.83	29.48	32.78

Continued

*Excluding commissions and taxes, as throughout book.

191

(Continued)

Year	PPP	Five High-Yield/ Low-Priced	Ten Highest-Yield	DJIA
1986	29.58	27.90	32.08	26.92
1987	3.33	11.06	0.61	6.02
1988	19.46	21.43	26.14	15.95
1989	12.86	10.49	26.53	31.71
Cumulative	4210.10%	2401.76%	1553.71%	499.35%

First, some observations on our two portfolios, leaving aside the PPP momentarily:

The five-stock portfolio outperformed the Dow 14 out of 17 years. It lost money in just one year, 1974, but then it was down only 3.75 percent while the Dow was off 23.14 percent!

Of the three years it underperformed the Dow, two—1978 and 1979—were virtually even (within a percentage point or so) with the average.

In only one year, 1989, did the five-stock portfolio significantly underperform the Dow. That was a year when consumer stocks that had seemed fully valued going into the year surprised everybody: Coca-Cola was up 73 percent, Philip Morris 64 percent, and Procter & Gamble 61 percent, for example.

So it wasn't that the yield strategy didn't work in 1989. It in fact produced a very respectable 10½ percent return. It was that the Dow in general went through the roof, with stocks like the aforementioned leading a 32 percent return!

THE TEN-STOCK portfolio produced less dramatic returns than the five-stock portfolio but was generally equal in the consistency of its outperformance.

In the losing year 1974, the ten-stock portfolio was down less than the five-stock portfolio (−1.28 vs. −3.75) and, of course, substantially less than the Dow's overall 23 percent decline. It underperformed in only five of the 17 years (including a negligible loss in 1978).

The larger portfolio's most pronounced underperformance was in the years 1989 and 1987, when it returned .61 percent and the Dow, reeling from the October crash, was up only 6.02 percent. The stocks that went into the crash fully valued simply regained value more quickly afterward.

In both portfolios, but especially in the five-stock portfolio, there were years when the outperformance was particularly striking (see Appendix B).

A WORD about the Penultimate Profit Prospect, which I've defined as the second lowest-priced stock of the ten highest yielders.

Here's the detail on it, with the Dow's performance noted as a comparison:

Year	PPP Stock	Total Return	DJIA
1973	Allied Chemical	73.41%	−13.12%
1974	Chrysler	−41.70	−23.14
1975	Woolworth	157.24	44.40
1976	International Harvester	55.08	22.72
1977	American Can	4.29	−12.71
1978	Goodyear	1.01	2.69
1979	U.S. Steel	−10.08	10.52
1980	U.S. Steel	50.57	21.41
1981	Goodyear	27.25	−3.40
1982	Sears	95.26	25.79
1983	Exxon	36.05	25.65
1984	Chevron	−2.82	1.08
1985	Goodyear	26.35	32.78
1986	Texaco	29.58	26.92
1987	Union Carbide	3.33	6.02
1988	Primerica	19.46	15.95
1989	Allied-Signal	12.86	31.71
Cumulative		4210.10%	499.35%

First of all, I wouldn't put my grandmother in one stock. But I'm not doing this just for fun, either; I present this research quite seriously.

It dramatizes that an out-of-favor Dow stock priced low enough has very favorable odds of becoming a winner.

If you have unessential funds, a good set of nerves, and ironclad discipline, to the extent history is a guide, you can make out with the PPP strategy as the above results clearly show. You might want to consider having two or three portfolios, including the PPP stock.

Why not simply the lowest-priced high yielder? Why select the second lowest? Am I just playing with numbers? No. The lowest-priced Dow stock has tended over the years to be a company in financial difficulty rather than a company out of favor due to other circumstances, usually lower earnings.

WHY HIGH YIELD PRODUCES OUTPERFORMING RETURNS

Bear with me for a quick review of Equities 101.

A stock's dividend yield—what I'm calling simply yield—is the annual dividend paid by a company as a percentage of its market price. A stock selling for $100 that pays $1 each quarter in dividends has a yield of 4 percent. The major newspaper stock tables give the anticipated yield—that is, they show the latest quarterly dividend multiplied by four and calculate the yield on the assumption that the same dividend will be paid for the ensuing year. We're of course using the same yield and the assumptions that go with it for our purposes.

Not all companies pay dividends, so not all stocks have yields. Stocks that don't pay dividends tend to be either smaller companies that plow their earnings back in to finance their faster growth rates or companies that are short on cash. The usual reason for being short on cash is lousy earnings. Earnings, and the anticipated future levels thereof, are the prime determinant of stock prices, whether a company pays dividends or not. But earnings and cash flow are not the same thing. Earnings are just part of cash flow, or the cash a company actually generates from all its activities (mainly operations, but also borrowed money, or new stock issued and other things done to raise cash).

Earnings and cash flow also differ because accounting rules permit companies to make certain deductions from earnings, such as depreciation of plant and equipment, depletion of natural resources (like an oil well), and the establishment of reserves for bad debts and other contingencies. Because these charges reduce earnings (and therefore taxes) but do not require the expenditure of cash, they are an important factor in differentiating between earnings and cash flow.

Professional stock analysts make a big thing of cash flow per share. Particularly since the law forbids the payment of dividends from capital—that is, it limits dividend payments to earnings or retained earnings—net cash flow (cash left over after obligations requiring cash are satisfied) is important in predicting a company's ability to pay or increase dividends in the future. That has obvious relevance to the value of the stock.

Cash flow explains a reality that is key to the dividend yield strategy: earnings can go down and dividends can go up. What I'm saying, simply, is that stock prices fluctuate with earnings expectations—the investing public has a short-term obsession with earnings—but are ultimately sustained by dividend payments made possible by cash flow. The significance of this will become clearer in a minute.

High yield is a contrarian indicator—a way to identify bargains—because it is telling us that the investing public has doubts about the stock, usually doubts about the company's immediate earnings prospects or about whether it's still eating nails for breakfast financially. What is happening is that the stock price has gotten low in relation to the dividend.

You might ask why, if such uncertainty exists, a company

doesn't lower or discontinue its dividend, thereby conserving cash and addressing whatever the problem might be. If we were looking at the London stock market we'd find that is exactly what happens. Even the alpha stocks—the U.K. equivalent of our blue chips—regularly adjust their dividends to reflect their earnings.

But American companies have a thing about consistent dividend payment. Annual reports boast of x years of consecutive (if not increased) dividend payments. When real financial problems cause a company to suspend its common stock dividend, it can take years to live it down, to restore the investment community's confidence in the stock as a solid investment.

In the United States the dividend is a sacred cow. A company would do almost anything to avoid lowering or suspending a dividend.

What does all this mean to us? First, the risk of earnings and stock price fluctuations is far greater than the risk of a suspension or lowering of dividends. Historically, dividends have accounted for 40 to 50 percent of the total return on the Dow stocks as a group, so this cherished continuity of dividends is of more than passing importance to Dow stockholders.

In the 17-year period we've been focusing on, only three of the *present* Dow stocks ever suspended their dividend—Bethlehem Steel, Navistar and, for technical reasons, Texaco. Only three ever reduced a dividend—USX, General Motors and Union Carbide. The rest have a record of consecutive and usually rising dividends.

This relationship—or nonrelationship, in most cases—of dividends and earnings can be seen by comparing the two statistics as they are shown for each year in the stock charts that accompanied our discussions of individual companies.

Look at Woolworth, for example. In 1976 it earned $1.81 a share and paid a dividend of .60. In 1977 it earned $1.40 (less) and paid .70. In 1981 and 1982, it earned .81 and .70, respectively, and paid out .90 both years. There are many other examples.

The point can be dramatically illustrated in a larger way. Barron's has a table each week showing the return on the Dow Jones Industrial Average as a whole—in other words, treating the aggregate of 30 stocks the way you'd look at a single company.

It shows that for the period between 1974 and 1985 earnings went down from 99.04 to 96.11. The Dow Jones Industrial Average rose, however, from 616 to 1547 during the same period—not quite tripling, but a major gain.

The key to this seeming contradiction? Dividends. Dividends nearly doubled during the period, rising from 37.72 in 1974 to 67.04 in 1985. Dividends were driving the market!

You can take it right up to the moment. The Dow earnings in 1988 were 215.46. During the week of May 28, 1990, Dow earnings were 207.84. The DJIA at the end of 1988 was 2168.-57. It closed at the end of May 1990 at 2820.92—up 30 percent. Crazy? Not really. Dividends for the period rose from 79.53 to 113.07—up 30 percent.

The fact that dividends are the driving force in the blue chip segment of the market and that there tends to be a high level of constancy to dividend payments by such companies explains why our yield strategies are not only singularly effective but quite conservative.

WHY LOW PRICE ENHANCES HIGH YIELD

Wall Street has a concept known as the small firm effect. It essentially observes that small stocks register higher percentage gains on average than large stocks.

Small and large refer to market capitalization, but it happens also to be true that smaller-capitalization stocks generally have lower prices than higher-capitalization stocks. That was why, you'll recall, the price-weighted DJIA tended to perform like the broad market value-weighted indexes; big-cap stocks had the highest prices and small-cap stocks the lowest prices, generally speaking.

Much of what is involved in the small firm effect has limited, if any, relevance here: the tendency of smaller firms to have more growth potential; the tendency of smaller companies as a group to include a higher proportion of financially distressed firms, whose price gains are dramatic when their fortunes recover; and the tendency of small firms, again as a group, to be neglected by the analytical community with dramatic price gains when they are "discovered."

Another factor, and the one of most relevance here, is simply the phenomenon that the less expensive a stock is, the more it is prone to greater percentage moves:

TOTAL RETURN COMPARISON

Year	10 Lowest-Priced	5 Lowest-Priced	DJIA
1973	1.89%	28.96%	−13.12%
1974	−13.98	−3.35	−23.14
1975	50.66	70.07	44.40
1976	42.32	48.07	22.72
1977	−9.62	−12.73	−12.71
1978	−8.70	−3.72	2.69
1979	12.44	13.93	10.52
1980	27.63	32.84	21.41
1981	−7.26	4.71	−3.40
1982	23.39	13.20	25.79
1983	55.25	68.01	25.65
1984	−7.94	−20.00	1.08
1985	20.06	13.00	32.78
1986	−3.19	−24.70	26.92
1987	33.59	58.74	6.02
1988	22.06	23.56	15.95
1989	15.92	4.57	31.71
	699.62%	1009.75%	499.35%

The column showing ten stocks is really there to assure you that we're not just playing with statistics. Ten stocks over a

17-year period is a meaningful sample. And when the five most expensive of those are taken out, the improvement in total returns is formidable.

1. Pick the ten highest-yielding Dow stocks if you want to protect yourself against the remote possibility of three Manville Corporations occurring in one year. (Manville Corporation, formerly Johns-Manville and a Dow stock until August 1982, was the world's largest producer of asbestos. Faced with massive lawsuits alleging the company was responsible for debilitating and often fatal lung diseases, it declared bankruptcy in 1982. Manville stock, which had been as high as $150 in 1977 (retroactively adjusted), plunged to under $20. The Manville story and its current status is discussed in Appendix A.)
2. Pick the five of the ten high yielders with the lowest prices if you want the cheapest way to buy in to a portfolio providing the highest returns.

And if you're looking for income as well as the safety of blue chips, with the exception perhaps of the PPP in some years, that comes as an automatic part of any basic method.

3. Consider the PPP if you are comfortable without portfolio diversification and want even higher returns and minimal pace of admission.

CHAPTER 8

Beating the Dow—Advanced Method

UP FOR something a little chewier? In the following pages I will share some advanced methods of beating the Dow. These strategies are interesting for different reasons.

Several, such as those based on market timing and seasonal phenomena, enhance the Basic Method on a risk-adjusted basis. They would have you invested in stocks only part of the time and in risk-free or lower risk investments the rest of the time. The advantages include less period-to-period variability of returns, and the virtual elimination of negative returns. Although absolute dollar returns may be lower when compared to a fully invested position, they become superior when adjusted mathematically for the lesser exposure to risk.

Another advanced strategy—investing in stocks with the lowest price to book value ratios—appeals to investors who feel more comfortable relating a stock price to underlying asset values than to earnings or dividends.

Other contrarian strategies that have had well-publicized success in broader stock universes, such as low price to earnings ratios, low price to sales ratios, and prior year poor performers, have, when applied to the Dow universe, beaten the Dow but by lesser margins than high-yield strategies. The explanation for this has been the historical stability of Dow stock dividends and their percentage importance as a part of total returns. Were

U.S. companies ever to go to a system (such as that in the U.K.) whereby dividends float with earnings, these strategies could be more effective than those based on dividend yield.

To show that a strategy of investing in stocks with the worst analysts' earnings forcasts not only beats the Dow but beats a strategy based on the best earnings estimates is just too much fun to resist—and it's useful as well. You'll see what I mean.

Investing in Dow stocks with the greatest relative strength is another advanced method that has been highly effective. As we will see, however, it involves trading off some of the peace of mind a larger portfolio would provide.

As a final exercise, I subjected the 10 highest yielders to a series of Dow-beating screens in an effort to get the best of all worlds. Such complexity has to enhance our simple methods, right? Well, you'll see.

Read on.

AT THE beginning of *Beating the Dow,* I introduced O'Higgins' Law—there is a natural human tendency to complicate things in direct relationship to their importance.

Look at weight control, to take an example outside the realm of finance and investment. Hundreds of books have been written on complex methods of weight reduction and control. We all know that the way to lose weight is to eat less and exercise more. (Remember the old joke: Place your hands against the dining room table and push.) But who wants to hear it?

The way to accumulate wealth is to work hard and spend less than you make. But who wants to hear that? People would rather pay millions to buy books, tapes and videos and attend expensive seminars claiming to reveal the secret road to riches. The investment field is no exception. In fact, because so many people are worried about money, we probably have more con artists pitching miracle cures for your investment ills than in any other field.

Thousands of stockbrokers, financial planners, investment

letter writers, financial columnists, securities analysts, mutual fund salespeople and investment advisers live off an unsuspecting public's belief that the world of finance and investing is beyond their comprehension. Nothing could be further from the truth. The truth is that, for the most part, the activities of investment "experts" are detrimental to investment success.

For those who may still disbelieve, perhaps a brief look at what the investment experts do will show what a waste of time it is to use complex strategies to beat the Dow.

INVESTMENT RESEARCH

Back in 1971, because the company I worked for, Spencer Trask, was considered the number one research firm in the country, there were thousands of institutional investors eager to pay big bucks for the privilege of listening to our analysts. Being young and gullible at first, I bought the party line and went busily around propagating the gospel according to Spencer Trask. There were fifty high-quality growth stocks, the gospel went, that could be bought and held forever regardless of price.

You'll recognize what I'm talking about. It's our familiar nifty fifty, the "one-decision" investment approach that had worked very well since the late sixties and continued to work well through 1972, my first full year in the business. But the past, as I've observed more than once in these pages, is seldom heeded in the investment business, and one should reserve a special wariness for trends of such long duration that they have become confused with permanent reality.

So it was that the 1973–74 bear market went after the nifty fifty with a vengeance. While the Dow Jones Industrial Average lost 47 percent of its value in under two years, many of our "one decision" glamour growth stocks declined by 75 percent or more. Table 8.1 illustrates the debacle.

TABLE 8.1

PERFORMANCE OF TEN ONE-DECISION STOCKS IN THE 1973–74
BEAR MARKET

Company	1972–73 High	1974 Low	% Decline
American Express	64.75	17.38	−73.2%
Avon Products	140.00	18.63	−86.7%
Disney	112.38	15.63	−86.1%
Honeywell	170.75	17.50	−89.8%
Howard Johnson	34.88	4.00	−88.5%
Polaroid	149.50	14.13	−90.6%
RCA	45.00	9.25	−79.4%
Simplicity Pattern	176.63	18.00	−89.8%
Westinghouse Electric	54.88	8.00	−85.4%
Xerox	171.88	49.00	−71.5%
		Average	−84.1%

The shellacking my clients' portfolios took in 1973 and 1974 made me wonder: if we were the best research firm in the country, how did the clients of the worst one make out?

PREDICTING EARNINGS

Most stock analysts believe the way to beat the Dow is to forecast a company's earnings per share. There are different ways of doing this. Some analysts use the top-down or macro method, which looks first at the overall world economy, then at particular countries where the company's products are sold, then at the industry, finally focusing on the individual company. Other analysts prefer a bottom-up or micro method looking only at particular companies without regard to the outside world. In either case, the record of the analytical community is generally pretty dismal.

Looking at the 1973–74 period again (Table 8.2), we see that

TABLE 8.2

EARNINGS AND P/Es FOR TEN GLAMOUR GROWTH STOCKS, 1972–74

	1972–73 High	*EPS 1972*	*P/E 1972*	*1974 Low*	*EPS 1974*	*P/E 1974*	*EPS % 1972–74*
AXP	64.75	5.16	12.55X	17.38	6.54	2.66X	26.7 %
AVP	140.00	2.16	64.81X	18.63	1.93	9.65X	−10.7 %
DIS	112.38	2.62	42.89X	15.63	3.06	5.11X	16.8 %
HON	170.75	4.38	38.98X	17.50	3.93	4.45X	−10.3 %
HJ	34.88	.90	38.75X	4.00	.81	4.94X	−10.0 %
PRD	149.50	1.30	115.00X	14.63	.86	17.01X	−33.9 %
RCA	45.00	2.05	21.95X	9.25	1.45	6.38X	−29.3 %
SYP	176.63	3.21	55.02X	18.00	1.77	10.17X	−44.9 %
WX	54.88	2.24	24.50X	8.00	1.57	5.10X	−29.9 %
XRX	171.88	3.16	54.39X	49.00	4.18	11.72X	32.3 %
	Average		46.89X			7.72X	−9.32%

instead of the continued growth trend so confidently predicted in 1972 to justify price earnings ratios of 46.9, seven of ten "desert island stocks" (as the nifty fifty were also called, because you could be stranded for 10 years or more without having to worry about your stock portfolio) had earnings declines of 10 to 45 percent, while the group as a whole saw earnings plummet almost 10 percent. So much for predictable growth.

Scrutinizing analysts' projections for the 30 DJIA stocks since 1973, we find an *average* margin of error of 47.9 percent per year (Table 8.3) when comparing what the analysts predicted the Dow companies would earn and what those companies actually reported a year later.

It is not as though we were looking at statistics biased by inexperienced or incompetent analysts. Why do Wall Street analysts, who earn six-figure salaries ranging upwards of $500,000 and have computers and large staffs at their service, do so badly? There seem to be several reasons.

One is that, at year end, the analysts don't even know what

TABLE 8.3

IBES CONSENSUS EARNING ESTIMATES
ANNUAL MARGIN OF ERROR

Year	Margin of Error	
1974	off	36.6%
1975		54.1
1976		46.7
1977		25.3
1978		24.2
1979		74.8
1980		42.5
1981		38.4
1982		153.3
1983		42.1
1984		28.0
1985		56.3
1986		60.2
1987		23.5
1988		33.7
1989		26.2%
16-Year Average	off	47.9%/year

the accountants will ultimately determine earnings were for the year just ended. In the past ten years, they have been off an average of 18 percent, with only two weeks left in the year. How can they accurately predict where earnings are going if they don't know where they've been?

Another reason is their tendency to extrapolate trends from historical earnings experience. This problem has been greatest in the case of cyclical, basic manufacturing companies. Analysts have a poor record of anticipating cyclical downturns and recoveries over the years.

A third, and perhaps most important reason, has essentially to do with conflict of interest. We have had the dramatic example of Donald Trump managing to get an analyst who was negative on the Trump enterprises fired from his brokerage firm—an extreme case, but it serves to point up a more subtle yet pervasive problem, which is summed up well by Thornton O'Glove in *Quality of Earnings*:

> The pressure on analysts to "be positive," particularly when writing up firms which the investment banking part of the firm is wooing, can be intense. This is especially so when the analyst has earlier been positive on the stock. Being negative makes enemies of managements; switching positions can be murder on the brokers and institutional salesmen, those people and fiduciaries with whom customers deal. "If you put out a negative on the stock, people who own the stock hate you. And the people who don't own the stock don't care," was the conclusion of one analyst, while another, who claims never to have issued a sell recommendation in his 20 years of experience in the business, added, "It's very, very difficult to go before fifteen or twenty salesmen at 9:00 A.M. Monday morning and tell them to sell something you were recommending."

The conflict that exists between the brokerage firm as researcher and as investment banker was well illustrated during the high-tech, new issue craze in 1983. According to Zacks Investment Research, a Chicago organization similar to the International Broker's Estimate System (IBES), the balloon burst then not because profits were bad but because they came in so far under expectations. O'Glove quotes Zacks as saying, "The analysts just started out way too optimistic, possibly because they are pushing stocks or have investment banking relationships with their companies."

Analysts also tend to become enamoured of the companies they follow. They develop close personal relationships with executives and financial public relations people, who, of necessity, are their prime sources of information.

Analyst-company relations are a key factor in the generally mediocre record the profession has. The Securities and Exchange Commission requires that the same information be available to all analysts, and one way companies protect themselves is to channel a party line through an investor relations representative.

With everybody getting the same numbers, the consequences when the numbers happen to be wrong are obvious.

ADVANCED METHOD #1:
THE TEN WORST EARNINGS ESTIMATES

Where to get the information you need: mid-December Investment Outlook issue of *Business Week* magazine.

What to do:

1. Using extra columns (or pages) in your portfolio planning worksheet, calculate the percentage earnings gains expected by the consensus of Wall Street analysts for each Dow stock.
2. Rank the stocks from 1 to 30, giving a 1 to the stock with the highest estimated percentage gain.
3. Buy the 10 *lowest* ranking stocks.

The results: See Table 8.4.

The significance: You outperform the Dow rather impressively, wouldn't you say? But you'd do better with any of the Basic Methods. The significance of this exercise is that it proves the fallibility of fundamental analysis as a tool to predict stock performance. It bears out the value of keeping it simple.

TABLE 8.4

THE TEN DJIA STOCKS WITH THE LOWEST EPS
ESTIMATES

Year	Total Return	DJIA
1973	−14.51	−13.12
1974	−10.52	−23.14
1975	39.21	44.40
1976	39.15	22.72
1977	−3.50	−12.71
1978	−1.82	2.69
1979	7.99	10.52
1980	29.48	21.41
1981	1.32	−3.40
1982	9.54	25.79
1983	55.25	25.65
1984	3.91	1.08
1985	42.96	32.78
1986	27.38	26.92
1987	−14.27	6.02
1988	20.59	15.95
1989	25.34	31.71
Cumulative	729.35%	499.35%

PREDICTING P/ES

But even if earnings were predictable, it still wouldn't help us much, because the key variable in the price of a stock—the price to earnings ratio—is even more unpredictable than its earnings.

Let's look at two examples of how useless it would be to know future earnings from either a macro (total stock market) or a micro (individual stock) point of view.

Let's imagine ourselves gazing into our crystal balls at the end of 1965 to determine what the DJIA as a whole would be earning nine years later. Starting with 1965 earnings of $53.67, we see earnings remaining fairly flat until mid-1972 ($58.87) and then taking off—rising 69.4 percent to $99.73 by September 1974, a mere 1¼ years later!

If you had known that the Dow's earnings were going to rise by 85.8 percent over a nine-year period or, even better, by 69.4 percent in only 2¼ years, couldn't you have assumed that stocks were a pretty safe bet with that kind of fundamental support?

Look what in fact happened. Instead of rising from December 31, 1965, to September 30, 1974, the Dow dropped 37.3 percent from 969.26 to 607.87. In the 27-month period between June 30, 1972, and September 30, 1974, the loss was an almost identical 34.6 percent.

Taking it down to individual stocks, suppose that in early 1973 someone had told you that the earnings for the bluest of blue chip stocks, IBM, were going to more than triple over the next ten years. Wouldn't you have felt pretty comfortable about buying or holding shares in such a fast-growing, high-quality company, one dominating a very attractive industry? As Chart 1 shows, however, poor IBM and its hapless shareholders would have seen their shares erode by 23.8 percent by 1982 in the face of a 235 percent earnings jump!

They say a compass pointing south is as useful as a compass pointing north, as long as you're onto it. The only way I have found to make constructive use of analysts' research is to take the mid-December Investment Outlook issue of *Business Week* each year, compute the percentage earnings gains expected by the consensus of Wall Street stock analysts, then buy the stocks these overpaid soothsayers predict will do worst in the coming year!

Table 8.4 shows what an investment strategy based on analysts' worst estimates would have produced in total returns.

If you had applied the erroneous analyst indicator consistently since 1974, you would have made almost twice as much money betting against the experts as betting with them (see Chart 2).

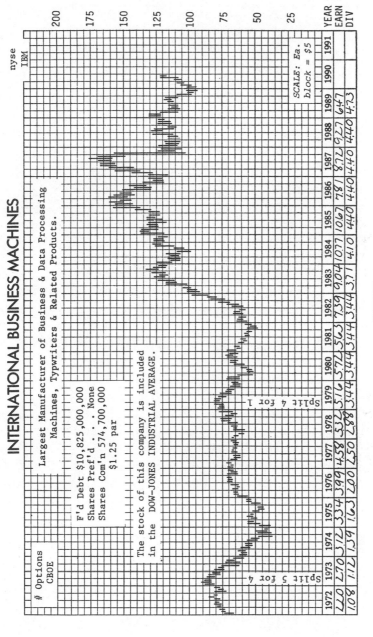

INTERNATIONAL BUSINESS MACHINES

nyse
IBM

Largest Manufacturer of Business & Data Processing
Machines, Typwriters & Related Products.

F'd Debt $10,825,000,000
Shares Pref'd . . . None
Shares Com'n 574,700,000
$1.25 par

The stock of this company is included
in the DOW-JONES INDUSTRIAL AVERAGE.

Options
CBOE

Split 5 for 4.

Split 4 for 1.

SCALE: Ea.
block = $5

	1972	1973	1974	1975	1976	1977	1978	1979	1980	1981	1982	1983	1984	1985	1986	1987	1988	1989	1990	1991
YEAR																				
EARN	2.20	2.70	3.12	3.34	3.99	4.58	5.32	5.16	5.72	5.63	7.39	9.04	10.77	10.67	7.81	8.72	9.27	6.47		
DIV	1.08	1.12	1.39	1.63	2.00	2.50	2.88	3.44	3.44	3.44	3.44	3.71	4.10	4.40	4.40	4.40	4.40	4.73		

CHART 1

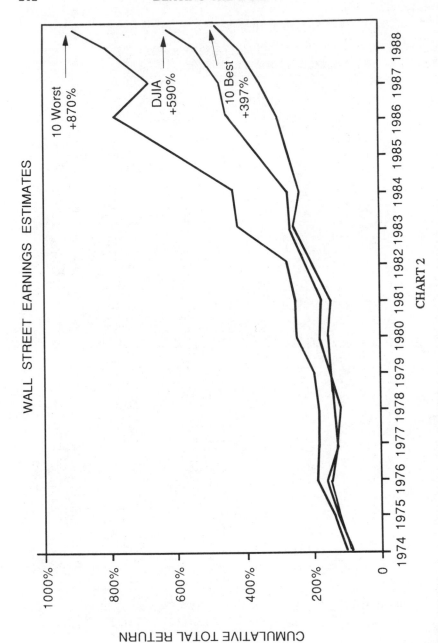

WALL STREET EARNINGS ESTIMATES

10 Worst +870%

DJIA +590%

10 Best +397%

CHART 2

Still, however, even though you would have beaten the Dow handily (and 75 percent of the pros), you wouldn't have come close to the returns shown in Beating the Dow—Basic Method.

I trust I've demonstrated the futility of trying to predict earnings and, more importantly, price earnings ratios. How about some other methods we sophisticated investment professionals use to beat the Dow?

VALUE INVESTING

We touched briefly on this approach to investing in Chapter 4. Very popular among analytical types, it is the method made famous by Graham and Dodd, whose book *Security Analysis* is a widely read classic on fundamental analysis.

Value investing attempts to determine the basic value of a company and to compare it with the current market price of the company's stock. "If you can buy a dollar for 40 cents," Ben Graham used to say, you don't have to worry about what the stock market's going to do. Graham is said to have been fascinated by the fact that the worth of private companies is evaluated in terms of book value, but once a company goes public, attention shifts away from book value to earnings.

The problem with this approach is that value, like beauty, is sometimes in the eye of the beholder. One analyst's bargain may be another's overvalued sale candidate.

One quick way to discover "value" is to look at the ratio of a stock's market price to the value of its net assets, or book value per share.

Unlike the dividend yield and ratio of price to earnings, book value is not shown in the newspaper stock tables. It is, however, easily found in the reports of popular stock services, such as Standard & Poor's and Value-Line Investment Survey, which most public libraries have. It is also in *Barron's* and highlighted in corporate annual reports.

Book value per common share is the value of a company's assets less what it owes to various kinds of creditors and less the par value of its preferred stock, divided by the number of its outstanding common shares. The significance of book value is that it is an indication of what the common shareholders, as owners, would have left over for themselves after all the assets were sold or converted to cash and everybody with a prior claim was satisfied. I say "an indication" because book value, when it comes to property, plant and equipment, does not pretend or even intend to measure market value. Such fixed assets are shown at their original cost less accumulated annual depreciation charges. Depreciation is an accounting concept. The government, to encourage companies to keep their facilities modern, allows them to "recover" the cost of such assets by taking annual deductions from their income and thus paying less in taxes.

So the original purchase price of fixed assets is continually reduced until it is either replaced, starting the whole process over again, or gets down to a figure representing salvage value.

My point is that book value, to the extent it reflects fixed assets, is unreal. The resale value of the assets, called liquidation value since such assets are normally sold at auction, could be less if, say, the equipment is obsolete or in really bad shape. On the other hand, with inflation, it may be worth now what it originally cost, or even more. Real estate, particularly, is typically worth much more than its book value because it has actually appreciated while, for accounting purposes, it has been depreciated.

Assets other than property, plant and equipment tend to have book values more closely approximating their market values. Cash is cash, accounts and notes receivable are adjusted for potential losses, so they should be worth pretty close to the book figure. Inventory can be tricky, depending on what it is and the accounting valuation method used, but it has to be reflected at the lower of cost or market value, so it can usually be viewed as a conservative figure.

The bottom line is that book value is not just a meaningless accounting figure. It is, in fact, a pretty good clue to what a company would be worth in liquidation and, where assets have appreciated during the time they were being depreciated, can represent substantial hidden values.

A portfolio of Dow stocks selected because their price to book value ratios are relatively low has historically beaten the Dow. Table 8.5 shows how the ten Dow stocks with the lowest ratios of price to book value compared with the Dow from 1973 through 1989.

Once again, though, we find ourselves with an advanced strategy that beats the Dow impressively but is left in the dust by Beating the Dow—Basic Method.

TABLE 8.5

THE TEN DJIA STOCKS WITH THE LOWEST
PRICE-TO-BOOK VALUE RATIOS

Year	Price/Book	DJIA
1973	5.71%	−13.12%
1974	−7.15	−23.14
1975	51.18	44.40
1976	45.22	22.72
1977	−13.82	−12.71
1978	−6.05	2.69
1979	12.45	10.52
1980	22.03	21.41
1981	−2.40	−3.40
1982	21.78	25.79
1983	56.91	25.65
1984	−6.39	1.08
1985	19.79	32.78
1986	6.91	26.92
1987	29.39	6.02
1988	33.36	15.95
1989	21.07	31.71
Cumulative	1018.27%	499.35%

ADVANCED METHOD #2: PRICE TO BOOK VALUE

Where to get the information you need: You will find book value per share in *Barron's* (separate from the stock tables), in corporate annual reports, and in the reports of popular stock services, such as Standard & Poor's and Value-Line Investment Survey, which most public libraries have. Stock prices, of course, are in the New York Stock Exchange Composite Listings of daily newspapers.

What to do:

1. If a price to book value ratio is not provided, you must compute it. It is simply the market price of the stock divided by the book value per share of that stock.
2. Using a column of your portfolio planning worksheet, list the price to book value ratios of each Dow stock.
3. Rank the stocks from 1 to 30, giving the highest ratio a 1.
4. Buy the 10 *lowest* ranking stocks.

The results: See Table 8.5.

The significance: This strategy produces one of the better margins of outperformance, more than doubling the Dow's cumulative total return over the past 17 years.

    Low price to book does not produce returns comparable to our high-yield strategies, but some investors find comfort in the knowledge that the market price of a company is low in relation to the value at which its assets could probably be liquidated.

    Analysts looking at long-term trends prefer the linear, year-to-year comparability of book value figures to statistics that are more variable, such as those tied to earnings, sales or dividends.

MARKET TIMING

We touched earlier on this topic, but it's worth a closer look if only because we investment professionals waste so much time at it. The aim, of course, is to guess which way the stock market is going so we can jump in and out of stocks and be at risk only when we are sure the market's going in our favor.

The shrewder market forecasters limit themselves to very long predictions and use lots of qualifiers, such as "on the one hand . . . on the other hand."

One problem with market timing systems is that once they're discovered and become popular, they never work quite as well again. Another is that the stock market, perverse beast that it is, tends to make its major moves very· quickly and without warning, leaving most market timers scrambling to get "in sync" with the market well after the fact. Nonetheless, some market timing methods have impressive histories of success.

HALLOWEEN INDICATOR

I live on a golf course, and maybe that's one reason I'm so fond of a seasonal technique we call the Halloween indicator, so named because it would have you in the stock market starting October 31 and through April 30 and out of the market for the other half of the year. For me it means I can spend half the year working on my slice, and the other half worrying about the market.

I ran a series that compared the annual gains in the Dow Industrial average from 1925 through 1989—just capital gains, not dividends—for the six months between October 31 and April 30 and for the full year. It revealed that 85 percent of all capital gains occurred from November to May. The figures, on a compounded annual basis, were 4 percent versus 4.63 percent.

I then took the ten highest-yielding Dow stocks and did calculations that assumed you were invested in them for the six months between November and May and had your money in Treasury bills for the other six months of the year. The Treasury bill rate is a widely available statistic, which is why I used it instead of a money market fund. As a practical matter, money market funds would pay a higher rate, so the figures would look even better.

For the years from November 1977 through April 1990, the ten highest yielders bought and sold on that seasonal basis and including two dividends would have produced a cumulative total return of 752.94 percent, or 17.9 percent per year. The comparable in-and-out return for the DJIA was 521.86 percent, or 12.9 percent per year.

Interestingly, the total return on the DJIA if you had simply held it for 12 months each year and not switched to Treasury bills would have been a lower 420.14 percent, or 12.5 percent per year for the same period. What that tells us is that you would not only have gotten your gains from November through May, but you'd have avoided losses by being in T-bills for the other six months.

Running the same exercise for a five high-yield, low-priced portfolio, our return would have been 762.18 percent, or 18.02 percent per year, ten percentage points better than the ten high-yield stock portfolio.

Table 8.6 shows a summary of the above data. Significantly, the period covered is one when the DJIA itself rose more sharply than in any period since the 1950s.

There are several notable observations to be made about these results, especially when compared with the calendar-year returns shown earlier for the high-yield portfolio alternatives. First, with the exception of 1990, you would have had positive returns in every year, including years when the DJIA had negative returns. Second, there is less volatility—that is, a lesser degree of variance between annual returns. (Statisticians use the term standard deviation.) Third, and perhaps most important: your money is at risk only half the time—T-bills and money market funds are just about risk-free.

TABLE 8.6

HALLOWEEN STRATEGY

INVESTED 11/1–4/31 / T-BILLS 5/1–10/31

Year	DJIA Full Year	DJIA Using Halloween Strategy	10 High-Yield Using Halloween Strategy	5 High-Yield/ Low-Price Using Halloween Strategy
1977	(12.71%)	.94%	14.96%	19.01%
1978	2.69	8.99	11.05	9.77
1979	10.52	16.73	22.62	28.24
1980	21.41	7.99	6.24	6.25
1981	(3.40)	19.51	38.62	32.42
1982	25.79	8.29	9.12	15.99
1983	25.65	32.00	35.27	40.20
1984	1.08	2.94	8.10	17.59
1985	32.78	10.80	13.13	19.43
1986	26.92	36.14	25.47	19.97
1987	6.02	27.15	24.27	17.49
1988	15.95	7.23	10.62	8.69
1989	31.71	19.56	20.35	12.35
Cumulative	406.09%	499.66%	763.85%	826.53%
Annualized	13.28%/yr	14.76%/yr	18.04%/yr	18.67%/yr

Statisticians use mathematical means to make returns comparable on a risk-adjusted basis, and if those methods were applied here there would be an astounding benefit to the returns you'd gain using the high-yield strategies (or any of the other strategies we have covered) from November through April and being out of the stock market the rest of the year.

What explains the Halloween phenomenon?

Before I attempt to answer that question, let me explain that market analysts, most notably Yale Hirsch, publisher of the *Stock Traders Almanac* and author of a popular book about seasonality and market timing, *Don't Sell Stocks on Monday,* have exhaustively established that certain months have historically been significantly better for the market than others, some being egregiously bad.

For example, Hirsch has determined that in the 35½ years through June 1985 the hottest month has been April, with 464.06 Dow points gained, and the worst month May, with 324.38 Dow points lost during the same period.

February has historically been lousy but November, December and January consecutively good. And so on. But it would be too hard to switch in and out of all these months. If you kept ducking in and out of the market to avoid months in which the probabilities are against you and took advantage of those with a favorable history, you'd be like a one-armed paper hanger trying to keep track of it all and you'd get eaten alive by commission expense.

I've determined that the best half-year to be in the market is November through April—that period encompasses the best months and avoids the worst months.

Why are some months better than others? There are different but logical theories to explain each month. November, December and to a lesser extent January are good months for capital gains because it is then that new money is put into corporate and private pension funds in lump sums. That money is dollar-averaged into the market over a period of months, creating more buying than selling and thus lifting prices.

April has always been a good month for the market, but it was especially favorable between 1981 and 1987, when everybody could take a tax deduction for money put into Individual Retirement Accounts (IRAs). Since the 1986 Tax Reform Act was passed, only certain taxpayers are allowed deductions. Everybody can still enjoy the tax deferment of IRA income, though, so there is still a big influx of cash into the market before the April 15 deadline.

What's the bottom line? Using the Halloween strategy every year since 1976, combined with the five high-yield/lowest-priced strategy, would have produced 13 years of steady gains without a single losing year and done twice as well as the Dow. But it still would have underperformed our fully invested strategies outlined in Beating the Dow—Basic Method.

ADVANCED METHOD #3: THE HALLOWEEN INDICATOR

Where to get the information you need: This is a market timing method, which can be used with any strategy, although for the best returns you would probably want to combine it with the Basic Method high-yield portfolios.

You would thus find your prices and yields in the newspaper stock tables as of November 1.

From May 1 through October 31, you will be out of the stock market and invested in a money market fund. The yields of such funds are published in the financial sections of newspapers, usually on Thursdays or Fridays.

What to do:

1. Simply perform the same exercise outlined in the Basic Method, except that instead of buying and selling annually, your portfolio is structured as of November 1 and sold as of April 30.
2. An account with a money market mutual fund can be opened easily, and it is quite likely one is offered as part of your existing discount brokerage arrangement.

The results: Table 8.6 shows the results of applying this seasonal approach to the ten highest-yielding stocks portfolio and the five high-yield/lowest-priced portfolio.

The significance: This method has several advantages over the Basic Method portfolios held for 12 months.

1. With the single exception of 1990, you would have had positive returns in every year, including years when the Dow had negative returns.
2. There is less variability when returns are compared from year to year.
3. Your money is at risk (a money market fund is assumed to be risk-free) only half the time. Although your absolute returns were higher historically on a fully invested basis, your returns on a risk-adjusted basis were much higher using the Halloween strategy.

PRESIDENTIAL ELECTION CYCLE

One of the most reliable market indicators over the years has been the presidential election cycle, and there's an obvious reason why: presidents do their dirty work in the first 1½ years of their administrations and spend the latter 2½ years softening up the electorate for the next election. Since it's the pocketbook issues that usually make the difference, the implications for the stock market are clear.

Figure 4 compares the Dow stocks' performance for the respective stages of presidential administrations going back to the 1½ years at the end of the last Truman administration. It shows that in virtually every administration the market was weak in the first 1½-year period and strong in the latter 2½-year period.

The exceptions, such as the beginning of the Eisenhower administration and the latter Reagan/Bush period, had their explanations in unusual economic circumstances. From 1952 to 1954—the postwar period—industrial capacity was increasing to meet high consumer demand, and a figure of unprecedented popularity, Eisenhower, was generating high optimism about

PRESIDENTIAL CYCLE

Time Period	2 1/2 Yrs In/1 1/2 Yrs Out	D.J. Ind Avg
June 1950-Dec 1952	+39.6%	+39.6%
Dec 1952-June 1954		+14.3%
June 1954-Dec 1956	+49.8%	+49.8%
Dec 1956-June 1958		−4.3%
June 1958-Dec 1960	+28.8%	+28.8%
Dec 1960-June 1962		−8.9%
June 1962-Dec 1964	+55.7%	+55.7%
Dec 1964-June 1966		−0.5%
June 1966-Dec 1968	+8.5%	+8.5%
Dec 1968-June 1970		−27.6%
June 1970-Dec 1972	+49.2%	+49.2%
Dec 1972-June 1974		−21.3%
June 1974-Dec 1976	+25.2%	+25.2%
Dec 1976-June 1978		−18.5%
June 1978-Dec 1980	+17.7%	+17.7%
Dec 1980-June 1982		−15.7%
June 1982-Dec 1984	+49.2%	+49.2%
Dec 1984-June 1986		+56.2%
June 1986-Dec 1988	+14.6%	+14.6%
Dec 1988-June 1990		+32.8%
Cumulative	+1610.5%	+1277.2%

FIGURE 4

almost everything. The strong market in the first years of the second Reagan administration and now the new Bush administration reflect the thrust of a raging bull and confidence (naïve, in my opinion) that the government has finally mastered the art of managing economies and preventing unfavorable economic cycles from occurring.

Prior to the Eisenhower era, the only bad presidential year in 175 years was 1931, when the market slide that had begun in 1929 was nearing its bottom.

Yale Hirsch has done all kinds of interesting work correlating market patterns with politics, and I would much rather recommend his book than steal his thunder.

One caveat, though, before we leave the subject: don't buy the popular myth that the market does better when Republicans are in the White House. In the last 45 years, the market has done three times better under Democrats than under Republicans. But that is not an argument for voting Democratic. The Republicans have done much better controlling inflation. So take your pick.

ADVANCED METHOD #4: PRESIDENTIAL ELECTION CYCLE

Where to get the information you need: This is another market timing method that uses the same information and produces the best results when applied to the Basic Method high-yield strategies.

What to do: Simply follow the procedures for structuring the high-yield portfolio you prefer, but be invested in the stock market only in the last 2½ years of a presidential administration.

In the other (first) 1½ years, put your money in a money market fund.

The results: See Table 8.7

The significance: This method has the advantages of no negative years when the ten- and five-stock yield portfolios are used. Although returns beat the Dow impressively, they are inferior on an absolute basis to the fully invested strategy. Again, however, you are at risk only a portion of the time. On a risk-adjusted basis, you are better off with this seasonal method.

TABLE 8.7

TOTAL RETURN COMBINING PRESIDENTIAL CYCLES WITH BASIC
METHOD, 1973–1989

Year	PPP (2nd Lowest Price of 10 (PPP) High-Yield)	5 High-Yield/ Low-Priced	10 High-Yield
1973	6.93%	6.93%	6.93%
1974	8.00	8.00	8.00
1975	157.24	70.07	55.87
1976	55.08	40.79	34.81
1977	5.12	5.12	5.12
1978	7.18	7.18	7.18
1979	−10.08	9.91	12.37
1980	50.57	40.53	27.23
1981	14.71	14.71	14.71
1982	10.54	10.54	10.54
1983	36.05	36.11	38.73
1984	−2.82	12.64	7.64
1985	7.72	7.72	7.72
1986	6.16	6.16	6.16
1987	3.33	11.06	.61
1988	19.46	21.43	26.14
1989	8.37	8.37	8.37
Cumulative	1702.28%	1463.44%	1064.05%

YEAR-END TAX LOSS VICTIMS AND THE JANUARY EFFECT

Year-end tax selling is another opportunity to profit with the Dow stocks. Taxable investors look for stocks to sell at year end in order to create tax-deductible losses, and they ain't about to sell their best performers.

That means you can make out by identifying the year's poorest performers (the 12-month high-lows in the newspaper stock tables are a quick way of doing it, but it's better to track them from the end of the last calendar year) and buying these tax-loss "victims" before the final day on which, for tax purposes, profits can be taken for the year.

My studies show that for the last 15 years, the Dow's five worst losers rose an average of 5.3 percent between the two-week period between that December deadline and the fourth trading day in January.

There are other factors, in addition to tax selling, that explain this phenomenon. Since most corporations and money managers operate on a calendar-year basis, the end of the year is also the time for "window dressing" done by realizing capital gains or simply getting stocks with poor results out of the year-end portfolios. Corporations and individuals also tend to sell stock for the purpose of raising holiday cash for bonuses and for holiday spending. Since such seasonal selling depresses prices without altering the fundamentals of the stocks concerned, bargain hunters (like you and me) are there in early January to take profits.

ADVANCED METHOD #5: YEAR-END TAX LOSS VICTIMS AND THE JANUARY EFFECT

Where to get the information you need: Most stock tables show 12-month highs and lows along with daily prices.

What to do:

1. Using your portfolio planning worksheet, rank the stocks in order of how far they have dropped from their 12-month highs. Do this before the December deadline date for taking tax profit and losses. Your tax accountant will know when this is—usually it's in the third week.
2. Buy the five worst losers.
3. Sell these stocks before the fourth business day of January.

The results: For the last 15 years, the Dow's five worst losers rose an average of 5.3 percent during the above two-week period. Annualized, that's some return!

The significance: This seasonal timing technique has a history of producing profits in the Dow universe. The tendency of stocks to decline in late December and rise in the first days of January can also be used to time purchases and sales when using the Basic Method strategies.

MEDIA INDEX

When headlines scream bull or bear or magazine covers picture one or the other, you are well advised to run in the opposite direction. In June 1990 *Barron's* ran a picture of two bears with a headline that read: "Endangered Species: Bears in a Bull Market." The only thing I could make of that was confusion and uncertainty, which did seem accurately to describe the market's mood then.

I get a lot of magazines and all the financial newspapers, so I have made something of a game of using them as a contraindicator. For example, back in October 1983, I happened to

notice one Saturday morning that seven publications had headlines announcing the bankruptcy of the airline industry. I could
hardly wait until Monday morning. I bought four airline stocks
when the market opened. Between October 3, 1983, and February 27, 1985, I had made 57 percent on the four stocks. The
Dow in the same period had gained 4 percent.

In 1984, headlines proclaimed doomsday for the nuclear
utilities industry. I bought the best nuclear plays and between
October 25, 1984, and February 27, 1985, gained 16 percent
while the Dow gained 4.5 percent.

In November 1980, the name of the game was oil. Buy, buy,
buy said one headline after another. I did a little short selling
on that occasion and was rewarded with a 25.3 percent decline
between November 21, 1980, and April 26, 1983. While the oils
were plummeting, the Dow was gaining 21 percent.

The October I booked my short-sale profits, the headlines
almost to a fault said get out of oil. I bought. Between October
26, 1983, and February 27, 1985, my oil stocks gained 10.3
percent and the Dow gained 5.9 percent.

I could go on and on. Headlines announcing the Death of
Equities in August 1979 were followed by a 57.7 percent gain
in the Value-Line composite index between then and April 30,
1983. When Rebirth of Equities was the headline in April 1983,
the Value-Line started a decline of 6.6 percent until December
31, 1984.

In his bestseller *Winning on Wall Street,* analyst and adviser
Martin Zweig describes his *Barron's* ads indicator. He counts
the number of bullish and bearish ads that appear weekly in
Barron's, the most popular medium for ads placed by investment advisers.

Actually it's more a matter of keeping track of how many or
how few bullish ads there are, since advisers know that bearish
ads don't pull. Zweig figures if you can count as many as 20
bullish ads, you're probably looking at a bear market. If you
count seven or less bullish ads and any bearish ads, consider

buying. The ads are a reflection, he reasons, of two important areas of sentiment: the advisers themselves, and the investing public as the advisers read it.

ADVANCED METHOD #6: MEDIA INDEX

Summary: This contrarian timing method relies on such indicators as magazine covers, newspaper headlines and ads placed by investment advisers, primarily in *Barron's.*

It is the least scientific of our advanced methods, but if it gives you a clear reading of market psychology you can make out like a bandit by acting the opposite way.

TACTICAL ASSET ALLOCATION

This strategy has been very much in vogue in recent years, and got a boost when most asset allocators avoided the October 1987 crash. It involves shifting percentages of portfolios among stocks, bonds or cash, depending on the relative attractiveness of the respective markets.

For example, if the tactical asset allocator's model indicates that stocks are expensive relative to bonds or Treasury bills, he will sell some or all of his stocks and put the proceeds into bonds and/or T-bills.

A relatively easy way for an investor to assess the relative attractiveness of those three markets would be to compare current rates on high-grade bonds to the earnings yield of the DJIA. These figures are all published in *Barron's.*

A strategy using this calculation at every year-end since 1972 and shifting 100 percent of the portfolio from stocks to bonds when *Barron's* 10 Best Grade Bonds yielded more than the earnings yield of the DJIA and then reversing the procedure

when the opposite was true would have outperformed the Dow
but (you guessed it!) underperformed Beating the Dow—Basic
Method. Table 8.8 tells the story.

TABLE 8.8

TACTICAL ASSET ALLOCATION COMBINED WITH BASIC METHOD,
1972–1989

Year	2nd Lowest Price of 10 High-Yield (PPP)	5 High-Yield/ Low-Priced	10 High-Yield Total Return
1973	1.14	1.14	1.14
1974	−41.70	−3.75	−1.28
1975	157.24	70.07	55.87
1976	18.65	18.65	18.65
1977	4.29	4.47	.93
1978	1.01	1.65	−.13
1979	−10.08	9.91	12.37
1980	50.57	40.53	27.23
1981	27.25	.01	5.02
1982	95.26	37.36	23.58
1983	4.70	4.70	4.70
1984	16.39	16.39	16.39
1985	30.90	30.90	30.90
1986	19.85	19.85	19.85
1987	−.27	−.27	−.27
1988	10.70	10.70	10.70
1989	16.23	16.23	16.23
Cumulative	1464.60%	985.82%	747.24%

ADVANCED METHOD #7: TACTICAL
ASSET ALLOCATION

Where to get the information you need: Barron's will give you
the figures you need: 1) the current earnings yield on the

Dow Jones Industrial Average; 2) current rates on high-grade corporate bonds.

What to do:

1. Compare the two above figures at the end of each year.
2. If *Barron's* 10 Best Grade Bonds are yielding more than the DJIA, put your entire portfolio in bonds.
3. If the Dow is yielding more than the best-grade bonds, put your money in the Basic Method strategy of your choice.
4. Repeat the exercise the following year.

The results: See Table 8.8. Where the return is the same for all three Basic Method strategies in a particular year, the portfolio was in bonds.

The significance: You outperformed the Dow, but not the Basic Method fully invested in stocks. To the extent that bonds are safer than stocks, there is an advantage in terms of risk. In my opinion, however, the risk involved with the Dow stocks is far outweighed by their potential for capital gains, as is evident in the historical return comparisons.

OTHER CONTRARIAN STRATEGIES

Almost every investment professional claims to be a contrarian. That's because we all know that in the investment business, at least, it pays to be contrary. I have alluded to contrarianism throughout *Beating the Dow*. A contrarian tries to figure out what the majority are thinking and doing so the opposite path will be clear to see. Since the majority is usually wrong (crowds are stupid, is another way of putting it), a contrarian is more likely than not to beat the Dow. There are, however, some

TABLE 8.9

THREE CONTRARIAN STRATEGIES 1972–1989

Year	10 Stocks with Lowest Price/Sales Ratio	10 Stocks with Worst Price Performance the Previous Year	10 Stocks with Lowest P/E Ratios Total Return
1973	−18.55%	14.33%	18.29%
1974	−3.54	−7.48	−6.16
1975	57.91	52.30	54.35
1976	47.82	36.99	27.24
1977	−6.14	−16.31	−7.10
1978	1.81	−5.38	2.00
1979	7.60	15.27	15.27
1980	18.14	15.04	21.54
1981	−4.34	−5.55	5.67
1982	18.09	14.40	9.16
1983	59.32	55.31	37.77
1984	−2.77	.05	12.56
1985	21.14	20.29	30.52
1986	1.68	5.45	35.18
1987	16.71	30.94	−16.08
1988	37.00	30.91	30.72
1989	17.96	28.99	14.04
Cumulative	805.65%	717.70%	689.32%

serious practical problems with contrarianism. One is that it's not always that easy to determine what one should be contrary to. It's not as if contrarians had polls or surveys to give them readings on matters of interest. Another is that the majority can be right for a long time before its sheeplike behavior is brought to task. If a majority is right long enough, most contrarians will either be wiped out, lose faith, or lose clients. Usually it is all of the above.

Three easy ways to take a contrarian position successfully are to invest in 1) stocks that have performed poorly, such as a group of the 10 Dow stocks that performed most poorly the previous year; 2) the 10 DJIA stocks with the lowest P/E ratios; or 3) the 10 DJIA components with the lowest price to sales ratios. (Price to sales can be viewed as a variation on price to earnings, the rationale being that sales are more constant and less vulnerable to ephemeral "glitches.")

As Table 8.9 shows, all three strategies beat the Dow by a long shot. But they can't lay a glove on Beating the Dow—Basic Method.

ADVANCED METHOD #8: OTHER CONTRARIAN STRATEGIES

Where to get the information you need:

1. Price earnings ratios are part of the stock tables in *The Wall Street Journal, The New York Times,* and other newspapers with comprehensive financial sections.
2. Price to sales ratios may have to be calculated. The ratio relates the share price (daily newspaper) to sales per share—the most recently available sales figure divided by the number of shares outstanding.
3. Previous year's performance is calculated by taking the difference between the market price of a share at the beginning of the previous year and the price at the end of the year.

What to do:

1. On your worksheet, rank the Dow stocks in terms of P/E, P/S, and previous year's performance.
2. Structure portfolios comprising the *low* ten stocks in each category.
3. Repeat the exercise the following year.

The results: See Table 8.9.

The significance: These three contrarian strategies have been demonstrated to produce superior total returns in different universes of stocks and are shown here, applied to the Dow stock universe, as a matter of interest.

Again, all outperform the Dow, but none comes close to the Basic Method.

TABLE 8.10

RELATIVE STRENGTH ANALYSIS

Year	*Total Return 1 to 3 Strongest of 5 High-Yield/ Low-Priced*	*DJIA*
1973	51.02%	−13.12%
1974	8.00	−23.14
1975	77.48	44.40
1976	39.10	22.72
1977	3.21	−12.71
1978	−6.72	2.69
1979	−12.09	10.52
1980	39.23	21.41
1981	27.25	−3.40
1982	95.26	25.79
1983	42.71	25.65
1984	13.92	1.08
1985	15.53	32.78
1986	32.22	26.92
1987	5.92	6.02
1988	10.93	15.95
1989	5.52	31.71
Cumulative	3529.87%	499.35%

RELATIVE STRENGTH

The flip side of contrarianism is relative strength, also called momentum analysis. This approach to investing monitors potential investments and their price action relative to one another or to some other benchmark or index.

The momentum buyers aim to jump aboard just as the stock is taking off. Unlike the contrarians or the value investors, they want to be where the action is. They don't want to be sitting in dull, listless stocks while other people are thriving on the hot stocks of the moment.

Although there are various ways of measuring relative strength, the easiest method appropriate for the Dow universe is simply to compute the previous year's percentage change for each Dow component and then rank them in descending order.

By identifying the stocks in the 5 high-yield/lowest-priced portfolio that were gaining relative strength, I obtained the results shown in Table 8.10.

The total return, a cumulative 3529.87 percent for our 17-year period, is the best any advanced strategy has produced. Its limitation is that because we are applying the relative strength test to five stocks, not all of which necessarily had gains, it results in portfolios ranging in size from one to three stocks. Again, you may prefer the greater security of a larger portfolio.

An investor willing to risk single stock exposure for any length of time would probably prefer the significantly higher return of the Penultimate Profit Prospect discussed in Beating the Dow—Basic Method.

ADVANCED METHOD #9: RELATIVE STRENGTH

Where to get the information you need: Relative strength rankings are published in the stock tables of *Investor's Daily* but are related to all stocks and are not as useful as other methods for ranking the Dow stocks relative to each other. Our method simply uses the beginning and ending prices for each year, available in newspapers and stock guides.

What to do:

1. Compute the previous year's percentage changes for each Dow component, ranking them in *descending* order.
2. Referring to the portfolio planning worksheet where you did your Basic Method calculations, identify those stocks in the five-stock, high-yield/low-priced portfolio that were gaining relative strength.
3. Structure a portfolio of the identified high-yield/low-priced/relative strength stocks.

The results: See Table 8.10.

The significance: This portfolio produced a cumulative total return of 3529.87 percent, the best return of any strategy we have considered, with the exception of the Basic Method PPP.

The drawback here is that by the time you have purified a five-stock portfolio in terms of relative strength, you wind up with a portfolio ranging in size from one to three stocks.

Since this means there will be years when you have no diversification, isn't PPP with its 4210.10 percent return preferable?

MULTIPLE SCREENING

It is natural to wonder what would happen if the portfolio strategies that have beaten the Dow most impressively were combined, theoretically taking the best of each world and creating sort of a contrarian cocktail, with a twist of relative strength.

I did this exercise by taking the ten highest yielders each year, screening them using price to book, price to earnings, price to sales, worst earnings estimates, and relative strength, and giving each stock a score.

For example, take General Motors in 1989, which had a score of 4. In addition to being a high yielder, it also qualified in terms of worst earnings estimates (one point), low price to book (two points), low price to earnings (three points), and low price to sales (final score, 4 points).

Tallying everything up for the 17 years, I took the five top scorers for each year. Since I included ties that occurred in some years, I wound up with portfolios ranging from five to seven stocks.

Table 8.11 shows the result—a cumulative total return nearly four times the Dow.

But Beating the Dow—Basic Method, put through the wringer, emerges victorious.

The final lesson of *Beating the Dow* is that analysis beyond a point becomes counterproductive. In investing, simplicity beats complexity.

ADVANCED METHOD #10: MULTIPLE SCREENING

Where to get the information you need: This method combines six separate strategies already covered, so the data you need have been compiled.

What to do:

1. Start with your basic list of the ten highest-yielding Dow stocks.
2. Refer to your price to book value portfolio, and put a

checkmark next to the high yielders that also appear as low P/B stocks. Any stock with a checkmark now has a score of 1.

3. Refer to your price to earnings portfolio and put a checkmark next to the high yielders meeting the ten lowest P/E criterion.
4. Do the same thing with your price to sales portfolio.
5. Check off any high yielder that was gaining relative strength.
6. Refer to your ten worst earnings estimates portfolio and put a checkmark next to any high yielder appearing on it.
7. Identify the five highest scorers (the highest possible score is 5), including additional stocks where there are ties.

The results: See Table 8.11.

The significance: Although it produces the small advantage of a sixth or seventh stock in some years, the total return on this most complex of portfolio strategies—one that theoretically should combine the best of worlds—is inferior to our Basic Method five-stock high-yield/low-priced portfolio.

TABLE 8.11

5–7 SURVIVING
HIGH-YIELDERS* 1972–1989

Year	High-Yield + Total Return
1973	18.36%
1974	−5.96
1975	56.26
1976	37.76
1977	4.47
1978	−.05
1979	5.56
1980	33.09
1981	2.11
1982	31.70
1983	43.36
1984	3.53
1985	31.12
1986	30.98
1987	4.88
1988	30.61
1989	22.96
Cumulative	1929.38%

*10 highest yielders were screened using five additional criteria. Highest scorers (including ties) produced a portfolio of five to seven stocks.

Conclusion

THE PARALLELS between the early 1970s and the first half of 1990 are striking: a two-tiered market led by blue chip growth stocks with the broader market declining; and a Dow Jones Industrial Average that was flirting with a record high of 3000 before Iraq invaded Kuwait. That sent oil prices skyrocketing and raised the possibility of a deepening recession combined with higher inflation.

Had you invested in super-safe 30-year U.S. government bonds between 1972 and 1974, the worst bear market since 1932, your portfolio would have declined 16.57 percent.

Had you been holding the Beating the Dow—Basic Method five-stock high-yield/low-priced portfolio during that historic bear market, you would have had a positive total return for the two years of 12.50 percent.

The blue chip companies with their vast resources and profit incentive were making the adjustments required to survive and prosper in difficult times.

IT'S WIDELY acknowledged that the investment alternative with the greatest wealth-building potential is common stocks. But common stocks have discouraged many individual investors because of their volatility, particularly in recent years, and because the professional establishment has led people to believe that investing is too complex a business to be left to the average person.

The result has been that individuals seeking the returns available only through common stocks have flocked to mutual funds and investment advisers of various sorts.

But as we have seen, 75 percent of these professionals fail to match, much less beat the market.

In *Beating the Dow,* I have demonstrated how the individual investor can consistently outperform the market and most professionals by rather awesome margins using the simplest investment methods with the most conservative common stocks.

The key to these returns has been buying these stalwart stocks when they are inexpensive relative to each other—when the institution-dominated investing public has, as is typical, overreacted to an earnings forecast or a news development and made a strong stock cheap. Of equal importance has been the individual investor's ability to follow a disciplined approach rather than having to respond to the quarterly expectations and liquidity requirements of a client community.

Beating the Dow has demonstrated the efficacy of its simple strategies going back to 1973, a 17-year period that has encompassed bear, bull and sideways markets, as well as moments of frightening volatility. This historical experience has proved that buying the highest-yielding Dow stocks year in and year out outperforms the Dow in all kinds of markets. Indeed, by automatically enforcing a contrarian discipline, the strategies in *Beating the Dow* actually capitalize on the volatility institutional trading causes.

Mutual funds and other professional investors, who must operate in a larger universe of stocks and have high overhead and limited flexibility, cannot enjoy the rich benefits of my simple, conservative investment approach.

In turbulent economic times, there is always talk of a flight to quality, referring to a movement of funds from investments of a more speculative character to those offering greater safety.

With equities, this means the blue chips. *Beating the Dow* doesn't fly to quality; it begins and ends there.

We have shown that the Dow stocks are the smart place to be in the 1990s for both large and small investors. Large institutional investors need these high-capitalization stocks to meet the responsibility they have to provide shareholders with liquidity. On the other hand, an individual investor, by focusing on the Dow universe, can achieve dramatic returns without having to be an expert.

While the long-range investment potential of these viable companies is virtually certain, short-term profit opportunities can be exploited by playing these stocks against each other using the simple methods we have described.

At a time when even banks are looking shaky, *Beating the Dow* provides a safe and highly effective way for individual investors not only to participate in the wealth-building potential represented by the stocks of these vital multinational enterprises but also to benefit from their enormous adaptability and resilience.

John Neff, one of the great living contrarian investors, had a pithy bit of wisdom when he said, "Get 'em while they're cold."

Beating the Dow is unique in bringing these worthy ideas into the gilt-edged world of the 30 Dow Jones industrials. Like an exclusive club, the silver is heavy, the linen starched, and the leather soft. But there's no lack of action in the squash courts. There's plenty in this venerable club to keep the investment heart pumping.

The ultimate lesson of *Beating the Dow* is Keep It Simple. The investment world has become complex to the point where analysis can be counterproductive. It's like a photograph blown up so you see detail you never imagined—but where you can't recognize the faces.

So it has become for the analysts trying and failing to predict corporate earnings, the economists divided on whether we are in recession or recovery, and the technical analysts trying to predict the direction of the markets, only to discover ever-new support and resistance levels.

Sometimes the best way to read the weather is to stop studying the barometer and look out the window.

The investment returns we achieved with the strategies outlined in Beating the Dow—Advanced Method were, by any conventional standard, superior. In several cases, they reduced risk.

But the best returns—I don't mind calling them phenomenal returns—were obtained by methods ingenious for their simplicity. *Beating the Dow* is proof that in investing, simplicity can beat complexity.

Recent Deletions and Substitutions in the Dow

A BRIEF review of changes and substitutions in the average since August 1976 is useful. It focuses our attention on exceptional situations, of which two are particularly notable: the greatest turnaround in Dow history and the most dismal *non*-turnaround in Dow history. I'm talking about Chrysler and Manville Corporation, respectively.

Here, first, are the facts:

Date	Deleted	Substituted
August 9, 1976	Anaconda	Minnesota Mining
June 29, 1979	Chrysler	IBM
June 29, 1979	Esmark	Merck
August 30, 1982	Manville Corporation	American Express
October 30, 1985	General Foods	Philip Morris
October 30, 1985	American Brands	McDonald's
March 12, 1987	Owens-Illinois	Coca-Cola
March 12, 1987	Inco Limited	Boeing

It's probably worth noting that the Dow Jones Company doesn't hire a hall and send out invitations when it makes a change in the average. To the contrary, it all takes place very quietly. According to *The Wall Street Journal:*

A company is selected for the list by the editors of the Journal. There is no consultation with the Securities and Exchange Commission, the New York Stock Exchange, or the company itself. The selection is made from companies with large market value, extensive ownership by individuals and institutional investors, consistent earnings and dividends and a leading position in an important industry. The idea is that each of the 30 stocks serves as a proxy for other companies in the same market sector and therefore that the 30-stock index serves as a proxy for the market as a whole.

It can be inferred, with the obvious exception of Dow companies that merge with each other, that the policy guiding deletions uses the same criteria as that determining selections. We can often only surmise what the *Journal* editors had on their minds in any particular case.

ANACONDA

Anaconda Company, an old and leading producer of copper in the United States and Mexico, operated mining, smelting and refining facilities. It also mined lead, zinc, silver, gold and uranium. Through its subsidiaries, Anaconda Wire & Cable Company and the American Brass Company, it was a leading fabricator of copper and brass. Anaconda was also among the nation's largest producers of aluminum.

It joined the Dow in 1959, replacing American Smelting, which was essentially in the same industry.

On March 31, 1976, 27 percent of Anaconda was bought in a cash tender offer by Atlantic Richfield (ARCO) and on January 12, 1977, the company was merged into a subsidiary of Atlantic Richfield pursuant to a Plan and Agreement of Reorganization dated July 26, 1976.

Before its deletion from the Dow, Anaconda had been having trouble. In 1971 its Chilean investments were expropriated, causing a $350 million writeoff net of insurance claims. A relatively high-cost producer in a cyclical industry, its profit margins were highly volatile. Low copper and aluminum prices, operating problems in uranium, and generally poor operating conditions caused a loss in 1975, and Anaconda stock had dropped from a 1969 high of $66 to a 1975 low of $14.

With analysts projecting recovery, Anaconda was the object of takeover attempts by Crane and Tenneco until Atlantic Richfield emerged. With the stock selling at $21, ARCO paid $27 a share for 27 percent of Anaconda, then subsequently exchanged stock and cash for the remaining shares in a transaction that worked out to $32 a share.

ARCO thought it had acquired an inflation hedge in Anaconda, but poor copper conditions persevered and ARCO ultimately restructured it out of its system.

CHRYSLER

Chrysler's near-death and revival (with an assist from the United States government) have become a part of America's industrial folklore and made its scrappy saviour Lee Iacocca a symbol of tough, no-nonsense management.

A Dow stock between 1928 and 1979, Chrysler became one of the original "big three" after Walter Chrysler quit GM to turn around the failing Maxwell Motor Car Company and rename it after himself. But the 1970s were bad times for the American auto industry, and Chrysler, always the weak sister, was the hardest hit. The decade had begun with the oil embargo and gas shortages. GM was quick to respond with smaller cars and gained market share, as did imports. But Ford and Chrysler still offered gas guzzlers, the latter with unappealing designs to boot, and lost market share. A series of price increases further aggravated the situation. New car sales dropped 20 percent in 1974 alone.

By 1978 Chrysler was on the verge of bankruptcy when it turned to Iacocca, recently fired from Ford after a personal feud with Henry Ford II. Iacocca took his considerable persuasive powers to Washington, where he convinced the Carter administration that a Chrysler bankruptcy would exacerbate an already troubled economy. Washington responded with $1.2 billion in loan guarantees in 1979 which, together with labor and lender concessions, gave Chrysler a new lease on life.

By the mid-1980s, with well-received new models, an improved economy, voluntary export restraints by the Japanese competitors and cost cutting combined with industrywide price increases, Chrysler was well on its feet and making advance payments on its government-backed loans.

Although dropped from the Dow June 29, 1979 (replaced by IBM, returning for the second time since its own 1956 deletion), investors who held on to their Chrysler saw it peak at just under $50 before the 1987 market crash. On a split-adjusted basis, the stock had seen a low of under $2 from a 1973 high of $20. It resumed paying dividends in 1984 and has been increasing them every year since.

ESMARK

In 1973 Esmark Incorporated, the new name of Swift & Company, a Dow stock since 1959, acquired Playtex, a maker of bras and other women's undergarments. In 1979, Esmark was deleted from the Dow.

The old Swift & Company, the nation's leading meatpacker, had already become a conglomerate, with interests in petroleum (Vickers Energy Company), fertilizers, adhesives, specialty chemicals, dental equipment, automotive additives and sound systems and, of course, undergarments and personal products.

And it was just warming up. Before he sold Esmark to Beatrice Foods in 1984 for $60 a share, Donald Kelly, the colorful Chicago Irishman who was Esmark's chairman between 1977 and 1984, had made some 50 acquisitions. The last one was Norton Simon, itself a conglomerate with interests in cosmetics and apparel (Halston), foods (Hunt, Wesson), beverages (Canada Dry), liquor (Johnny Walker Scotch, Tanqueray gin) and publishing *(McCall's, Redbook)*.

Meanwhile the food industry in general was both consolidating and diversifying, a trend that culminated in the late 1980s with Philip Morris/General Foods/Kraft and RJR Nabisco.

Esmark, as noted, was bought out by Beatrice, which finally was taken private by Kohlberg Kravis Roberts & Company in the largest such leveraged buyout ($6.2 billion) until then.

I suppose the Dow Jones Company figured Esmark had lost its identity, that the food industry was undergoing fundamental changes, and that since the Dow had no real representation in the growing health care field, the substitution of Esmark with Merck made sense.

Esmark stockholders had nothing to worry about. The shares, in the high teens (split-adjusted) before the deletion, rose quite steadily following the 1981–82 recession to the $60 level at which Esmark was tendered to Beatrice.

MANVILLE CORPORATION

Manville Corporation, I think, was put on earth to prove that no rule is pure. Huge companies, even Dow stocks, can go down for the count. Even Manville may yet struggle to firm footing, but as I write things seem to be going from bad to worse.

In the mid-1970s *Moody's Handbook of Common Stocks* said of Johns-Manville, as it was then called, "Earnings tend to move with changes in the national economy, but diversification has helped to stabilize results. The stock is high-grade."

Manville, a Dow stock since 1930, was the world's largest

producer of asbestos, which was widely used for insulation and as a fire retardant in the construction industry and had a variety of industrial applications. Although diversified in such areas as fiberglass and plastic pipe, asbestos was Manville's core business.

Asbestos also happened to be extraordinarily profitable, earning three times the operating margin of any other Manville activity. That may have had something to do with management's obliviousness to mounting evidence that asbestos was the cause of severe, even lethal diseases, mainly of the respiratory system.

Although Manville had been putting warning labels on its asbestos products since 1964 and had won earlier lawsuits, by the early 1980s suits were being filed against the company at the rate of 425 a month. In August 1982 Manville filed for Chapter 11 bankruptcy and the stock was deleted from the Dow.

The stock, which (retroactively adjusted for capital restructuring done as part of its release from bankruptcy) had been as high as $150 in 1977, plunged to under $20.

The bankruptcy reorganization plan provided that Manville transfer 80 percent of its stock to a Personal Injury Settlement Trust, which it also funded with cash and a promise to pay $75 million a year starting in 1991. In addition, the trust has the right after 1992 to 20 percent of Manville's profits if it needs the money to settle claims.

In exchange for that, Manville received court protection from claims against the corporation and was allowed to emerge from bankruptcy in November 1988. In 1989 the company netted $173 million from sales of fiberglass, forest and specialty products.

As of March 1990 the trust had received 152,000 claims and settled more than 22,000 at an average of $42,000 for a total of $935 million. It had also paid over $200 million in fees to three dozen lawyers representing plaintiffs. Strapped for cash, the trust announced that tens of thousands of victims, many terminally ill, would not be compensated until well beyond the year 2000.

Facing more than $5 billion in potential liabilities and with assets of $2.8 billion, the trust is now looking at bankruptcy as an alternative. There is even talk of reopening the question of a corporate bankruptcy.

Meanwhile, Manville Corporation stock has been under $10 for several years.

Let Manville be a reminder that with stocks, risk is always present, which is what makes a portfolio so important. With Dow stocks, the probability of long-term losses is small. Small but, as Manville proves, not nonexistent.

Quoted last year in *Financial World,* Manville CEO Tom Stephens said: "The key to survival in today's climate is to live by tomorrow's risk." Manville now puts warning labels on its plywood; sawdust might be dangerous to people's health.

If Manville's experience registered on other companies, as it must have, investors may have less in the future to fear from the risk of product liability suits.

GENERAL FOODS

General Foods was deleted from the Dow because it was acquired in October 1985 by Philip Morris. General Foods stock, which prior to takeover speculation had been selling at $40 to $60 a share, was tendered at $120. Not a bad deal at all for holders of General Foods.

AMERICAN BRANDS

At the time of the above substitution, *The Wall Street Journal* ran an article pointing out that the combination of Philip Morris and General Foods would overweight the average in the tobacco products and processed food sectors.

The *Journal* therefore deleted American Brands, formerly American Tobacco. American Brands is best known for Lucky

Strike and Pall Mall cigarettes and Jim Beam bourbon, but it also makes Swingline staplers and owns Franklin Life Insurance Company. It was a Dow stock from the very beginning.

The substitution of McDonald's increased the Dow's representation in the service sector.

American Brands, for those who might have remained holders, proceeded generally upward from around $27 (retroactively adjusted for a two for one split in 1986) to a 1989 high of over $80.

OWENS-ILLINOIS

This leading producer of glass containers, plastic bottles, corrugated boxes and other packaging products, a Dow stock since it replaced National Distillers in 1959, was taken private for $2.1 billion in March 1987 by Kohlberg Kravis Roberts, the same gang that did the Beatrice Foods deal. Holders were offered $60.50 for shares that had traditionally been high at half the price (adjusting for a two for one split the previous year).

INCO LIMITED

This venerable Canadian company is best known as the world's leading producer of nickel, but it also produces copper, silver and platinum and has other metals processing activities.

Under its former name, International Nickel Company, it became a part of financial folklore by raiding ESB, Inc. (formerly Electric Storage Battery) in 1974. Considered an ungentlemanly act at the time and the more surprising because Inco was aided by the indisputably white-shoe Morgan Stanley & Company, the move started the modern wave of hostile takeovers.

In *One Up on Wall Street,* Peter Lynch cited International

Nickel, which officially became Inco in 1976, as first a growth stock, then a cyclical, and then a turnaround. He pointed out that it had sold for $48 in 1970, $25 in 1971, $14 in 1978, and $8 in 1982.

Inco, which has a virtually exclusive franchise on nickel in the free world (as Lynch says, nobody in Japan or Korea can invent a nickel mine), has nonetheless ridden the roller coaster of precious metals prices through the years.

Since its replacement in the Dow by Boeing, which brought needed transportation sector representation to the average, Inco, after a $10 special dividend, emerged from the 1987 market crash to soar to a 1989 high of $38 ($48 if you were still holding and counted your special dividend). It then leveled off in the mid-$20 range, where it is today.

So stocks deleted from the Dow have generally fared well.

A Look at the Major Outperformers

ALTHOUGH WHAT I said about its taking four Manvilles to lose money with a five-stock high-yield/low-priced portfolio in 1982 is absolutely true, I must admit I lucked out again. I certainly don't want to make light of anything as serious as the risk of stock ownership and the value of diversification.

Sears, Roebuck, the cheapest stock after Manville, gained 95.26 percent that year, and Woolworth, the next cheapest, gained 53.75 percent—two retailers starting from the bargain basement of a stock market that was anticipating recovery from one of the worst recessions in history.

It is entirely within the realm of possibility that a five-stock portfolio under other circumstances would have lost heavily, although the previous year (1981) Manville dropped over 34 percent and the five-stock portfolio gained 5.02 percent, still outperforming a Dow that went underwater by −3.02 percent.

The fact that in the last 17 years there is no example that really justifies the ten-stock alternative doesn't change an indisputable fact: stocks are vulnerable to risk, and diversification helps reduce that risk. It's a question of how well you sleep at night. As long as that's clear, the choice is yours.

There were several years when high yield outperformed the Dow to an exceptional extent, and it will be both useful and fun to take a close-up look at them.

The first example were the years 1973 through 1976, when, to recap page 191, the five high-yield, low-priced stock portfolio outperformed the Dow as follows:

Year	5 High-Yield/ Low-Priced	DJIA Total Return
1973	19.64%	−13.12%
1974	−3.75	−23.14
1975	70.07	44.40
1976	40.79	22.72

The individual five-stock portfolios in those years and the performance of their components is shown below:

Year	Stock	Total Return
1973	American Can (Primerica)	−10.04%
	U.S. Steel	28.62
	General Foods	−11.75
	Allied Chemical (Allied-Signal)	73.41
	Bethlehem Steel	17.96
Average:		19.64%
1974	Chrysler	−41.70
	United Aircraft (United Technologies)	48.75
	Johns-Manville (Manville Corp.)	25.45
	Goodyear	−8.82
	Woolworth	−42.42
Average:		−3.75%
1975	Chrysler	39.66
	Woolworth	157.24
	Westinghouse	43.55
	Anaconda	32.41
	Goodyear	77.48
Average:		70.07%

Year	Stock	Total Return
1976	Texaco	27.27
	International Harvester (Navistar)	55.08
	Westinghouse	39.10
	Standard Oil of California (Chevron)	46.95
	International Nickel Company (Inco)	35.54
Average:		40.79%

The years 1973 and 1974 were bad years for the market as a whole. The Dow, which closed 1972 at 1020.02, closed 1973 at 850.86 and 1974 at 616.24 before beginning its recovery the following year. In 1973 only eight of the 30 Dow stocks rose, and in 1974 only seven, and they were different stocks.

Our 1973 portfolio was led by U.S. Steel, then exclusively a steel company, Bethlehem Steel, and Allied Chemical, then still a chemical company. That these three companies led the group reflected a short-lived market theory known at the time as the shortage thesis.

Somewhat simplistically put, the economic boom that began in 1963 and continued through 1966, before leveling off, left supplies of basic raw materials such as chemicals and steel in short supply. Prices began rising in the early 1970s and earnings of these companies peaked in 1974.

The other two companies in the 1973 portfolio, American Can and General Foods, both being "defensive" food or food-related stocks, were simply off less than other stocks that affected the average negatively.

In 1974, the economy began sliding into stagflation, with unemployment over 7 percent and inflation over 10 percent. The Arab oil embargo had gone into effect in 1973, creating fuel shortages and causing factory closings.

Two companies in our 1974 portfolio benefited from the fuel crisis—Johns-Manville, which sold fuel-saving insulation materials, and United Aircraft, whose jet engines were in demand from an aircraft industry that was switching to fuel-efficient planes. These gains, of 25.45 percent and 48.75 percent, were enough in a generally depressed Dow to offset the dismal results of Chrysler and Woolworth, which both lost over 40 percent. Goodyear raised its dividend that year despite lower earnings, and was off only 8.82 percent.

Nineteen seventy-five brought raging inflation, but by midsummer the market had turned around. Chrysler and Woolworth, the prior year's worst losers, bounced back. The latter, an inflation-sensitive stock, gained 157 percent and was clearly the dominant factor in the outperformance.

Westinghouse, which, as we saw in an earlier chapter, had almost gone under and was the worst-performing of all the Dow stocks in 1974, showed a 43.55 percent gain as the market took note of its survival. Anaconda was the object of several suitors and rose on takeover speculation as well as anticipated higher metals prices. Goodyear's earnings were up, and it was doubtless still benefiting from the prior year's dividend increase.

In 1976 the Dow broke 1000. Jimmy Carter had been elected to bring the economy and inflation under control. Instead inflation went to even higher levels in the next three years, giving us our first double-digit prime rate.

Our five-stock portfolio that year was led by International Harvester (now Navistar), which was anticipating a cyclical recovery that never materialized. The anticipated recovery also explains the rise in International Nickel (Inco). Westinghouse continued to recover. Otherwise, the action was in the oil stocks, namely Texaco and Chevron, which were now benefiting from the higher prices resulting from the Arab embargo of 1973.

As a general comment on the 1970s, the bull markets were led by the nifty fifty, which were seen as solid investments offering sure growth potential. The bear markets were caused by depressed basic industry stocks that were caught in the shift to a service economy.

In 1980, our five-stock portfolio returned 40.53 and the Dow returned 21.41.

At the onset of the 1980s, everyone was obsessed with energy and the technology required to produce or save it. Oil prices, which had gone from $18 a barrel in 1976 to $35 in 1980 (spurred by the Iranian revolution in 1979), were about to tumble.

Texaco, which was putting less of its profits into exploration than its competitors, was anticipating higher earnings in 1981 (when other oil companies were looking at declines) and led the portfolio in 1980 with a 74.72 percent gain.

Manville, with its fuel-saving insulation, gained 10.55 percent. U.S. Steel, which had suffered a deficit in 1979 of nearly a half-billion dollars, came back in 1980 and was up 50.57 percent. Bethlehem Steel, anticipating higher 1981 earnings, was up 32.43 percent. Goodyear, down in 1979 on earnings, recovered and was up 34.37 percent.

In 1982 the five-stock portfolio outperformed the Dow 37.36 percent to 25.79 percent.

The retailing stocks, Sears and Woolworth, were characteristically strong in a market anticipating economic recovery. Sears soared 95.26 percent to offset Manville's 26.52 percent decline.

Westinghouse, having increased its dividend the previous year, enjoyed a 59.51 gain as it continued its steady recovery. The outperformance was also helped by the fact that Bethlehem Steel and United States Steel took major writeoffs in a year that they figured couldn't be much worse anyway; that depressed their stocks and curbed the exuberance of a Dow that otherwise was up on favorable economic forecasts.

Bibliography

Arbel, Avner. *How to Beat the Market with High-Performance Generic Stocks.* New York: New American Library, 1986.

Blamer, Thomas, and Shulman, Richard. *Dow Three Thousand: The Investment Opportunity of the 1980s.* New York: Simon & Schuster, 1982.

Bruck, Connie. *The Predator's Ball: The Inside Story of Drexel Burnham and the Rise of the Junk Bond Raiders.* New York: Penguin Books, 1989.

Cobleigh, Ira U. *Happiness Is a Stock That Lets You Sleep at Night.* New York: Donald I. Fine, 1989.

Downes, John, and Goodman, Jordan Elliot. *Dictionary of Finance and Investment Terms.* 3rd ed. Happauge, N.Y.: Barron's Educational Series, 1991.

Dreman, David. *The New Contrarian Investment Strategy.* New York: Random House, 1983.

Fisher, Kenneth. *Super Stocks.* Homewood, Ill.: Dow Jones-Irwin, 1984.

Graham, Benjamin. *The Intelligent Investor.* 4th rev. ed. New York: Harper & Row, 1986.

Hirsch, Yale. *Don't Sell Stocks on Monday: An Almanac for Traders, Brokers and Stock Market Investors.* New York: Penguin Books, 1986.

Kaufman, Phyllis C., and Corrigan, Arnold. *How to Choose a Discount Broker.* Stamford, Conn.: Longmeadow Press, 1987.

Lynch, Peter, with Rothchild, John. *One Up on Wall Street.* New York: Simon & Schuster, 1989.

Malkiel, Burton G. *A Random Walk Down Wall Street.* New York: W.W. Norton & Company, 1990.

Mattera, Philip. *Inside U.S. Business: A Concise Encyclopedia of Leading Industries.* Homewood, Ill.: Dow Jones-Irwin, 1987.

Naisbitt, John, and Aburdene, Patricia. *Megatrends 2000: 10 New Directions for the 1990s.* New York: William Morrow, 1990.

O'Glove, Thornton L., with Sobel, Robert. *Quality of Earnings: The Investor's Guide to How Much Money a Company Is Really Making.* New York: The Free Press, 1987.

O'Neil, William J. *How to Make Money in Stocks: A Winning System in Good Times and Bad.* New York: McGraw-Hill, 1988.

Peters, Thomas J., and Waterman, Robert H., Jr. *In Search of Excellence: Lessons from America's Best-Run Companies.* New York: Warner Books, 1982.

Rolo, Charles J., and Klein, Robert J. *Gaining on the Market: Your Complete Guide to Investment Strategy.* Rev. ed. Boston: Little, Brown & Company, 1988.

Rosenberg, Claude N., Jr. *Investing with the Best: What to Look For, What to Look Out For in Your Search for a Superior Investment Manager.* New York: John Wiley & Sons, 1986.

Stillman, Richard J. *Dow Jones Industrial Average: History and Role in an Investment Strategy.* Homewood, Ill.: Dow Jones-Irwin, 1986.

Train, John. *The Midas Touch: The Strategies That Have Made Warren Buffett America's Pre-eminent Investor.* New York: Harper & Row, 1987.

———— *The Money Masters: Nine Great Investors: Their Winning Strategies & How You Can Apply Them.* New York: Harper & Row, 1980.

———— *The New Money Masters: Winning Investment Strategies of: Soros, Lynch, Steingard, Rogers, Neff, Wanger, Michaelis, Carret.* New York: Harper & Row, 1989.

Walden, Gene. *The 100 Best Stocks to Own in America.* Chicago: Longman Financial Services Publishing, 1989.

Weiss, Geraldine, and Lowe, Janet. *Dividends Don't Lie: Finding Value in Blue Chip Stocks.* Chicago: Longman Financial Services Publishing, 1988.

Zweig, Martin E. *Winning on Wall Street.* New York: Warner Books, 1986.

Index

Index

Dow Jones Industrial Average (DJIA) (cont.)
Philip Morris Companies, 118–21
Primerica Corporation, 121–26
Procter & Gamble Company, 127–29
Sears, Roebuck & Company, 129–32
Texaco, 132–36
Total Returns in Percentages, 51–52
Union Carbide Corporation, 136–39
United Technologies Corporation, 139–42
USX Corporation, 142–45
Westinghouse Electric Corporation, 146–49
Woolworth Corporation, 149–52
compared with other popular indexes, 38–43
cumulative total return, 1973–1989, 188–89, 191–93
finding bargains among, 15–16
history of, 31–35
limitations of, 43
list of, 14
preeminence as a market indicator, 44
recent deletions and substitutions in, 245–53
American Brands, 251–52
Anaconda Company, 246–47
Chrysler, 247–48
Esmark Incorporated, 248–49
General Foods, 251
Inco Limited, 252–53
Manville Corporation, 249–51
Owens-Illinois, 252
weighted and unweighted, 39
Dow Jones Transportation Average, 42
Dow Jones Utility Average, 42
Dow Theory, 42–43
Drexel Burnham Lambert, 165
Du Pont de Nemours and Company, E. I., 80–82
address and telephone number of, 153

Earnings, 194–95
cash flow differentiated from, 195
difficulty of predicting, 172–73
dividends and, 195–96

Earnings (cont.)
forecasting, 204–9
yields and, 195
Eastman Kodak Company, 43, 83–86
address and telephone number of, 153
Efficient market hypothesis, 28
Electronic Data Systems (EDS), 94
Equity fund, determining your, 175–76
Esmark Incorporated, 248–49
Experts (investment professionals; stock analysts)
forecasts of earnings by, 204–9
short-term focus of, 25–26, 203–4
Exxon Corporation, 3, 40, 86–88
address and telephone number of, 153
Exxon Valdez (tanker), 3, 86

Federal Communications Commission (FCC), 64
Federal Reserve Board, 158, 159
Fidelity Brokerage Services, 180
Financial services industry, 43–44
First National Brokerage Services, 181
Five high-yield/lowest-priced stock portfolio, 186, 255–59. See also Basic Method portfolio
cumulative total return, 1973–1989, 188–89, 191–93
Forecasting
earnings, 204–9
price to earnings ratio, 209–13
Fundamental approach (value investing), 20, 21, 213–16

General Electric Company, 43, 88–91
address and telephone number of, 153
General Foods, 120, 251, 257
General Motors Corporation, 44, 82, 91–95
address and telephone number of, 153
Getty, Gordon, 134
Getty Oil Company, 134–35
Getty Trust, 134
GM Hughes Electrics Corporation (GMHE), 94
Gold, 10, 12
Goodyear Tire & Rubber Company, 95–98, 258, 259

For additional information contact:

Michael B. O'Higgins & Co.
601 New Loudon Road, Suite 160
Latham, NY 12110
(518) 786-1854